D1616731

CONSTITUTIONALISM

Recent Titles in
Contributions in Legal Studies
Series Editor: Paul L. Murphy

CONSTITUTIONALISM

The Philosophical Dimension

Edited by

Alan S. Rosenbaum

Contributions in Legal Studies, Number 46

Greenwood Press
New York • Westport, Connecticut • London

Library of Congress Cataloging-in-Publication Data

Constitutionalism: the philosophical dimension.

(Contributions in legal studies, ISSN 0147-1074 ;
no. 46)
Bibliography: p.
Includes index.
1. United States—Constitutional law—Philosophy.
2. Constitutional law—Philosophy. I. Rosenbaum,
Alan S. II. Series.
KF4550.C594   1988   342.73'001   88-5634
                          347.302001
ISBN 0-313-25671-3 (lib. bdg. : alk. paper)

British Library Cataloguing in Publication Data is available.

Library of Congress Catalog Card Number: 88-5634
ISBN: 0-313-25671-3
ISBN: 0147-1074

First published in 1988

Greenwood Press, Inc.
88 Post Road West, Westport, Connecticut 06881

Printed in the United States of America

The paper used in this book complies with the
Permanent Paper Standard issued by the National
Information Standards Organization (Z39.48-1984).

10 9 8 7 6 5 4 3 2 1

To my dear friend George Leibacher

Contents

Acknowledgments

As the editor, I wish to express my gratitude for the enthusiastic commitment with which the contributors greeted my initial invitation in the planning of this volume. It was their continuing cooperativeness and promptness at each stage in the volume's preparation that facilitated its timely completion. I am most pleased by the overall quality of the contributors' papers, which I believe justifies, once again, the esteemed professional reputations these scholars enjoy.

To Professors Robert Sweeney, Berkley Eddins, and Arthur Landever, I owe a special "thank you" for their willingness to review the manuscript and to offer some critical suggestions. Of course, the responsibility for any shortcomings that may remain is mine alone. My friend George Leibacher is owed a debt of gratitude. His inestimable critique of and his abiding confidence in my works have always contributed to their quality.

I express my deep appreciation to Dr. James Sabin and Ms. Mildred Vasan of Greenwood Press for their faith and encouragement in this project from the beginning. Finally, it is my secretary and typist, Brenda Kohout, who richly deserves my praise and appreciation. She always approached my endless stream of requests, despite her other tasks, with kind attention and care, giving it the highest priority. For this I am grateful.

Preface

This collection of essays is intended to be an enduring, scholarly commemoration of the bicentennial of the Constitution of the United States. The distinguished contributors give testimony in their writings to the high regard they have for a "critical" clarification and amplification of a philosophical understanding of the American Constitution and of the idea of constitutionalism in general.

Each of these papers has been written specifically for this volume. In addition, all contributors have a well-established expertise in the areas their respective chapters cover.

The topics and classical philosophers' views examined in this volume were selected mainly on the basis of what would likely be of greatest current interest to professional philosophers and to the philosophically minded scholar. Undoubtedly, certain themes of special concern to many prospective readers have been only peripherally discussed or deliberately omitted, such as systematic explorations of the Bill of Rights; federalism; "judicial restraint" (or "activism"); differences between rules, principles, and policies (in the context of judicial discretion). This is so because they are the more usual focus of recently published reflections on issues concerning constitutionalist thought in America. The editor does not regard these themes as any less significant than those chosen. Rather, the intention is to concentrate upon areas of compelling philosophical inquiry relating to constitutionalism that are neglected in the current professional literature but for which increasing demand has become evident.

Those classical philosophers selected for inclusion here are those the editor believes arouse the greatest curiosity in the philosophical community today concerning their ideas of constitutionalism. On the other hand, some equally prominent classical philosophers such as Aristotle, Thomas Hobbes, Karl Marx, and Jeremy Bentham have been to some degree arbitrarily excluded. The reasons, beyond the limitation of space imposed by the publisher, are that both Aristotle's and Marx's views have been incorporated in some limited fashion into essays already featured (for example, by Peter Stillman and Mark Tushnet). For our purposes, the literature in philosophy and jurisprudence is replete with discussions about the influence of Hobbes' concept of unrestricted political sovereignty and Bentham's utilitarianism, particularly upon the "command theory" of John Austin. These, also, have been omitted, regrettably. But the British tradition is nevertheless well represented in essays on John Locke (by Leslie Armour) and David Hume (by Wade Robison).

In any case, the chief virtue of this volume lies in its contemporary interpretive essays about (1) what some of the leading modern classical philosophers in the American, British, French (see Guy Lafrance's chapter), and German (see the chapters of Mary Gregor and Peter Stillman) traditions have said about constitutionalism, and in some cases the historical influence their ideas have enjoyed, and (2) important and timely philosophical-legal issues involving constitutionalism. The book's format corresponds in Part I and Part II to (1) and (2) above.

Introduction

The Constitution of the United States of America was ratified in 1790, and a Bill of Rights was added to it in 1791. The bicentennial celebrations of the signing of the Constitution in 1787 have drawn to a close. What remains is the continuing need to educate ourselves further about the Constitution's provisions, about the values and standards behind these provisions, and about the idea of constitutionalism as it functions in our contemporary world. The set of philosophical inquiries contained in this volume are systematic reflections upon a variety of important normative matters relating to constitutionalism. It is intended to serve the dual educational function of presenting information and stimulating critical thought and dialogue about the meaning and role of a constitution.

THE PERFECTION OF A CONSTITUTION

We underscore the recollection that the American Constitution was the outcome of a "great compromise," as Andrew Reck's paper outlines, a conciliatory product of the most advanced thinking of which the framers were capable at the time. It took three years and much debate for the Constitution to be ratified. Therefore it is a mistake to consider it as an object of uncritical worship, as if the original document was "perfect" (that is, unflawed), or as if all the framers were of a single mind, or as if all provisions were sufficiently unambiguous, precise, relevant, and complete to handle all future contingencies and developments with minimal interpretation and innovation. Of special interest in this regard are the papers by Mark Tushnet and Jeffrey Reiman, which include lively critiques of either other "non-originalist" theories[1] or of "originalism," the theory of constitutional interpretation and judicial decision making most recently popularized and variously defended by Attorney General Edwin Meese, Chief Justice of the Supreme Court William Rehnquist, and Robert Bork.[2]

Twenty-six amendments to the Constitution, the inclusion of provisions for amendment, and a vast array of differences among experts' opinions about the "original intentions" of the framers and the criteria of constitutional interpretation , bespeaks the practical limitations of the Constitution. Former Supreme Court Chief Justice Warren E. Burger stated that the Constitution was "the best thing of its kind that was ever put together," and President Reagan has called it "the impassioned and inspired vehicle by which we travel through history."[3] The effect of these expressions of unqualified praise is to cloud its genuine historical meaning and value. Their words suggest that the Constitution is best regarded as beyond fault and criticism. In contrast, Associate Supreme Court Justice Thurgood Marshall answered such overstatements by noting some crucial defects in the original document, the worst being the continuation of slavery. In fact, the need for affirmative action legislation in our day to supplement the Thirteenth and Fourteenth Amendments, and with respect to women's rights the Nineteenth Amendment,[4] indicates how elusive fulfillment of the constitutional promise of "moral equality" and "equal opportunity" can be. The early conception of this "promise" is rooted significantly in the political writings of John Locke on the subjects of "natural law" and the "social contract," as Leslie Armour's chapter discusses.

An illustration of a different weakness in the Constitution involves the system of checks and balances and the "separation of powers" doctrine, the seminal formulation of which is found in Montesquieu's writings and is elaborated upon by Guy Lafrance's paper. Both James Madison and Alexander Hamilton, two important framers of the Constitution, appear to have accepted the philosopher David Hume's view that only a system of government such as this can best control the unholy mix of personal ambition and political power.[5] Wade Robison's paper explores what its author regards as Hume's overall contribution to American constitutionalism. The "warmaking" power of Congress and the Chief Executive as Commander-in-Chief of the Armed Forces are functions clearly separated by the Constitution where each is intended to provide a check on the other and to maximize popular support for military operations. The classic democratic rationale for requiring a president to consult with congress in this matter is to guarantee official accountability.[6]

Although Madison may have envisioned the supremacy of the legislature in a republic,[7] the presidency has gradually come to control foreign affairs involving the armed forces. Richard Falk, in his paper, charts the evolution of this development and thus confirms the fears the framers had of an "unchecked" presidency. Furthermore, he explains how constitutional design may have made the "imperial presidency" inevitable and what may be done to correct this imbalance. It is an irony of the political conservative impulse today, typically associated with some version of "originalism," to prefer a strong chief executive, particularly in foreign affairs, at the expense of congress; the net effect of this preference being loss of official accountability as originally intended.

The prosecution of the Vietnam war by Presidents Kennedy, Johnson, and Nixon occcurred without a formal congressional declaration of war. Schemes for covert assistance to the Nicaraguan Contras by President Reagan's staff (as revealed in the Iran-Contra congressional hearings) were carried out in defiance of the intent of the Boland Amendment prohibiting such unauthorized aid. And President Reagan's deployment and "defensive" use of American military forces in the volatile Persian Gulf region during the Iran-Iraq war has been done to date without explicit compliance with the War Powers Resolution Act,[8] which requires that the President consult with, and report to, Congress whenever he engages in an exercise of war power. The Constitution itself does not specify clearly under what circumstances the President may, without congressional authorization, deploy armed forces and to what degree he may both make and execute policy.[9] What this implies for the American constitutional democracy is that the Constitution has not provided practical guidelines for settling the ongoing dispute about prerogatives between the branches of government. Hence, the failure of executive accountability can be seen as an obvious constitutional imperfection, however unavoidable it may be when the powers of government are separated.

A parallel problem involving military personnel is the issue of whether or not, and how far, the ordinary rights of citizens (that is, civilians) should extend to those who serve in the armed forces during peacetime. Peter French's chapter focuses on this problem in light of the fact that the Constitution has no provision for a standing army or navy.

The Constitution is not a perfect document, but it may be claimed that it is "perfectible." Weighing heavily in favor of its perfectibility is the flexibility the document allows for application to novel situations and problems (for example, the amendment process). Whether the Constitution will be able to fulfill its purpose in the face of challenges or threats to basic rights arising from some new technologies is the topic addressed by Rosemarie Tong. Milton Fisk discusses the fate of a constitution in a private property system when attempts to preserve constitutionalism (that is, basic property rights) require that property be modified. The persuasive fact that the Constitution has endured as "basic law" for over 200 years continues to testify to its overall strength.

Ultimately, any final evaluation of the Constitution must be made with respect to how effective the document has been in guiding society toward fulfillment of its constitutional ends. In a constitutional democracy, the dissent and conflicts that inevitably arise, owing to the premium publicly placed on independence of thought and action, require a continual reexamination of the "constitutional" foundations of society which foster competing visions of the ideal society. In his Afterword, Jeffrie Murphy urges us to consider the relationship between morality and religion in the context of American constitutionalism. He raises the contentious question about how well-founded a constitutional system is that authorizes the promotion of certain moral values while at the same time officially separating itself from all religious conviction.

CONSTITUTIONALISM

Modern constitutionalism in the western democracies has generally involved the idea of a civil society organized and governed on the basis of a written body of "constitutional" law.[10] A "democratic" constitution embodies a conception of the fundamental rights and obligations of citizens and establishes a judicial process by which rights claims may be litigated. The function of a judiciary is to interpret the constitution and to authorize enforcement of its decisions. Pragmatically, it seeks to strike a "delicate balance" between the rights and freedoms of "the governed" and the exigencies of effective government.

Constitutionalism has evolved to mean the legal limitations placed upon the rightful power of government in its relationship to citizens. It includes the doctrine of official accountability to the people or to its legitimate representatives within the framework of fundamental law for better securing citizens' rights. Behind the doctrine lies the axiom that the people as a whole are the best judges about what is (not) in their own interest.

This is not the sole meaning and purpose of a constitution, however, for in nations with different traditions, social tensions, and distinctive configurations of political power, constitutionalism is understood differently. In this regard, Peter Stillman's essay on Hegel's theory of constitutionalism is significant because it depicts a countermove, taken most seriously by Hegel's own contemporaries in Germany, to the succession of classical liberal theorists (many of whom are included in this volume). Although none of the scholarly writings of which I am aware attribute to Hegel any discernible impact upon non-German constitutionalism, his influence upon Karl Marx was substantial, and his writings appear to have exercised some influence upon a prominent consultant to the designers of the Federal Republic of Germany's post-war constitution.[11] The philosopher Immanuel Kant's influence is far more general and lasting than Hegel's, particularly as a legacy from the Enlightenment conception of a human dignity born of the capacity of rational choice, of which he was its most outstanding articulator. A dignity accrues to the human capacity of rational choice which constitutionalism ought to respect in its conception of the ideal relationship between citizen and state. Mary Gregor's chapter is a distinguished contribution to this book because it describes Kant's constitutionalism in the abiding light of his moral philosophy which, perhaps more than other modern philosophies, continues to influence how we conceive of the moral value of personhood and so of the moral purpose of a constitution.

A "constitution" may simply refer to a nation's "basic law." It may seek official legitimation of the actual unlimited power of a nation's policymakers (for example, such as the Supreme Soviet in the USSR).[12] It may be a nation's "ideological manifesto"; an existing government's attempt to legitimize itself; or, a nation's birth certificate.[13] Also, a constitutional framework may be agreed upon in order to transform an authoritarian political system into a constitutional democracy.

Accordingly, in some societies with long, nondemocratic traditions, such as Korea, Nicaragua, and the Philippines, the quest for democracy has assumed the form of constitutionalism. The constitution becomes the legal structure and process for establishing domestic stability and peace, national unity and, ultimately, political legitimacy. The most immediate goal is to replace violent confrontations with a legal and political process for dealing with grievances.

Although all written constitutions are designed to impose a certain pattern of government "and to mold the nation in that image,"[14] a constitution remains merely a statement of its framers' intentions unless the preexisting government and the military establishment in a newly "constitutionalized" society are both sufficiently powerful *and* determined to bind all crucial warring factions to, and to be bound by, the provisions of the constitution. Unlike the American Constitution, which actually instituted a new government, the proposed Korean Constitution, for instance, must be approved by the very same government it has been fashioned to replace. In general, governmental institutions and officials who are permitted to operate legitimately or officially "above the law," will inevitably pursue their own agenda at the expense of their society's best interest. A democratic and just constitutional "rule of law," with its provisions for respecting citizens' rights and establishing "due process" and official accountability, is supposed to prevent precisely this tyranny. Most nations today have at least a written constitution, due in no small measure to the success of the American experience in constitutionalism.

In conclusion, the American Constitution is a remarkable document that has invigorated the idea of constitutionalism as the most rational and usual way for a government to be formed and to conduct its business. Although the English "constitution" is unwritten (that is, it is not a single charter, but rather an evolved product of ancient custom, statute, and authoritative decisions), both the American and English constitutional systems continue to be emulated by many nations in their vision of a "rule of law."

Notes

1. For instance, see Michael Perry, "The Authority of Text, Tradition, and Reason: A Theory of Constitutional Interpretation." in *Authority Revisited: NOMOS XXIX*, eds. J.R. Pennock and J.W. Chapman (New York: New York University Press, 1987), 221-253.

2. See Edwin Meese, "Toward a Jurisprudence of Original Intention," 2 Benchmark 1 (1986); William Rehnquist, "The Notion of a Living Constitution," *Texas Law Review* 54 (1976) 693; and Robert Bork, *Tradition and Morality in Constitutional Law* (Washington D.C.: American Enterprise Institute for Public Policy Research, 1984).

3. *New York Times*, 7 May 1987, 14.

4. The following citation illustrates why the Constitution had to be amended and supplemented. On the presumption that suffrage is not a privilege accruing to federal citizenship, the Supreme Court upheld a statute restricting the right to vote to males only. See *Minor v. Happersett*, 88 U.S. (21 Wall.) 162,22 L.Ed. 627 (1874).

5. See Morton White, *Philosophy, The Federalist, and The Constitution* (New York: Oxford University Press, 1987), 97-99.

6. See Alan S. Rosenbaum "Presidential Accountability," *The Gamut*, No. 22, Fall, 1987.

7. *The Federalist* No. 48, 321-6; also , see Wilfrid E. Rumble, "James Madison and the Value of the Bill of Rights," in *Constitutionalism: NOMOS XX*, eds. J.R. Pennock and J.W. Chapman (New York: New York University Press, 1979), 142-3.

8. 50 U.S.C. Secs. 1541-48.

9. Louis Henkin, *Foreign Affairs and The Constitution* (Mineola, NY: Foundation Press 1972), 50-1.

10. Two distinguished studies which trace the evolution of modern constitutionalism are: Charles H. McIlwain, *Constitutionalism: Ancient and Modern* (Ithaca: Cornell University Press, 1983); and Edwin C. Corwin, *The "Higher Law" Background of American Constitutional Law* (Ithaca: Cornell University Press, 1979).

11. Namely, Carl Friederich. See, Paul Sigmund, "Carl Friederich's Contribution to the Theory of Constitutionalism-Comparative Government," in *Constitutionalism: NOMOS XX*, eds. Pennock and Chapman, 32-40.

12. As a noted legal authority has observed, the Soviet Constitution does not provide for "judicial review" to check the power of the Supreme Soviet. See Louis Henkin, *The Rights of Man Today* (Boulder, CO: Westview Press, 1978), 66-70.

13. For a fuller discussion of these claims, see, Henkin, *The Rights of Man Today*, 31-5.

14. Martin Edelman, *Democratic Theories and The Constitution* (Albany: State University of New York Press, 1984), 35.

PART I

The Idea of Constitutionalism:
Classical Foundations

1

John Locke and American Constitutionalism

Leslie Armour

Armour believes the issue of the nature and degree of Locke's influence upon American constitutionalism in both theory and practice centers on Locke's doctrine of equality of opportunity. Armour's interpretation of Locke's theory and its impact is distinguished from Nozick's "conservative" libertarian view and from Macpherson's "leftist" claim regarding the primacy of the doctrine of property. Further, Armour's critique of the individualism in Locke's theory is especially attractive because it amplifies the weakness he finds in any constitution that minimizes or ignores the claims of the community and so does not prevent the destruction of the natural environment.

LOCKE, HIS CONSTITUTIONALISM AND HIS READERS ON THE LEFT AND ON THE RIGHT

Lockean Constitutionalism

Everyone agrees, I think, that the American constitution—not just the document which is often given that name but the whole body of what might be called American constitutional practice—is pervaded by a Lockean spirit, though Locke was never an unchallenged authority and many others influenced the constitutional draftsmen. Here, I want to explore Locke's central political idea, an idea which I shall call "constitutionalism," and to examine the way in which it takes shape in Locke's philosophy and in the form which Americans have given to the basic framework of their public life.

It is "constitutionalism"—the view that men may safely be left free provided they agree to conduct themselves within the limits of certain rules—which, more than anything else, has animated American political and legal life. And it is the acceptance of this thesis that accounts for the deep attachment many American thinkers and ordinary citizens of otherwise very different political persuasions have for their Constitution.

The requirements for the rules which Locke thought necessary to guarantee a peaceful political life and a tolerable public authority break down into ten distinct clusters. If I read Locke correctly, these rules must (1) place clear limits on the powers of government, (2) provide a legal system with ultimate power to arbitrate disputes, (3) incorporate a principle of majority rule, (4) divide political powers so that the law making and executive powers are not in the same hands, (5) create a measure of equality of opportunity, (6) guarantee the availability of knowledge necessary for the social process to proceed in an orderly fashion, (7) recognize a set of "natural rights" which protect citizens from interference with their justified individual ends, (8) protect the state against ambiguous allegiances on the part of its citizens, (9) protect freedom of religion while recognizing man's ultimate duties to God and to the created universe, and (10)—despite (9)— leave the citizens free to choose their own *ultimate* ends.

I would argue that all of these demands have been significantly met by American constitutional and political practice. Some appear literally in Locke's books and in the document whose two hundredth anniversary we are celebrating. Others are the result of interpretation. Locke does not use the words "equality of opportunity"; he speaks instead of leaving "enough and as good for others."[1] Though it pervades most of Locke's other work, the concern about the availability of knowledge is mainly only implicit in the *Two Treatises of Government* and the *Letter Concerning Toleration*.

Some of these principles are the chief sources of American pride—hardly anyone in American political life would dispute the necessity of a wide dispersion of knowledge if political life is to be successful and tolerable. There has been long national effort to promote it as well as a constitutional struggle, not wholly over, to secure its reasonably equitable availability. Equality of opportunity has become settled doctrine at least within the public discourse of widely admired American political figures of the left, the center, and the moderate right.

Others of Locke's principles have given rise to serious problems and even to occasional injustice. The demand for protection against ambiguous allegiance has been hotly disputed. In recent times the objection to double allegiance has usually been proffered against communists and not against the Catholics whom Locke distrusted; but the issue has always been one to which many Americans are ready to respond and its tolerance is still, I think, an exception made uneasily. The obvious tension between recognizing duties to God and freedom of religion has always troubled many Americans and continues to do so.

Divergent Readings—Left and Right

I shall deal with each of these "constitutional requirements" in turn, but first it is important to notice that, apart from the details of the ten demands for kinds of rules, the position I am advocating differs quite sharply from two current popular readings of Locke—one advanced from the left and one from the right.

From the left—above all in the writings of C. B. Macpherson[2]—it is argued that Locke's constitutionalism is a derivative and not very important aspect of his thought. The real core of his doctrine is a conviction about what Professor Macpherson calls "possessive individualism." The name makes Locke and the Lockeans sound more than a little avaricious but the theory behind it is that Locke's political philosophy centers on his doctrine of property. When Locke says that the "great and chief end of men's uniting into commonwealths . . . is the preservation of their property,"[3] he means that this is the chief end for which political society is organized and he also means to denigrate other ends.

This makes for a simple reading of Locke and provides a "motive" in the light of which all of Locke's other claims can be interpreted. But I shall argue that the discussion of property is originally entered into by Locke in order to illustrate the meaning of the claim that everyone who takes wealth from nature or from the community must abide by the principle that "enough and as good for other"[4] must always be left. He says that no constitutionally justifiable rights are ever rightfully lost in the transition from the state of nature to that of the organized political state ("for no rational creature can be supposed to change his condition with an intention to be worse")[5]. This right to "enough and as good" must continue even though it can no longer literally be a right to occupy land once all the land, or all the good land, has been occupied. Since the original rule is simply a claim about equal opportunity to use the resources of nature, its transformation must result in a generalization of that principle itself. I contend that the "great and chief end" in Locke's view is the end for which men originally "*unite into* commonwealths" and *not* the end for which political society is *maintained.* Indeed Locke describes the ends for which society is maintained as including both personal liberty and a stable community.[6]

From the right—especially in the writings of Robert Nozick[7]—comes the view that Locke's aim is the creation of the "minimal state" which again safeguards property rights and, as much as possible, leaves all other issues to the citizens. This view does not imply that Lockeans promote greed and does not intend to associate them with capitalism considered as an end in itself but simply holds that the whole cluster of natural rights is best protected by restricting the state to this necessary minimum. Against this view is, once again, Locke's insistence on certain sorts of equality, his insistence that God does not intend us to let our neighbors starve, his view that widespread participation in the civil process is a good thing in and of itself, and his view (which has roots in his natural theology) that there are real limits to what we can do with and to nature, with and to ourselves, and what we can inflict upon others. Locke thus sides with modern liberalism in holding that men and women must choose their own ultimate ends, but opposes it in thinking that human choice is limited by a higher authority.

Locke's insistence on the fact that there is a limit imposed on what human beings may do—even if all of them are agreed—distinguishes him from much of the mainstream of traditional *left* liberalism in American thought as much as it distinguishes him from the new conservatism, sometimes called "libertarianism." The idea, that though God has no constitutional role, He is nevertheless to be considered when we ask about the limits of permissible human behavior, associates Locke with a long line of deist, Christian and Jewish reformers from the eighteenth century to the present day (from the Jeffersonians to many contemporary environmentalists)—who have wanted to set limits to the human urge to govern the universe all by themselves. It connects Locke, as well, with the older tradition of paternalistic conservatism that tended to see the most grandiose of human pretensions as the pride which goes before a fall. Locke's admitted interest in property, the priority he gives to freedom, and his natural theology certainly pit him against the Marxist left even if Macpherson's analysis is not sustained. His taste for majority rule pits him against all claims to aristocratic pretension and against many kinds of "elitism" which form the barely hidden agenda of a vocal fraction of the political right. But it remains true that, though neither right nor left in any of their obvious forms can claim the endorsement of Locke, virtually everyone in the mainstream of American political life has been able to draw *some* comfort from him.

THE ROOTS OF LOCKE'S CONSTITUTIONALISM

Locke's constitutionalism has at least six roots—his metaphysics, his epistemology, his belief in natural law, his natural theology, his observations on political life (especially in England) and his understanding of the English history of his time.

If one is to understand the reception of Locke in the United States, one needs to see that though Locke's views of the world, of knowledge, of God and of natural law have had their ups and downs amongst professional philosophers and are perhaps now mainly out of fashion, they can be understood in such a way as to make them (with the exception of Locke's belief that he could *demonstrate* the existence of God) correspond rather closely with what most Americans probably take to be either "common sense" or the natural beliefs of most men and women.

This is not to say that Americans understand these propositions as Locke himself did, nor to suggest that the correct reading of Locke is a simple matter, but only to point out that some version of these Lockean doctrines seems to have had a natural appeal to the American mind. The political experience of most Americans in the eighteenth century was quite close to that of most Englishmen and the American Revolution can be construed, amongst other things, as the simple demand of the colonists for the normal rights of Englishmen. The political experience of the two groups has diverged considerably since then, but American political life, governed more by specific decision and less by tradition than its English counterpart, has continued much more in the Lockean vein. Indeed, one may think of American political life as closely regulated by specific constitutional provisions and constantly involved in attempts to arrive at a precise understanding of the "rules of the game," in contrast to the British tendency to keep the constitution vague and to rely on the fact that the people who really matter have an instinctive grasp of what is and is not acceptable and have no serious need for a precise explication of the rules. Locke belonged to the middle class which hoped to have a turn at making the rules and, therefore, demanded the rules be spelled out.

Metaphysics and Politics

Hobbes, faced with those political events which largely animated Locke—the "Puritan" revolution of 1640 and its aftermath—came to the conclusion that human beings were mere "matter in motion." He also believed that man had, within him, no ultimate natural principle of self-limitation. Beavers, when they have dammed everything in sight, do not then dream of conquering the dry-land world of tigers. But, propelled in constant motion, human beings move on to the "war of all against all." Hobbes admitted not all men were by nature greedy and pushy, but he believed that those who were not would be made insecure by those who were. The only solution possible was a powerful state which could keep the human animal in check.

Locke had a different view: Men are more than "matter in motion." They are thinking things—though that is not their most important character. Their most important character is given by the fact that they have souls. They are also talking animals animated in part, by reason and so they will tend to strike bargains with one another.

As John Yolton reminds us, despite the fact that Locke once entertained the possibility of "thinking matter," Locke was *some* kind of mind-matter dualist.[8] Locke's metaphysics is, however, subtle and, despite the ink which has been spilled over it, not so very well understood.

The first thing to notice is Locke's metaphysics centers on the notion that the ultimate substratum of reality consists of substance. Substances *have* properties and relations, but they are not themselves properties and relations. Thus Smith may be thin, grouchy and a Republican or fat, jolly, and a Democrat. But it is not the thinness of Smith that is grouchy nor the fatness of Smith that is jolly. As a consequence, of course, one cannot say anything about substances as such nor form clear ideas of them in any direct way. For if one could say anything about them, what one said would describe some quality and a clear idea would be that of another quality.

According to Locke, one may, however, characterize substances indirectly by the company they keep. For, after all, substances do have, or manifest, qualities. There are material substances. Matter is the "substance and solidity" of body. "Body" is matter together with its extension[9] and both are rather mysterious. We cannot, he says,[10] really understand how motion is "communicated by [matter]" nor how it holds together or is divided. But there *are* material substances. There are spiritual substances also. Though we do not know if any spiritual substances exist without bodies,[11] we do know that some characteristics (colors, tastes, sounds and smells, which he calls secondary qualities) vary with changes in the observer and from observer to observer while others (size, figure and motion) can be established in a more objective way. Material substances are associated with (but do *not* consist of) primary qualities; spiritual substances *account for* the changes of perception; and secondary qualities arise out of the interaction between them.[12]

Locke admits that just how all this complex activity comes about is difficult to envisage. But though spiritual and material substances are distinct kinds and entertain, as it were, distinct kinds of qualities, they are all substances and substances *not* simply clusters of their qualities. There is no reason why *substances* should not interact even though they have distinct kinds of qualities.

Men and women are neither beasts nor angels. Their material properties give them a footing in this world, but their spiritual properties—which include the capacity to reason—give them a larger outlook. Indeed, as spiritual substances they can entertain ideas of anything of which there can be an idea, including God.

It is, indeed, through their knowledge, including their knowledge of the existence of God, that human beings are able to find for themselves the natural limits to their activities which Hobbes had claimed to be conspicuously lacking. Aristotle had claimed that men are not born with enough knowledge to guide their lives and Hobbes agreed with him. Locke goes further. It is a much emphasized tenet of his philosophy that men have no innate ideas whatsoever and therefore must be taught. The need for teaching is a foundation of the community. Most of all, however, the limits on men's behavior must be imposed through learning.

But Locke's men and women are still rather dangerous—though not so dangerous as Hobbesian creatures would be—if one confronts them in the state of nature. Commentators sometimes wonder why Locke thought it necessary to pass from the wholly unpolitical "state of nature" to the political condition. But the reason is obvious. Men are tamed only through knowledge.

Locke's Theory of Knowledge

Locke's belief that men are trainable and so more tractable than Hobbes thought comes from his metaphysics. Ultimately, his sense of community comes, as we shall see, from his ideas of natural theology and natural law. But the contrasting individualism which creates the tension in his philosophy comes, above all, from his theory of knowledge.

If there are no innate ideas and every man must gain his knowledge from his own experience, then everyone will be different since every experience is different. Furthermore each person will, to some extent, be the prisoner of his own experience, able to understand others only by inference and effort.

There is one exception to the claim that all knowledge comes from experience. Knowledge of the existence of God comes through "demonstration." Natural reason provides it and this piece of knowledge is what ultimately unites men and women into a single unity.

It is worth noticing that most Americans would take Locke's view of knowledge for granted, even if their philosophers might not. Most people believe that the bulk of human knowledge is empirical, that natural science is founded on experience and provides, on the whole, in matters outside religion, the best guide to the facts about life. They would also agree that theological knowledge is different.

Natural Law

The concept of natural law in Locke is rather confusing. It seems obvious that there are three distinct senses of "natural." One relates to Locke's idea of the "state of nature," one to "natural law" in the scholastic tradition in which certain rights arise from man's "nature" as a rational being, and one derives from the notion that the natural condition of man is to be subject to God.

Locke's point about the "state of nature" is not chiefly historical but logical. It concerns the status of a person who has not given his consent to a political organization (either tacitly by choosing to live in an organized society or literally). Such a person has, as his or her own, all the "rights" which we popularly associate with the state—including the right to make, interpret and enforce laws. It is natural that a person alone should have such rights, for there is no one else who could claim them. It is, generally speaking, Locke's thesis that one can claim anything as a right unless someone ("someone" includes God) is able to posit a counterclaim. Thus, I have a right to use the land so long as no one else has put his labor into it, so long as "enough and as good" is left for others, so long as I don't waste it, *and* so long as God's original rights as creator are not violated.

But there are other rights which are not to be understood in this way. My right to express my opinions and to have them tolerated does not depend on anyone else's claims or counterclaims. It depends only on my being a reliable citizen, not given to ambiguous allegiances, and able to exercise reason. These rights stem from our very natures as rational creatures.

Finally, however, some rights—including the right to have left for me "enough and as good"—evidently depend upon the fact that everything, originally, belongs to its creator, God, and that God, like the crown, maintains a residual interest in them. Just as the crown can appropriate land for the public good, so God has a right to demand our cooperation for the public good. One may not ignore or fail to provide for any of His creatures.

Natural Theology

Locke believed that he knew his own existence by intuition, God's by demonstration and that of all other things, if at all, through experience.[13] His own existence he thought could not really be doubted, for it is involved in all his thoughts.

God is clearly a special case. First of all an infinite, omnipotent, omniscient and perfect being cannot enter directly into experience. To be omniscient is to know everything—infinitely many things. And no finite set of information has any evidential bearing on claims about infinity. Yet Locke believed that if God did not exist, we could not have any knowledge and so the existence of God must be logically prior to the occurrence of knowledge.

> A man finds himself in *Perception* and *Knowledge*. . . . and we are certain now, that there is not only some Being, but some knowing intelligent Being in the World.[14]

What kind of argument is this? Locke is at pains in the *Essay,* and elsewhere, to claim that knowledge would be impossible but for God. There are various interpretations, but one that makes sense and shows some of the force of Locke's argument is that of Thomas Hill Green, amongst the most influential, along with Mill and Spencer, of Victorian political philosophers.

Green reminds us that Locke held a causal theory of perception. Perceptions are to be trusted because we have reason to think they have causes and these causes have a regular pattern. The best knowledge (of the world) depends on these causal assertions. These perceptual events cannot simply be regarded as events whose significance is exhausted by their description. For, as Hume was later to argue, nothing would follow from their existence by way of inference to any other events. In that case we could not have any scientific knowledge since scientific knowledge consists of finding law-like patterns in series of events. He says:

> If events were merely events, feelings that happen to me now and the next moment are over, no "law of causation" and therefore no knowledge would be possible. If the knowledge founded on this law [of causation] actually exists, then the [argument] . . . rightly understood . . . is valid . . . [15]

Locke, in any case, has to believe in laws of nature. If such events "merely happen," then they are not evidence for anything beyond themselves. There are two other alternatives. One is that they are logically necessary—that is, that we can discover in them logical laws of inference in terms of which they could not have failed to happen. But this is not the case. You can deny contingent facts, *whatever* they are, without committing a *logical* mistake.

How, then, can the events which are our sensations be evidence for the existence of anything and how can they enter into scientific laws? The only option left is to ask if they exist as a matter of policy—if "some Being" (as Locke calls God) created them so as to manifest an intelligible policy. If so, knowledge would be possible.

But in point of fact knowledge exists and so knowledge must be possible. Which is to say that empirical science works and gives us better knowledge than anything else. If it is possible only because God exists, then God exists.

If, as Green thinks, this is what Locke had in mind, it would still seem plausible to many people. And once God's existence has been demonstrated, much of Locke's political program follows. If anyone has a claim on property if he creates it, then God as creator of everything has a prior claim on the objects of nature, and men are restricted in their use of it to purposes not inconsistent with those of the diety. For Locke, that means sharing and the creation of an adequate community.

Locke, the English Revolution, and English Political Practice

The events of the 1640's led the self-confessed "timid Mr. Hobbes" to fear that man was reverting to his natural, violent, animal state and that civilization was in peril. It seems to have convinced Locke, on the contrary, that men love to organize, make deals with one another, reward their friends and punish their enemies, and generally to connive with one another for personal advantage.

None of this especially alarmed Locke, who himself enjoyed, at times, the rewards of patronage and, at other times, suffered the penalties of exile and relative poverty. He was annoyed by, but did not despair at, the complex of dubious motives which caused Oxford to deny him a medical degree which he much wanted. He enjoyed the spectacle of other men conniving for advantage, and himself managed to emerge, in the end, on the right side of poverty though hardly, as is sometimes alleged, rich. (Locke's income rarely exceeded 300 pounds a year. At the end of his life when he lived with the Masham family at Oates, he paid one pound a week in rent and a shilling extra for his horse—even then hardly a rich man's rent.)

The causes of the "English Revolution" are still much debated. The arrogance of Charles I, the desire of the shopkeeping and trading classes to take power from the aristocracy, the Catholic issue, the insecure position of the lower orders of the "gentry" at a time when their patrons seemed to be losing power, the loose arrangements between the executive and the legislature, and even the question of Sunday football, all played their parts. Subsequent maneuverings led to the Restoration and the Act of Settlement through which William and Mary became the British monarchs, reigning finally at the behest of parliament.

Locke drew the obvious moral from all this—human beings are capable of using political organization for almost any end. But it is obvious that it is profitable to belong to a large, well-organized group. What we need, therefore, are rules which will see to it that the advantages of political organization remain while its disadvantages are minimized. Locke did not suppose that the human boxing match could be turned into a tea party. But he hoped that the fighters would accept reasonable and prudent rules and agree to wear helmets.

If one compares him to a thinker like Karl Marx, the difference is that where Marx hoped to identify the causes of human conflict through the study of history and economics and then to eliminate them, Locke accepted conflict as simply part of the human process. He hoped to regulate it and, indeed, to make it humane and even profitable. Locke did not need to have his own theory of the causes of the English Revolution, for he hoped to add a new factor that would make such conflicts unlikely in the future, whatever their causes. The new factor was a working constitution.

Americans have tended to follow him. The American Civil War, for instance, has been ascribed to economic tensions between North and South, to the ideological differences between northern liberals and southern slaveholders, to the political ineptness of various figures both North and South, and it has been alleged that a variety of other factors (even British meddling) played a part. The elimination of poverty and racism, along with the industrialization of the South have, of course, been common American political goals, but these have almost always been advocated for their own sakes not because they will eliminate conflicts in the future. The avoidance of such confrontations has generally been entrusted to constitutional measures. Like Locke, most Americans have suspected that the elimination of one conflict tends only to make room for another. But conflicts can be controlled. The actual response to the Civil War was a cluster of constitutional amendments.

The failure of Marxism to take hold in the United States as it did in Europe is, to a large degree, simply explicable by the fact that the American, Lockean, outlook renders it irrelevant. If capitalists quarrel with their workers the problem is not to explain how the system makes it inevitable but to create labor legislation which will allow the rival parties to come to terms.

THE RULES OF THE CONSTITUTION

Locke's hope, then, was to find a set of rules which would enable human beings to live together and to determine the ultimate ends of their own lives while, at the same time, respecting the prior rights of God. Locke speaks of life, liberty and estates where the American Declaration of Independence speaks of life, liberty and the pursuit of happiness as the basic rights which a constitution ought to promote. The distinction has a point. Happiness, presumably, is an end which one might or might not choose. It is not that Locke is against happiness but rather that a constitution is not supposed to dictate or even perhaps suggest ultimate ends. No doubt, too, the authors of the Declaration were chary of the notion of property. The Lockean notion of property had radical implications as we shall see. Moreover, the facts that slaves were both persons and property was to form the foundation of the most devastating of all American political disputes.

The Limits of Government

Human beings are individual moral agents and therefore are entitled to their own ends. Each of us is a distinct center of knowledge whose actions, therefore, stem from a unique source. Additionally—and central to the *Second Treatise*—states morally derive their powers from the desire of the governed to form a state. No one, Locke says, would agree to form a state if it diminished the range of his effective rights. It may negate some rights (that is, the right to make one's own legal decisions), but it must result in an overall net gain. Hence, in the U.S. Constitution all rights and powers which are not assigned to the federal government are reserved to the states or to the people.

The Need for a Legal System

One of the great disadvantages of the state of nature is it provides no settled legal system. In the state of nature no one can tell which of his acts will be protected and which condemned and no one can act with confidence. Locke makes much of the idea of a *settled* system.[16]

This demand corresponds to the provisions for judicial review contained in the U.S. Constitution. I cannot find anything in Locke which specifically suggests the desirability of the very great (and final) powers which have ultimately come, through judicial action itself, to reside in the United States Supreme Court and, of course, there was originally much dispute about the extent of those powers vis-à-vis those of Congress. Nevertheless, if one has a formal written constitution someone must give it meaning and whoever does will have the final power. Within the structure envisaged by Locke and the authors of the U.S. Constitution, it is difficult to think of any alternative to the supreme court.

Majority Rule

Locke is clear that everyone who willingly enters into or who comes to accept a political society as preferable to the state of nature must accept the principle of majority rule.[17] This seems to follow from the fact that human beings are distinct individuals and none has natural precedence over the others, together with the fact that the ordinary disputatiousness of human beings makes absolute consensus unworkable as a plan for maintaining a stable society.

Locke sees two difficulties. One is that, though we must accept majority rule in matters in which legitimate decisions are to be made, even a majority may not interfere with the basic rights of anyone. The other difficulty is that majorities are not stable. While there tend to be long-term trends in political views, there are also violent short-term swings, and a society which responded to all of them might well be unworkable. Hence Locke's notion of majority rule is tempered.

The earliest amendments to the U.S. Constitution entrenched various basic rights and have prevented legislative interference with them. The Constitution can be changed, but only by an elaborate process which involves the states as well as the central government. The drafters and those who have since influenced constitutional practice provided various versions of what might be called "filtered" majority rule. Senators were once indirectly elected through the state legislatures and, though they are now directly elected, majority rule is tempered by the fact that each state has two senators, whether its population is large or small. Each state, as well, has a minimum number of congressmen. Though presidents are not directly elected, the electoral college system is not now regarded as a serious check on direct majority rule.

The Separation of Powers

The American theory of the separation of powers is often ascribed to other sources, but Locke devotes Chapter XII of the *Second Treatise* to it. His main argument is that human frailty may be too much tempted by the possibility of manipulating the laws to private advantage if the legislative and the executive powers are combined. The legislators are better employed watching over the executive—able to call a halt to what the executive does but not able to become the executive themselves.

He notices that besides the executive, legislative and judicial powers there is a fourth which he calls "federative."[18] The federative power is the power to enter into arrangements with other states and Locke remarks that it includes matters of war and peace. It is his natural instinct to call it "federative," for he supposed all mankind would naturally form a system of profitable liaisons if only it could. But he inclines toward putting this power in the hands of the executive.

In the American Constitution, though the power to make treaties and declare wars is withheld from the executive, the president has always had very wide powers and Locke's practical instinct seems to have been correct, whatever its theoretical weaknesses. Treaties must be ratified by the senate but, in reality, presidents can make all manner of deals under other names and can enter into events which look like wars without declaring them to be wars. Congress is left with little choice but to agree or leave the troops abroad without supplies.

Equality of Opportunity

Locke first states equality of opportunity as the principle that one may appropriate land by putting one's work into it so long as there is "enough and as good left in common for others,"[19] so long as one does not take more from nature than one can use before it spoils,[20] and so long as one provides adequately for those in need of charity.[21] Later, he envisages a situation in which all the land has been occupied and suggests that such total occupation is permissible.[22] Whether he thought this later state was beneficial to everyone or not is a matter of some dispute.[23]

As a result of Locke's account of the changes brought about by the ultimate occupancy of all the good land, C.B. Macpherson has claimed that the right to "enough and as good" is extinguished when political society[24] becomes effective. Robert Nozick seems to regard Locke's original pronouncement as of relatively little importance. This enables Nozick to justify modern capitalism, and Macpherson to maintain that Locke would also have endorsed a world in which nothing was necessarily left for the poor and the oppressed.

Yet Locke says that basic natural rights are never extinguished if the result is a net loss in overall natural rights and adds that "the power of society . . . can *never* be supposed to extend farther than the *common good*" [italics mine].[25] This surely implies that some form of "enough and as good" must continue.

The mystery disappears, I contend, if one thinks of the original claim as the claim to equality of opportunity. Everyone must have the same *opportunity* to work the land and so must have "enough and as good." What happens when all the land is occupied is simply that—as Locke actually says—the new society provides new opportunities. What is required, then, is that opportunity remain open.

In a developed society with a market economy, opportunity mainly stems from education and from the availability of capital. Nothing in the U.S. Constitution guarantees either, but in practice the states have all undertaken programs of public education and I think it is now unimaginable that any state would abandon these programs, though there were dreams of turning southern schools over to private foundations after *Brown et al. v Board of Education*.[26]

Though a small state college in eastern Montana gives many of the same degrees as Harvard, it takes great faith in the powers of its faculty to believe that they can overcome the disparity in resources well enough to provide the same opportunity. Yet the records show that graduates of even the most underfinanced universities succeed at all levels of human activity and, for those who proceed to graduate education, opportunities are much more nearly equal.

Inheritance acts against equality of opportunity both in terms of money and in terms of race and ethnic background, but equality amongst racial and ethnic groups now has enormous constitutional support. It is unlikely that a mass movement against it would be more than marginally successful in overturning American constitutional practice, though some losses have been sustained in recent years.

The notion that society should provide equal access to capital for prospective entrepreneurs has no constitutional support. Yet it has some legislative support—federal loans for education, federal guarantees of mortgage money, federal insurance schemes to enable bank depositors to withstand risks are examples. The prospect of constitutional economic rights—the right to access to capital in particular—appears dim. Yet it may well be that the next "leftward turn" in American politics will bring about a beginning. I think Locke would be pleased by such a thing.

Knowledge and Society

Because human beings are knowing and reasoning creatures, Locke supposes that the Hobbesian picture of the constant war within the human species—controlled only by a powerful state—is too bleak. We learn and can be educated. And this learning covers a very wide range of behaviors. Human beings can even unlearn as well as learn almost any behavior, for, according to Locke, they do not have any innate ideas. This being so, human societies will be structured largely by the kind of knowledge available within them and human government will be successful only if it is informed. Opportunity will depend on what one knows.

Lockeans have generally taken all this as axiomatic. Significantly, one of the first actions taken by the Continental Congress in 1774 was to secure borrowing privileges from the Library Company of Philadelphia. The congressional draftsmen did the same thing in 1787, and in 1789 they actually met on the premises of the New York Society Library. In 1800, the Library of Congress was created and it occupies a curious place in American constitutional practice.

It is the creature of Congress itself and its budget is not part of the executive budgetary process but subject to direct appropriation by Congress. It shares this privilege only with the various housekeeping matters that concern Congress. Yet the Librarian of Congress is appointed by the President. The library is in other ways special, too. Two recent historians have come to the conclusion that congress has never attempted to censor it. Librarians have never been discouraged from buying particular books nor been urged by congress to remove any books.[27] They also claim that the library has never been used for patronage appointments. "Never" is a strong word for an institution with a long and complex history but, even if later historians find some exceptions, the fact remains that the library is almost as independent as if it were the separate cognitive branch of government.

Research is to a large extent funded by the federal government so that universities—public and private alike— have become involved to a significant extent with all levels of government, and questions about their freedoms and public responsibilities have become questions of constitutional practice. In a country governed on Lockean premises it is almost inevitable that this should happen even though such matters as academic freedom are dealt with in only a general way through the constitutional amendments which specify particular human rights.

Natural and Constitutional Rights

One might have supposed that the most decisive and pervasive of Locke's influences would be found in the "Bill of Rights," the first ten amendments to the United States Constitution. In fact, those amendments are a mixed bag and derive in large part from the traditions of the English common law, from constitutional landmarks of the distant past, particularly Magna Carta, and from the recent experiences of the American legislators of that time. Locke's influence was diffuse and indirect.

The Declaration of Independence places "life, liberty, and the pursuit of happiness" out of the reach of the crown. But the original constitutional draftsmen did not follow this up. The first Congress, spurred on by George Mason of Virginia, made good this omission.

One can relate some of the original amendments to Locke's theories, and one can make a rough classification of them which suggests what was going on in the minds of the amendment writers. The first and fifth amendments contain the basic provisions for freedom of religion, speech, press, association and property, though the fifth also includes a set of rights intended to protect citizens from abuses of the law (forced self-incrimination, double-jeopardy). These rights can be related to Locke's original "natural" rights (the rights which one has as a person independently of any political association) or to his claims about the necessary conditions of political association.

They are either "natural" in the sense that it requires no political body to grant them to us—we have them merely from the fact that we are human beings; or they are "natural" in the quite different sense that no thoughtful person who took Locke's view of the importance of liberty would give up his state of nature except to a political organization which could guarantee his or her rights. The "natural" rights are nonetheless properly "constitutional" because they represent part of the framework of limitations which is necessitated by the mere fact that political organizations exist.

Since slaves turned out to be both properties and persons, the liberties granted to the individual clashed with protection to property. We know what Locke would have decided, for he said of slavery, "It is hardly to be conceived that an Englishman, much less a gentleman should plead for it seriously."[28] This is one of the reasons for not believing that the property-obsessed Locke described by Macpherson is the real Locke. But the American courts decided differently, and Locke's own view did not prevail until after the Civil War.

A second set of rights has to do not with substantive matters but with legal procedures. These include trial by jury, speedy trial and rules about witnesses. Chiefly they codify the underlying logic of the English legal system, though parts of the American Fifth Amendment—the protection against self-incrimination especially—were quite radical. In other legal systems derived from the English common law, the Canadian system for instance, protection against self-incrimination is limited and witnesses must answer incriminating questions though they may prevent the *use* of such information in subsequent prosecutions.

Locke might have been astonished to find the "right to bear arms" and the limitations on quartering troops in a constitution. But the right to bear arms had to do with the demand for citizen armies and was a protection against the use of mercenaries of the sort employed by George III, while the forced quartering of troops in private houses testified to an all-too-recent experience of revolutionary necessities.

Ambiguous Allegiances

To the continuing astonishment of his liberal admirers, Locke refused to tolerate atheists and men with ambiguous allegiances. Though he will tolerate "pagans" and "idolators," the *Letter Concerning Toleration* specifically rules out legal tolerance of those "who deny the being of God." Locke believed that Catholics tied to the political pretensions of the Pope and Moslems tied to the Caliphate were beyond the pale. Locke's text clearly refers to the excommunication of Henry VIII which was followed by a papal declaration to the effect that the faithful need not recognize him as king[29]. The objection to Catholics had nothing to do with religion. Locke believed that men could be trusted to behave reasonably and be granted very great liberties, but these liberties could not be tolerated in the face of divided allegiances. The ordinary citizen will behave patriotically because he prefers orderly society to the anarchy of the state of nature. But if he has to choose between two orderly societies to which he is committed, no one can predict how he will behave. Catholics, he thought, owed allegiance both to their own country and to the papal states.

This may seem quite absurd to us, but we should remember that the political pretensions of Popes have declined in modern times to almost nothing and that, in Locke's time, the disputes over the English and Scottish crowns had much to do with the rivalry between Catholics and Protestants. In England there were still Catholics who marched to a different drummer, and they were still capable of stirring up a good deal of trouble.

Nor was Locke alone in his feelings. Throughout American history there have been movements against "double allegiance." At most times dual citizenship has been denied to Americans and, in our own time, there have been demands (and some legislation) which aim at limiting the activities of communists or, in general, those who preach the violent overthrow of the government.[30]

The creation of the state of Israel is largely responsible for the softening of this attitude. In the context of the political and religious situation which arose out of the Second World War and the Holocaust, it seemed natural enough that a measure of dual allegiance should be felt by many Americans.

Atheists and Believers

Locke's case against atheists arises because his view of the claims of the community as opposed to those of the individual are clearly related to his natural theology. If one did not believe in God but was otherwise a Lockean, one might see no bar to the endless pursuit of self-interest apart from the need to guarantee a kind of minimal state which would protect his property. Indeed, Nozick's conservative Lockeanism is precisely what one would get if one ignored natural theology in building one's political theory.

Despite this, Locke warns against jumping to the conclusion that all those who disagree with one in religion are atheists. It is not clear where he would have drawn the line. I think he would have tolerated anyone whose religious beliefs provided a genuine framework for collective responsibility and who accepted that the world did not belong exclusively to human beings, but he did not want to say this clearly.[31]

An ambiguity and public belief has run through American life. The separation of church and state is supposed to be absolute, though it says "In God We Trust" on the currency and legislative bodies even have chaplains. While most people in countries such as England, France, and Sweden have given up overt religious practice, atheists are very often regarded with deep suspicion in the United States. Americans are, after all, Lockeans at heart even though they mostly realize their constitutional principles will not allow them to write that distrust into law.

The Ends of Life

Locke's ultimate view is that everyone must be free to choose the ends to which he will devote his life. The state cannot legitimately force anyone into a religion but it also cannot force anyone into a permanent occupation or force him to labor on behalf of others, except in the case of those convicted of an offense.

CONSTITUTIONALISM AS A TESTABLE
POLITICAL THEORY

Locke's Aims

For all its a priori notions about natural law and natural rights and its speculative accounts of the "state of nature," there is no doubt that Locke meant to propose an account of the circumstances under which human beings could live lives which they found acceptable and which provided such contentment as the conditions of life permit. He does not try to deduce the whole theory from some simple basic premise, though he has some basic axioms such as the premise that, all things being equal, one is entitled to own the things one has put one's work into. Rather, he seeks to take account of the complexities of political experience and then to suggest a mode of organization that will render it tolerable.

He has, as I suggested, more than one sense of "natural" in his theories of natural rights and natural law, and it would not have worried him very much to be told this. Basic to his theory is the notion that political life must be acceptable to the participants. Acceptability, however, has two dimensions for Locke. Superficially, a political system is acceptable if, indeed, people do not want to change it. But it must also be *morally acceptable*—that is, in conformity with one's moral convictions about one's duties to God and to other human beings and with a life which is morally permissible. One must take account both of the whole community and of the importance of the natural environment provided by the physical universe. Locke's God represents the claims of the totality.

Putting Locke to the Test

If one takes this view, one way of testing Locke's theory is to find out whether, if put into practice, it does lead to an acceptable life in one or both senses of that term. This is part of the fascination of discovering that the American Constitution and its surrounding practices do, to so large an extent, carry out the Lockean program. It has been in operation for two hundred years and very few Americans of any political persuasion would change the basic structure. In one of the senses of "acceptable" it certainly meets the test.

As to morality, it has begun to appear in recent years that American technology and culture are involved in a clash with nature in which nature may be losing. Yet it was Locke who insisted that no man had a right to "spoil" or "destroy" nature.[32] Still, the weakness of Lockean constitutionalism has been its difficulty in meeting the demands of the community interest, much less what one might call the universal interest. A theory which holds there are not really common ends for human beings, but only individual ends which the community must regulate to some degree in the interest of fair play, cannot cope with the possibility that there are communal ends which are not anyone's. But there *is* the problem of the community and its value as such, and there are legitimate interests, such as those of future generations, and legitimate obligations, such as our obligations to past generations, which are not necessarily tied to the interests of anyone now alive.

Locke tried to solve this problem by introducing the interests of another individual, God, as a counterbalancing device. But American constitutional practice has surely established that one cannot give God constitutional rights without interfering with the natural rights of the citizens, and so God has had to be content with an acknowledgment on the currency. Most Americans have never seriously asked themselves the question, what could replace God as a legitimate interest and be constitutionally acceptable? The answer which is shaping up is "nature." Respect for nature, if once we could define it, might have a chance at that role and, indeed, the "rights" of the natural environment may be coming into recognition. But this idea, too, surely has its roots in Locke.

There have been many attempts to duplicate the American Constitution and most of them have not worked. There are a good many military dictatorships whose constitutions, on paper, look like that of the United States. The piece of paper has no power. If what I have been arguing is true, namely that the whole body of constitutional practices is what counts and what Lockean theory demands, then there is a clear answer to this. The test is only valid if the whole body of practices or nearly the whole body is *available.*

Finally, however, there is a value decision to be made. The driving force behind the American Constitution has been the doctrine of equality of opportunity, and Locke himself, I contend, would have understood and insisted upon this.

Americans, indeed, have great sympathy for those who lack opportunity. By contrast, they have relatively little sympathy for those who do not take advantage of their opportunities, though, like Locke again, they keep reminding themselves of their charitable duties. Charity apart, lack of ambition, aversion to hard work, and failure to assess one's position realistically are all defects which Americans do not regard as being like blindness, lameness, or even mental illness.

Lockean constitutionalism does provide maximal opportunity combined with minimal interference by the community in the affairs of the individual. The alternative view is that it would be worth having more interference in order to act more compassionately toward the losers. No *empirical* test will settle this question.

Notes

1. John Locke, *Second Treatise*, section 27. There are many editions of Locke's *Two Treatises of Government*, first published in 1690 with changes in 1694 and 1698. They are divided into short, numbered sections and it is to these that the numbers in the subsequent footnotes refer. All references are to the corrected edition of 1764 which incorporated all the changes that Locke had made during his lifetime.

2. C.B. Macpherson, *The Theory of Possessive Individualism, Hobbes to Locke* (Oxford: The University Press, 1962).

3. Locke, *Second Treatise*, 124.

4. Locke, *Second Treatise*, 27.

5. Locke, *Second Treatise*, 131.

6. Locke, *Second Treatise*, 131.

7. Robert Nozick, *Anarchy, State and Utopia* (New York: Basic Books, 1974).

8. John Yolton, *Thinking Matter* (Minneapolis: University of Minnesota Press, 1983).

9. John Locke, *An Essay Concerning Human Understanding*, bk. III, ed. Peter H. Nidditch (Oxford: The Clarendon Press, 1975), chap. x, section 15. (I shall henceforth use the form Locke, *Essay*, III, x, 15 to indicate the book, chapter and section.) The Nidditch edition is the only reliable one. The original title read "Humane Understanding," but it meant "human" and not what "humane" means today.

10. Locke, *Essay*, II, xxiii, 26.

11. Locke, *Essay*, II, xxii, 30, 31.

12. Locke, *Essay*, IV, iii, 13.

13. Locke, *Essay*, IV, x.

14. Locke, *Essay*, IV, x, 5.

15. John Locke, *Works*, vol. I, ed. R. L. Nettleship, (London: Longmans, Green 1890) 128-129. For another analysis of the thrust of Locke's argument see Leslie Armour "La rationalite des questions sur Dieu: actualité d'un argument de Locke" in Thomas DeKoninck and Lucien Morin, eds., *Urgence de la philosophie* (Québec: Presses de l'Université Laval, 1986) 540-553. Locke's argument is related to problems raised by Ralph Cudworth and John Norris, but to raise questions about the details of its interpretation here would involve a major and unjustified digression.

16. Locke, *Second Treatise*, 125-127.

17. Locke, *Second Treatise*, 132 and 133.

18. Locke, *Second Treatise*, 145.

19. Locke, *Second Treatise*, 27.

20. Locke, *Second Treatise*, 31. ("Nothing was made by God for man to spoil or destroy.")

21. John Locke, *First Treatise*, 42. "We know that God hath not left one man so to the mercy of another that he may starve him if he please." It would be interesting to know what Robert Nozick makes of this. See also the passage in Locke's *First Letter on Toleration, Works*, vol. VI, (London: Thomas Tegg, W. Sharpe, et al., 1823) 10, where the magistrates are enjoined to take care of the "civil interests," which include the *health* of the citizens. If this is not a call for the "welfare state," it certainly at the very least enjoins the civil power to establish a framework under which *all* citizens *will* prosper.

22. Locke, *Second Treatise,* 35-37.

23. See the extended discussions in James Tully, *A Discourse on Property: John Locke and His Adversaries* (Cambridge: The University Press, 1980); and Neal Wood, *John Locke and Agrarian Capitalism* (Berkeley: The University of California Press, 1984).

24. Locke, *Second Treatise,* 35-37.

25. Locke, *Second Treatise,* 131.

26. *Brown et al. v. Board of Education,* 347 U.S. 483 (1945).

27. Goodrum, Charles A., and Helen W. Dalrymple, *The Library of Congress* (Boulder, CO: Westview Press, 1982).

28. Locke, *First Treatise,* 1.

29. There are many details of Locke's lifelong concern with the "Catholic Problem" in Maurice Cranston, *John Locke* (London: Oxford University Press, 1957).

30. The legal history of this issue shows a variety of opinions. *Dennis v. United States,* 341 U.S. 494 (1951) upheld the "Smith Act" which outlawed advocacy of the forcible overthrow of the United States government. The next year, in *Alder v. Board of Education,* 342 U.S. 485 (1952), the court took the same view. But in *Keyishian v. Board of Regents of the State University of New York,* 385 U.S. 589 (1967), the court took a quite different view. The times had changed, though four judges of the nine dissented.

31. Locke's discussion of atheists is chiefly located in the *First Letter on Toleration, Works* vol. VI, (London: Thomas Tegg, W. Sharpe, et al., 1823) 46-47; and in the *Third, op. cit.,* 414-416. Locke seems to have suspected Hobbes, despite the latter's claims, to be an atheist. Maurice Cranston, (*John Locke,* 62) gives evidence, however, of some "borrowing"from Hobbes by Locke but notes that Locke eventually claimed never to have read Hobbes carefully. Locke is generally similarly discreet about Spinoza, despite evidence of his efforts to find out about him and despite Locke's association with the Arminian Remonstrant theologian Philip van Limborch. (Spinoza was closely associated with the Remonstrants). Both Hobbes and Spinoza figured in Locke's library.

32. Locke, *Second Treatise,* 31.

2

Hume and the Constitution

Wade Robison

It is a traditional American aspiration that effective political authority and a citizen's political obligation be balanced against governmental accountability and respect for a citizen's basic freedoms. Robison explains that this "aspiration," as it influenced the framers of the Constitution, represented a major conceptual shift from earlier times in thinking about these matters. It is Robison's thesis that David Hume's (1711–1776) empiricist approach to political philosophy and, in particular, his critique of social contract theory, facilitated the conceptual revolution, culminating in the framers' notion of the ideal relationship which should arise between government and citizen. Also, Robison's examination of the political writings of Hume's precursors, Filmer and Locke, is a special feature of his essay; it provides a fuller conceptual basis for a deeper appreciation of Hume's contribution to American constitutionalism.

In his essay, "Whether the British Government Inclines More to Absolute Monarchy, or to a Republic," David Hume remarks on "a sudden and sensible change in the opinions of men within these last fifty years." He says,

> The mere name of *king* commands little respect; and to talk of a king as GOD's viceregent on earth, or to give him any of those magnificent titles which formerly dazzled mankind, would but excite laughter in every one.[1]

Hume penned these lines a little more than a half century after the "Glorious Revolution of 1688," and he says that "Had men been in the same disposition at the *revolution,* as they are at present, monarchy would have run a great risque of being entirely lost in this island."[2] In just a few generations, a view that, some might say, was the cause of the civil war in Great Britain had become an object of ridicule.

Hume is noting one of those odd occurrences in history. A proposition seems to one generation so obvious that it cannot be called into question. Those who try arguing for it are straining at the task since there are, to them, no other premises more obvious, from which this natural truth, as it were, could be derived. This natural truth then becomes so ludicrous to a succeeding generation that one need only mention it to "excite laughter."

Such odd occurrences mark great conceptual shifts. It was a natural fact for Aristotle that objects made of earth and water seek the center of the earth. What this fact means in Aristotelian physics is that no scientific explanation is needed or possible for why such objects fall to earth or why objects on the earth remain unmoving, any more than any explanation is needed in Newtonian physics for why an object continues moving uniformly in a straight line. We duplicate the naturalness of Aristotle's fact when—in response to a child's asking, "Why is that rock lying there?"—we say, "That's where it is supposed to be: it's a rock." It took a radical shift in our conceptual framework to make uniform motion in a straight line "natural" motion, requiring that all other motion be accounted for.[3] For someone to explain why a rock is on the ground by citing its natural tendency to seek the center of the earth would provoke in us a superior smile, despite our own unthinking use of a similar sort of explanation, especially in response to persistent children.

The anatomy and pathology of such conceptual revolutions are complicated and a subject of much dispute. One of their hallmarks is the difficulty, even the incapacity, of those on one side of a revolution to comprehend those on the other. The difficulty works in both directions. It is almost as difficult for us to understand how *natural* Aristotle's theory of physics was as it would be for Aristotle to comprehend modern physics. But such conceptual revolutions lie at the heart of our understanding of the world, and comprehending such revolutions lies at the heart of our understanding our history in this world. At the heart of the American revolution, I argue, is a conceptual revolution of monumental proportions, a Copernican revolution of political thought, greatly facilitated by David Hume.[4] That revolution is complex and not easily captured in a single line any more than Darwin's theory, for instance, can be captured in the line "humans are animals." But a story Archibald Cox tells catches its sense.

Of the Supreme Court's decision that President Nixon would have to hand over his tapes to Congress, Cox said that

... it really would have been disastrous if the decision had gone the other way, because what was at stake was whether our President has the qualities of a king or is under the law. Which reminds me: When I was introduced here one day to a visiting Swedish scholar, he attacked me with great excitement. "The chief of state can't be subject to the orders of the court," he said. "It can't be. It's unthinkable." I said, "Well, I'm sorry. It can't be *un*thinkable, because Americans have been thinking it for quite a while." And I really believe they have been *thinking* it from the beginning, but there had never been a hundred-percent test of it. Watergate finally buttoned it down.[5]

The contrast between what is thinkable and what is not, I suggest, captures Hume's contrast between what excites laughter and what does not. Sometime in the years between "the Glorious Revolution" and Hume's remark, the "natural fact" that the king was God's viceregent on earth became ludicrous. What was unthinkable—that he was *not* God's viceregent—became, in turn, a natural fact. At the heart of the American revolution is a wrenching away from an old way of thinking about political authority to a new conception, one which made the old way laughable.[6]

Revolutions are always messy affairs, conceptual revolutions are no different, and revolutions in political thought are especially contentious affairs. It is helpful to pick out of the concepts being changed that of political obligation. Before the "Glorious Revolution," the relation of political obligation was thought to be a natural one, some born to rule and others born to obey. However inaccurate the following tripartite division may be when mapped onto the actual maelstrom of ideas, the revolution may be thought of as consisting of three movements:

(1) Political obligation is a social artifact, not a natural relation.
(2) That social artifact is not created but develops naturally, its development sanctioning it.
(3) The form of the political society determines, causally, the form of political obligation and all political relations.

We owe (1) primarily to John Locke, though, I would want to argue, Hume's particular development of it was more congenial and thus, to use Cox's expression, buttoned it down. But for (2) and (3) we are primarily indebted to Hume.

We must start, however, with the enemy, the "natural fact" that kings are viceregents of God. We must come to comprehend how someone could find this a natural fact if we are to understand the full force of the conceptual revolution that occurred. For that, we need to examine the views of Sir Robert Filmer.

FILMER'S PATRIARCHA

Sir Robert Filmer is best known as John Locke's target, some would say strawman, in the first of the *Two Treatises of Government.* Here was a man who, in trying to justify King James I being an absolute monarch, concluded that since King James I was the eldest living direct male descendent of Adam, he was not only King of England and Scotland but also King of the World. One has to admire his panache, but "strawman" seems too mild.

Yet Filmer fastened on the basic problem of political theory: how can one justify political obligation? As a citizen, one can be obligated to do, or to re-frain from doing, what one would not, without that obligation, do or refrain from doing. One can, be obligated as a soldier to attempt to kill.

What kind of relationship could be so powerful that it could require one, as a citizen, to do what one would otherwise never do, as an autonomous moral agent? It would not be enough, Filmer thought, for that relation to result from someone gaining power over one by force of arms. Then one would be obliged, but not obligated to obey. The relation must produce a *moral* obligation, for only a moral obligation could override what one would otherwise never do as an autonomous moral agent.

Yet, if the relation between a citizen and a sovereign were a result of their *agreeing* that the one should rule and the other obey, the citizen could not be obligated any more than if the sovereign took command by force. Their rela-tion would be like that between, say friends who agree to sail together with one the captain and the other mate. If the first orders the second to do something he or she would never do except for the order—like jumping overboard in the middle of the ocean because "I'm the captain and I say so"—the agreement would just dissolve. Presumably Filmer thought, no agreement between persons could obligate someone to do what they other-wise, as moral agents, would never do, because they could simply change the relationship.[7]

Cox's Swedish scholar had the difficulty of conceiving how a sovereign, a king let us say, could be subject to the law he created. To conceive of a king being obligated to obey the law, we would have to conceive of a king issuing a command and not being able to exempt himself or rescind the command. But since he issued the command, he could change it—simply issue it again with a "but not me"—unless he were obligated not to. But if he were obligated not to, someone else he would be king. Who else could possibly obligate him?

I have been trying to reproduce the sense of obviousness that Filmer's reasoning had for him—a sense that should, if successful, make the last question rhetorical. In response, one should think, "Obviously, nothing could obligate a king to obey his own commands." Filmer thus says "in a monarchy the king must of necessity be above the laws" and "that which giveth the very being to a king is the power to give laws" so that he is "free of his own authority."[8] The judgment underlying this conception of a sovereign being immune from law is that what humans create can be changed by them.

A sovereign thus cannot be obligated by himself because being obligated presupposes, for Filmer, that one is not at liberty not to do what one is obligated to do. But if the law that creates the obligation is created by the sovereign, the sovereign is at liberty to change the law—and so is not obligated.

The same conception underlies Filmer's answer to the question, what kind of relation between the sovereign and the citizen is so powerful as to obligate citizens to obey? If the citizens are equal parties in creating the relation, they can change it—by, for instance, simply refusing to obey in a particular case. What is needed is some relation between the parties—between the sovereign and the subject—that is immune from being changed by the citizens, that, not being created by them, cannot be changed by them. Only then, Filmer believes, would citizens be morally obligated to obey the sovereign. So what is needed is some natural relation between the sovereign and citizens, and not just any natural relation will do, but only one in which one person is (naturally) obligated to obey the other person.

Filmer finds that relation in the one a father bears to his children. The relation is a natural one: neither the father nor the children can alter the children being children of that father. Each child has a natural father, each natural father has a natural child, and as long as the father and child live the relationship between them remains.

The relationship also may seem to be one in which children are obligated, not just obliged. We can sense something of what Filmer wants us to see when we remind ourselves of how we might respond, or have responded, when we see, or have seen, a father disciplining a child in a way that makes us uncomfortable—berating the child in public, for instance. One wants to interfere, but is reluctant. "After all," we may think, "I have no right to discipline the child—or the father—and who has a better right than the child's own father?"

Filmer thinks that what he calls the natural right a father has over a child is absolute, and he cites the example, among others, of Cassius putting his son "to death by throwing him down from the Tarpeian Rock, the magistrates and people standing threat amazed and not daring to resist his fatherly authority."[9] He also thinks a father has the right to lead his children into battle and to negotiate peace. He says, "these acts of judging in capital crimes [that is, having the right to kill a child], of making war, and concluding peace, are the chiefest marks of 'sovereignty' that are found in any monarch."[10] Thus, he concludes, a sovereign has the same relation to his subjects as a father to his children and so citizens are, as children, obligated to obey their sovereign.

Filmer's conception of political obligation is woefully lacking in internal coherence and explanatory power. He has at least the following problems:

(1) If being a parent matters to a father's having authority over his children, then, as Locke noted, what about the mother? Her relationship to their children is at least as natural as the father's.[11] But if being a father matters, why does sex make such a difference?

(2) We may feel that we may not interfere when a father chastises his child, the child must obey. But when the child grows into a full-fledged citizen, no longer dependent upon the father, the picture of a father castigating his now grown child no longer has the power on us that Filmer wants. Filmer needs to explain how an otherwise autonomous moral agent, an adult, can be morally obligated to obey another adult. One wants to ask why an adult should be obligated to obey his or her father merely because the person demanding obedience is his or her father?

(3) Filmer wants to explain how the citizens of England and Scotland are politically obligated to King James I, but King James I is not in any literal sense the father of his country and the argument Filmer uses requires that citizens obey *as* children, not just *like* children. Far from implying that King James I has political authority, Filmer's argument implies there are as many kings as fathers.

These three objections are enough to undermine Filmer's appeal to the father-child relation to explain political obligation, but Filmer has a very different sort of argument that, though it has problems of its own, does answer these objections. Filmer claims, on Biblical grounds, that God gave Adam dominion over the earth and everything on it, including Eve and all their progeny. For God to give Adam dominion means, for Filmer, that God gave Adam the right to rule. God's gift, combined with the British law of primogeniture (which Filmer assumes), means that the eldest living direct male descendant of Adam has that same right of dominion.

It is the *right* of dominion that is at issue here, not just the power to rule. Given Filmer's concern that might does not make right, and his consequent desire to ground political obligation on moral principle, it is clear that he is assuming that God has the moral right to command human beings. God's gift of dominion to Adam therefore is the gift of command. Adam became, as it were, God's viceregent on earth and his eldest living direct male descendent, by this line of argument, still is God's viceregent.

Far from implying that there are as many kings as fathers, this argument implies that there is only one legitimate ruler in the world. Filmer has an elaborate genealogical derivation showing, as luck would have it, the line of descent from Adam to King James I. Nothing before Noah matters, of course, Noah being, as it were, a new Adam. Still, the derivation beyond

Noah is a bit tricky, and one might doubt its accuracy. But there is no doubt, if Filmer is correct, that he has more than proved what he set out to prove: King James I is certainly King of England and Scotland if he is King of the World. This is some evidence, obviously, that the argument has gone astray somewhere.

This new argument also explains why being a *male* parent matters. Adam was given right of dominion over Eve as well as their progeny and everything on the earth. The argument also explains how a man need not actually be a father, and need not even be an adult, to have the right to rule. A child might be the eldest living direct male descendent of Adam and have the right to rule his father's brothers, for example, and everyone else, no matter what their age.

The primary difficulty with this new argument from God's gift to Adam is that there is not only one king of the world. We cannot trace the line of descent from Adam—even supposing there is one. In any case, Filmer needs a theory to explain why the French are obligated to obey the French king as well as why the English and Scotch are obligated to obey King James I.

Filmer appeals to the father-child relation to take advantage of our natural temptation to think a father has a right to tell a child what to do. He appeals to God's gift to Adam to provide backing for "the natural law of a father"[12] and to explain, among other things, how a king can rule those he has not fathered. The one appeal implies that there is but one king, the other that every father is a king. Filmer cannot have it both ways, and his theory of political obligation is thus incoherent.

Despite their competing conclusions, Filmer's two arguments share a crucial assumption. Whether each of us owes political obligation to Adam's eldest living direct male descendent or to our own father, we have no choice in the matter. One neither chooses to have a father nor chooses to be the eldest living direct male descendent of Adam. Filmer is assuming that one cannot impose obligations upon oneself.

One implication of this strong sense of obligation is that one is born obligated. One comes into the world already owing political allegiance—to one's father or to Adam's heir. Filmer thus begins *Patriarcha* by attacking the view that "mankind is naturally endowed and born with freedom from all subjection,"[13] and Locke thus begins the *First Treatise* by attacking Filmer's claim that *"no Man is Born free."*[14]

LOCKE ON POLITICAL OBLIGATION

Locke begins his *Second Treatise* by saying *"Adam* had not either by natural Right of Fatherhood, or by positive Donation from God, any such Authority over his Children, or Dominion over the World as is pretended."[15] So, he continues, unless "all Government in the World is the product only of Force and Violence," we must find "another Original of Political Power."[16]

The "Power of a *Magistrate* over a Subject," he continues, is not the same as that of "a *Father* over his Children" nor is it that of "a *Master* over his Servant, a *Husband* over his Wife, [or] a *Lord* over his Slave."[17] The relation is the sort created in a contract between equals, and, against the background of his attack on Filmer, we can see how fundamental is his commitment to the following premises:

(1) All persons are born free, and
(2) Persons can obligate themselves by contracting.

The main features of Locke's story of the "rise of Government"[18] can be quickly sketched. Since all are born free, they would be, were they without government, in a state of nature in which each is in "a *State of perfect Freedom* to order their Actions, and dispose of their Possessions, and Persons as they think fit, . . . without asking leave, or depending upon the Will of any other Man."[19] Disputes would arise, and, without government, each person would be judge in his or her own case. Life in such a state would be greatly inconvenient, Locke says, and the remedy is *"Civil Government."*[20]

One achieves the remedy by a double contract.[21] Persons first contract into what Locke calls the commonwealth, each person agreeing to abide by the principle of majority rule[22] and, "to preserve his Property, that is, his Life, Liberty and Estate,"[23] each giving up his or her right to decide in his or her own case. From the commonwealth, people contract into a political society, with a particular form of government.[24] Any form of government except absolute monarchy is an acceptable choice.[25] Absolute monarchy is ruled out because it does not guarantee to the contractors the preservation of their life, liberty, and estates and because the contractors cannot give up more than they began with, and they did not begin with such absolute power.[26]

Whatever the complications and objections to this conception of the "rise of Government," it constitutes a fundamental shift in how we are to conceive of political authority. This conceptual shift has two parts.

The first arises from Locke's claim that we are all born free, for the implication is that, as he puts it, we are "equal one amongst another without Subordination or Subjection."[27] With no *natural* subordination, no natural relation can be the basis of political obligation. We cannot appeal to the relation between a father and a child or to any other supposed natural relation between persons.

In particular, we cannot appeal to any natural aristocracy. One could object to Filmer's political theory and still think that political authority had a natural basis if one thought that some had a natural right to rule because they were, for example, especially wise politically. All arguments denying women the suffrage because, it is claimed, their minds are suited only to the politics of the kitchen depend upon this general presumption of a natural right, in this case of men, to rule. But in arguing that no one is born subjugated, Locke implies that no one has the natural right to rule. That some are born to rule—by their intelligence, or political acumen, or strength of purpose—is simply false.

The political equivalent of this claim is the denial to Congress in our Constitution of the power to grant titles of nobility (Article I, Section 9) and the explicit restriction of features like age and citizenship to the qualifications for office any citizen can meet.[28] Madison thus asks, regarding election to the House,

> Who are to be the objects of popular choice? Every citizen whose merit may recommend him to the esteem and confidence of his country. No qualification of wealth, or birth, of religious faith, or of civil profession, is permitted to fetter the judgment or disappoint the inclination of the people.[29]

The second part of the conceptual shift is that people, as equals, can create obligations by contracting with each other. Each party to the contract is subject to the conditions of the contract. Contracts are well entrenched in legal systems and there is no doubt at all that, *within* a legal system, one can obligate oneself by contracting with another person. The mechanism for enforcing such a contract is already in existence. The question is whether one can create the conditions for such a system by contract. Can one create the conditions for enforcing a contract by contract? This is the political equivalent of a computer booting itself.

Locke thinks that one can and that people have contracted from states of nature into political societies.[30] One immediate consequence of such contracts is that, despite the Swedish scholar Cox admonished, a Lockean sovereign is subject to law. For the contract is between all the parties of the commonwealth, including whomever is chosen to be sovereign—whether it be a single person, a group of persons, or the entire people—and all parties to a contract are equally subject to the contract. One contractor may be obligated to do one thing, and another, another, but in contracting into a commonwealth, all are contracting to protect their lives, liberty, and estates. Any failure of the sovereign to protect those interests breaks the promise and dissolves the political society.[31] As Hume says, in describing Locke's view, "this promise is always understood to be conditional, and imposes on him no obligation, unless he meet with justice and protection from his sovereign."[32]

Something momentous has occurred. What before was thought unthinkable, that the king be subject to the law, is now patently obvious. No one can become a king unless the citizens of a commonwealth agree to a form of government with a king and unless the king contracts as well, and so, far from being "of necessity . . . above the laws," as Filmer claims, a king is of necessity bound by the terms of the contract. A case for the divine right of kings can no longer rest on the inconceivability of a king's being subject to the law. Locke has made thinkable what before was unthinkable.

Locke's theory does have its difficulties, however, as Hume pointed out. Besides the difficulty of using a contract to create the conditions for enforcing contracts, Locke's theory faces a number of other problems.

(1) Locke bases a citizen's obligation to obey the sovereign on an obligation to abide by the terms of a contract, or promise, but, Hume asks, "Why are we bound to observe our promise?" We have no "original instinct of nature" to observe promises or to obey authority, he says, but are rather inclined "to indulge ourselves in unlimited freedom, or to seek dominion over others." Both these original inclinations are checked by our "subsequent . . . observation" of "the general interests or necessities of society."[33] Our obligation to obey the sovereign to fulfil our contracts rest on the same basis—our understanding of their necessity for order and our own security—and the one obligation cannot be justified by appealing to the other.[34] So, Locke's suggestion is theoretically dissatisfying.

(2) Once established, whether by contract or not, title of sovereignty in a monarchy, at least, passes to successive generations. Yet passage of title, Hume notes, is like "property in durable objects": we know that since it is passed from hand to hand, it must "have been founded on fraud and injustice."[35] Title becomes corrupted, but without diminishing the people's obligation. Their obligation thus cannot be founded on an original contract.

(3) If we look at the rise of governments, we find that citizens' obligations were not determined by contract. In fact, "were one to choose a period of time," Hume notes, "when the people's consent was the least regarded in public transactions, it would be precisely on the establishment of a new government."[36] The people distrust a new government, and "pay obedience more from fear and necessity, than from any idea of allegiance or of moral obligation." Only time creates obedience: "They imagine not, that their consent gives their prince a title: But they willingly consent, because they think, that, from long possession, he has acquired a title, independent of their choice or inclination."[37] So, Locke's theory cannot account for clear cases of political obligation.

Filmer's political world is to us a fairyland. We would take it as a sign of insanity for someone to claim the right to rule us all because he was the eldest living direct male descendant of Adam. But Locke's political world is as much a fairyland.[38] He means to describe how political authority is actually justified—in this world, our world—but if one were to come from another planet and, noticing the obedience of some to others, were to ask for the reason, it would never enter as a possibility that citizens had *contracted* into obedience. As Hume remarks,

> It is strange, that an act of the mind, which every individual is supposed to have formed, and after he came to the use of reason too, otherwise it could have no authority; that this act, I say, should be so much unknown to all of them, that, over the face of the whole earth, there scarcely remain any traces or memory of it.[39]

If this visitor were to ask people if they were obligated, he would discover that, at least in settled states, they think they are. If he were to ask why, they would not say they contracted into it and they would be astonished were he to suggest that as a possibility. If this visitor traced back lines of descent, he would discover that citizens say they are obligated to kings whose lineage is decidedly unclear and, could he travel back to see how governments actually arise, he would see nothing remotely suggesting a contract. Only if the visitor were committed to a system of philosophy that required a contract would he ever think to look for it.[40]

Locke is surely right that no natural relation can explain political obligation. But Hume thinks Locke's explanation bears little relation to the world we inhabit. Locke's empiricism has deserted him in political theory, and Hume is insistent that a theory of political authority must explain how we humans actually, in fact, are obligated. The conceptual difficulty he faces is that, like Locke, he thinks government a human artifact—"an invention of men"[41]—and yet thinks our obligation to obey does not rest on a contract.

HUME'S THEORY OF POLITICAL OBLIGATION

Locke's argument has four main stages: (1) the state of nature where people are inconvenienced and want security; (2) the initial unanimous contracting into a commonwealth where citizens agree to abide by majority rule; (3) the second contract to form a government of some sort; and (4) political society in which security is achieved or from which, if it is not, citizens revert to the commonwealth to try again. Hume cuts out the middle stages. Locke is correct that in a state of nature people can be inconvenienced and that they form a government for "mutual advantage and security."[42] But he is wrong, Hume claims, in thinking that contractual stages are needed between people being inconvenienced and forming a political society. History tells us otherwise.

People live in societies without government, Hume says, and that state "is one of the most natural states of men."[43] One may say they *agree* to do this, and mean that they contract, but they are simply living together. The idea of a "compact or agreement ... for general submission ... [is] an idea far beyond the comprehension of savages."[44]

People remain in that natural state until they are threatened by other societies or by internal dispute because, after many generations, they have come to have surplus wealth.[45] With the threat, they are led, by their need, to have some one among them with authority. The citizens do not *contract* with each other, but, Hume says:

> Each exertion of authority in the chieftain must have been particular, and called forth by the present exigencies of the case: The sensible utility, resulting from his interposition, made these exertions become daily more frequent; and their frequency gradually produced an habitual, and, if you please to call it so, a voluntary, and therefore precarious, acquiescence in the people.[46]

Though we humans have no natural inclination to submit to authority and, indeed, are naturally inclined to pursue our own short-term interests, the immediate threats to our security, and thus to even our short-term interests, force us to take the longer view and to see that it is to our advantage to submit.

Government thus arises naturally out of a natural state. It is a human invention that need not exist, but will, in the common run of events, evolve. People do come to live together without government; they do come to be threatened by outsiders or by internal disputes; a leader does come to the force; and, over time, people do come to feel obligated to obey the leader.

So the rise of government has a natural history—"*a* history" because we can generalize from what we know has happened in societies and "a *natural* history" because humans respond the same way everywhere to a problem caused by human nature: given that cause, the effect will follow. Government is a human artifact, but it rests on self-interest, not on any contract.

The general outline of Hume's solution to the conceptual problem left by Locke is straightforward. How can government be a human invention if there is no original contract, and how can citizens be obligated if they did not promise to obey? They can be obligated to obey if it is in their interest to do so, and they can come to see that it is in their interest to do so, that is, to create a government despite having natural inclinations towards short-term interests directly adverse to government.

We may see the fundamental difference between Locke's theory and Hume's by tracing out what the theories require when revolution is justified. For both, humans enter society to create a government for "mutual advantage and security," and for both there is a presumption against revolution since disorder will result with no guarantee of a better government.[47] But when our security is threatened, and revolution justified, Locke's theory requires that one note that a promise was made and has been broken. To quote Hume's summary:

> when instead of protection and security, they meet with tyranny and oppression, they are free'd from their promises, . . . and return to that state of liberty, which preceded the institution of government.[48]

Locke's theory requires the following sequence: the government is not providing security they promised to, the promise is broken so that I am no longer bound to keep my promise, therefore I am no longer bound to obey. Hume's theory cuts out the middleman: the government is not providing security, therefore I am no longer bound to obey. One need not, on Hume's theory, try to answer the factual questions of whether a promise was broken and an obligation consequently removed. One can appeal immediately to the loss of security.

Hume's theory has its own problems—not the least of which is the difficulty of explaining how citizens can come to be obligated by coming to have a habit of obedience.[49] But his firm insistence that theory be grounded in experience, and thus in history, and his rejection of any original contract—on both theoretical and historical grounds—has two important consequences.

First, the conceptual revolution we find in Locke was marred by his replacing Filmer's fiction of the divine right of kings with a new fiction of an original contract (two, in fact). Locke made it thinkable, indeed necessary, that a sovereign be subject to the law, but at the heavy cost of an undiscoverable—an empirically unobservable—contract and, were we to pursue the worry that a contract can create its own conditions for enforcement, at the risk of ultimate incoherence. That such a contract underlies government is implausible even if coherent. Hume's modification jettisoned the epicycles while saving the phenomena. He could account for what was important in Locke's theory—why we are entitled to rebel when the government does not provide us with security, for example—without committing himself to anything other than what anyone could observe.

Hume thus made the conceptual revolution in political thought intellectually respectable—rather in the way that Galileo's discovery of the moons of Jupiter made respectable the belief that the earth moves.[50] Copernicus made the idea fashionable, but anyone who accepted the view was faced with the difficult task of explaining, among other things, how the earth can move around the sun at the great speed it must (over 19 miles per second) without losing the moon which must somehow not only keep up with it, but go around it. The discovery of Jupiter's moons meant that a planet could revolve around the sun with satellites of its own—though one may not know how it could do that. Similarly, Locke's theory created an enormous problem for its proponents: where are we to find these supposed contracts that underlie our political obligations? By cutting out the contracts, while saving everything else of value, Hume allowed proponents of Locke's conclusions an intellectually respectable position. They might say, we may not know quite how we become obligated over time, but we are, and the basis of our obligation is our long-term self-interest in security. So Hume's surgery on Locke's theory had the effect of allowing anyone who might have been hesitant about a supposed original contract to accept the essential features of the revolution in political thought. As Archibald Cox would put it, it buttoned the theory down.

Second, and of more immediate importance, Hume's theory focuses concern on the very practical issue of how one can provide for mutual advantage and security. In Locke's theory, one focuses on the contracts—their features, their differences, how a contract can be implicit, conditions of enforcement, and so on. All these issues are generated wholly by the theory that we contract into a political society. One sees their attenuated versions in John Rawls's theory of justice—the concern about whether it is plausible to assume lack of envy, for instance. One's intellectual energy is expended in matters which seem to have little, if anything, to do with the practical problems of government.[51]

On Hume's theory, one's energy is focused directly on the issue of how to create a government which is to everyone's mutual advantage and security. That is a very practical concern, and, among other things, it forces one to recognize certain fundamental truths about human beings. The most important is that we "prefer the present to the remote."[52] So, though we recognize the need for a government, we also are always prone to undermine it to gain a present advantage. The solution, Hume suggests, is to take advantage of our human weakness. We should:

> render the observance of justice the immediate interest of some particular persons, and its violation their more remote. These persons, then, are not only induc'd to observe those rules in their own conduct, but also to constrain others to a like regularity, and inforce the dictates of equity thro' the whole society.[53]

Our practical problem then becomes that of figuring out how to arrange matters so that it is in the immediate interest of some to observe justice, and that problem is really a compound one: how are we to arrange matters so that some persons are in fact in authority to execute the laws and settle disputes, and how are we to protect ourselves from the weakness they share with us of preferring the present advantage to the more remote?

One need not have read deeply into the debates in the Constitutional Convention or in the *Federalist Papers* and various papers of the anti-federalists to see that this compound problem was the main problem.[54] The primary focus of concern is in the set of practical issues about how to arrange a government in such a way as to make it effective in providing security[55] and yet protect the governed from the governors.

THAT POLITICS MAY BE REDUCED TO A SCIENCE

Hume's theory of political obligation makes the focal issue of government a problem in design theory: how does one design a structure that is to the mutual advantage and security of citizens while not risking their liberty to those responsible for their security? This question presupposes, if not the truth of Locke's claim that all men are born free, at least that freedom is a value we should try to preserve in any government we create. That is a presupposition Hume shared with the Founding Fathers.

But there are two additional presuppositions: different designs for government are possible, and the particular design one chooses makes a difference. Having self-consciously modelled his philosophy of human nature on the Newtonian successes, Hume notes the implication that human artifacts can be the subject of the same scientific method. Politics, in short, is a science.

This claim runs counter to the view that, as Alexander Pope puts it:

> For forms of government lets fools contest,
> Whate'er is best administer'd is best.[56]

For Hume is claiming that the form of a government *does* make a difference. One piece of evidence for this view is that at one time in Poland the nobility had their own independent fiefs and acted in common only when each saw it to their own advantage to do so while the Venetian nobility had no source of wealth except what they gained as merchants in a wealthy and powerful city. They thus had a personal interest in advancing the interests of all.

Clearly the forms of the Polish and Venetian governments differ. In the one case there is a confederation, as it were, of independent princes, and, in the other, a joining together of dependent nobles for their mutual advantage. And, Hume points out, the results differ as well. Change the causes and the effects change. "A nobility," he says:

> who possess their power in common, will preserve peace and order, both among themselves, and their subjects; and no member can have authority enough to controul the laws for a moment. The nobles will preserve their authority over the people, but without any grievous tyranny, or any breach of private property; because such a tyrannical government promotes not the interests of the whole body, ... [57]

Form thus makes a difference, Hume is claiming, to some very fundamental features of our political life. Had we lived at the times in question, and could we have chosen where to live, we would have more liberty—and more security from invasion of our liberty—were we to choose Venice rather than Poland.

But what forms produce what effects? The question is a question for an experimental political science. Create different forms, vary the features, note the different effects. Such experimentation is not possible, but we humans have created different forms of government and we can thus "do" science by looking to history. We can examine various governments that actually existed—from the Greek city states to contemporary countries—and tease out the various effects of the different forms, isolating, as best we can from the complex features of any government, those characteristics that make a difference to what we most value.

Such an enterprise can be carried out without regard to any presuppositions about what is worth maintaining. The charting of effects can occur without valuing one effect more than any other. A Machiavelli would profit from such a study as well as a Locke. But since Hume accepted that freedom is a value that any government ought to foster, he was concerned to develop the theoretical implications of his theory vis-à-vis liberty. Two examples will suffice, I hope, to make clear his influence and the nature of his influence.

First, one problem facing those in favor of republican government is that such republics seemingly must be small because of the need for its citizens to gather together to vote, but that historically, in small republics, factions soon arose which denied minorities their liberty and tore the republic apart. That historical fact, combined with the vast extent of the thirteen states and the provisions for new states, made the future of a republican form of government for the United States look bleak. Hume recognized the general problem size presented, but pointed out that:

> Though it is more difficult to form a republican government in an extensive country than in a city; there is more facility, when once it is formed, of preserving it steady and uniform, without tumult and faction.
>
> ... however the people may be separated or divided into small parties, either in their votes or elections; their near habitation in a city will always make the force of popular tides and currents very sensible.[58]

The larger the size, in other words, the less the likelihood of factions being created which will upset the public order. One cannot find a clearer statement of the conclusion of Madison's argument in *The Federalist Papers*, Number 10. It has been argued, with good reason, that Madison drew his argument directly from Hume.[59]

Second, not only did Hume provide the founding fathers with specific arguments but, I suggest, his concern about securing liberty and his appeal to fundamental principles of human nature led him to adopt a *form* of argument that one finds repeated again and again at the Convention and in arguments for fundamental provisions of the Constitution. It is an argument which has as its aim the prevention of an abuse of power and as its premises a splitting of interests in such a way that, as Hume put it, it "renders the observance of justice the immediate interest of some particular persons, and its violation their more remote."[60]

An illustration will make the point clearer. The Convention met in Philadelphia, and the delegates had within easy view the state of the state of Pennsylvania. It had a single assembly, and it was pointed to as one example of the danger of popular assemblies assembling all governmental power.[61] In his essay "Of the Independency of Parliament," Hume considers just this problem in regard to Parliament. Since Parliament has the power of the purse, and the executive power requires, as he puts it, "an immense expense," what is to prevent Parliament from taking "from the crown all those powers, one after another; by making every grant conditional, and choosing their time so well, that their refusal of supply should only distress the government, . . . "?[62]

Hume's response is an ingenious one, a check of a unique sort. He says that "the interest of the body is here constrained by that of the individuals, and that the house of commons stretches not its power, because such an usurpation would be contrary to the interest of the majority of its members." Why? The crown has "offices at its disposal," and the self-interest of the individual members of the commons checks the power of the commons as a whole.[63]

We see here the same sort of argument that one finds again and again in both the Convention and in *The Federalist Papers,* for example. There is a careful marking out of interests and a structural arrangement that makes the interests compete. Madison thus raises a concern in regard to population being the basis for representation that states may be inclined to exaggerate the number of their citizens to gain greater representation. But, he points out, their population is also used as the basis for taxation.

> Were their share of representation alone to be governed by this rule they would have an interest in exaggerating their inhabitants. Were the rule to decide their share of taxation alone, a contrary temptation would prevail. By extending the rule to both objects, the States will have opposite interests, which will controul and ballance each other; and produce the requisite impartiality.[64]

HUME'S ACHIEVEMENTS

It is a familiar story that Madison spent time before the Convention reading up on various forms of government, perusing books sent to him by Jefferson,[65] and there was considerable recent experimentation in forms of government to study. Besides the Federal Government itself, as constituted by the Articles of Confederation,[66] those in the Convention had the examples of the thirteen former colonies—all of which had to create constitutions after the Declaration of Independence and many of which went through multiple constitutions trying to find the right mix.[67]

Nothing would be more appropriate, given Hume's theory, than that the founding fathers should look at such examples. From such living instances of government one could infer what effects would be produced by various features like, for example, a bicameral legislature. Given the aims they had of securing their liberty, they would be expected to pick and choose from among those various features a mixture that would produce the effects they desired.

One ought always to be chary to claim historical causal connections, and connections between ideas are themselves cause for even more caution. One may be able to trace specific lines of connection—as in Madison's use of Hume's argument about the extended republic—but even then one cannot be sure the same argument was not independently conceived. When one is making a general claim about the intellectual climate, about what historically allowed people to think a certain sort of way, to see a certain sort of problem or set of problems as fundamental, one has even more reason for skepticism.

Nonetheless, I think we will fail to understand the nature of the American political revolution if we do not see it as part of a conceptual revolution, a fundamental change in the very way we conceived of government. As Jefferson wrote in 1816, "The introduction of this new principle of representative democracy has rendered useless almost everything written before on the structure of government."[68]

Hume's achievement can be best understood in terms of what I call "conceptual space." Conceptual revolutions make conceptual space where none existed before. They make it possible to conceive something new. James Hutton's theory that geological change occurs gradually over long periods of time made conceptual space for Darwin's claim that the evolution of species occurs gradually.[69] Before Hutton, geological history was one of catastrophes—the flood, volcanic explosions, earthquakes. Without Hutton, or his successor to the view, Charles Lyell,[70] Darwin would have had to create that conceptual space himself and would be known as the theoretician of uniformitarianism. As it was, he could appropriate the concept to exploit in a new context. Locke's theory creates space for a new concept—the nature of the contractual conditions that underlie political obligation—and, because absolute monarchy is not a contractual choice, reconfigures an old concept on the nature of the government. Locke spent his intellectual capital primarily on the first concept. Hume's attack on the concept pushed it out of center stage[71] and so brought into the foreground the issue of how one creates security.

Hume is like an architect who, upon seeing a newly created building with a massive central pillar, realizes that, despite appearances, the pillar is structurally unnecessary: the edifice would stand if the pillar were removed, and appear more beautiful because one's focus would be directed to its more important structural features.

Hume was a conceptual revolutionary: he jumped aboard an ongoing conceptual revolution, removed what appeared to be its main concept, saved its implications, and focused concern on the solvable problem of designing a government. And that is the primary focus of the Founding Fathers: how does one create a government that provides security and secures our liberty?

Notes

1. David Hume, *Essays: Moral, Political, and Literary,* ed. Eugene F. Miller (Indianapolis: Liberty Classics, 1985), 51. Hereafter cited as *Essays.*

2. *Ibid.*

3. I mean here by "natural motion" no more than that. In Newtonian physics, for example, uniform motion in a straight line does not require any theoretical explanation but is, instead, the paradigm of motion, so that any deviation from *it* requires explanation. Saying that a motion is "natural" does not mean that such motion occurs in nature.

4. "What do we mean by the Revolution? The war? That was no part of the Revolution; it was only an effect and consequence of it. The Revolution was in the minds of the people, and this was effected, from 1760 to 1775, in the course of fifteen years before a drop of blood was shed at Lexington. The records of thirteen legislatures, the pamphlets, newspapers in all the colonies, ought to be consulted during that period to ascertain the steps by which the public opinion was enlightened and informed concerning the authority of Parliament over the colonies" (John Adams to Jefferson, 1815, quoted by Bernard Bailyn, *The Ideological Origins of the American Revolution,* [Cambridge, MA: Belknap Press, 1982] 1).

5. *The New Yorker,* 20 January 1975, 27–28.

6. One will simply fail to understand the history of the American political revolution, I am arguing, if one fails to understand the revolution in ideas. I am presupposing, therefore, a view about the nature of history—and thus, presumptuously, of how one ought to write history— even though, by not attempting to write history, I am saving myself the embarrassment of not living up to my own ideals.

7. I am presuming that this would be the form of Filmer's argument because I otherwise cannot make sense of what he says about political obligation, but the text of *Patriarcha* is bare of any self-conscious talk of such matters.

8. Sir Robert Filmer, "*Patriarcha,*" in John Locke, *Two Treatises of Government,* ed. Thomas I. Cook (New York: Hafner Press, 1947), 290. Hereafter cited as *Patriarcha.*

9. Filmer, *Patriarcha,* 266.

10. Filmer, *Patriarcha,* 255.

11. John Locke, *Two Treatises of Government,* ed. Peter Laslett (Cambridge: University Press, 1963), see esp. bk. II, sec. 52-53. Hereafter cited as *Two Treatises.*

12. Filmer, *Patriarcha,* 288.

13. Filmer, *Patriarcha,* 251.

14. Locke, *Two Treatises,* bk. I, sec. 2.

15. Locke, *Two Treatises,* bk. II, sec. 1.

16. *Ibid.*

17. Locke, *Two Treatises,* bk. II, sec. 2.

18. Locke, *Two Treatises,* bk. II, sec. 1.

19. Locke, *Two Treatises,* bk. II, sec. 4.

20. Locke, *Two Treatises,* bk. II, sec. 13.

21. The reasons for a double contract lie within the depth grammar of contract theory. For John Rawls, the double contract at least guarantees that consideration of justice cannot be trumped by any other considerations, practical or moral, for principles of justice are more deeply embedded than any other principles. See John Rawls, *Theory of Justice* (Cambridge: Harvard University Press, 1971) sec. 31. For Locke, the double contract guarantees among other things, that if there is a revolution, one reverts not to a state of nature, but to a commonwealth where one can, presumably, readily choose a new government—as the British did in the "Glorious Revolution."

22. Rawls, *Theory of Justice,* sec. 96, but see sec. 99.

23. Rawls, *Theory of Justice,* sec. 87.

24. Rawls, *Theory of Justice,* sec. 133.

25. If the contractors chose a direct democracy, they would be recreating the conditions of the Commonwealth and that would be unreasonable (though not irrational) because it would provide them with nothing to fall back on if the majority denied minority rights.

26. Rawls, *Theory of Justice,* sec. 135.

27. Rawls, *Theory of Justice,* sec. 4.

28. The one restriction on election that every citizen cannot meet is the requirement that the President be "a natural born Citizen, or a Citizen of the United States, at the time of the Adoption of this Constitution" (Article II, Section 1).

29. James Madison, Federalist Paper Number 57, in *The Federalist Papers,* ed. Gary Wills (New York: Bantam Books, 1982) 290.

30. I will not argue the point here that Locke is committed to making an historical claim about original contracts. I would argue on textual grounds that he is (see, for example, Locke, Two Treatises, bk. II, sec. 14-15). I would argue as well that he is committed to a general principle that one justifies something by appealing to its origins. His empiricist principle is not that ideas be derivable, but are in fact derived from experience. This same mode of thought, I would argue, affects his political theory. But the point is moot for what is at issue here.

31. The citizens would then revert to the Commonwealth to form a new political society.

32. Hume, *Essays,* 469.

33. Hume, *Essays,* 480-81.

34. My reconstruction of Hume's argument depends upon the assumption I think Hume is making that Locke must be talking not about the sort of contracts we meet in the law, which can be enforced by an already existing legal system, but about

a *Ding-an-sich* of a contract, one logically prior to any social system. Otherwise Hume could not be assuming that for Locke contracts are justified by the necessity for such a system.

35. Hume, *Essays*, 482. Hume would not accept Nozick's theory of justice. No string of transactions would produce a just outcome because fraud would enter in. Only if one had a powerful theory of what Nozick calls justice by rectification could Nozick's theory have a chance in what Hume takes to be the real world.

36. Hume, *Essays*, 474.

37. Hume, *Essays*, 475.

38. See in this regard David Hume's remark that when examining claims about, for example, "the two eternities, before and after the present state of things; into the creation and formation of the universe;" and so on, " we are like foreigners in a strange country to whom everything must seem suspicious, ... " See David Hume, *Dialogues Concerning Natural Religion,* ed. Nelson Pike (Indianapolis: Bobbs-Merrill Co., 1970), 12. Similarly, when one enters into Locke's theory about an original contract, I see Hume as claiming that it is like entering into a strange country, one with no clear connection to our own.

39. Hume, *Essays*, 470.

40. Hume thus says about an initial contract that "no one, whose judgment has not been led astray by too strict adherence to a system of philosophy, has ever yet dreamt of ascribing it to that origin." See David Hume, *A Treatise of Human Nature,* ed. Selby-Bigge (Oxford: Clarendon Press, 1960) 542—hereafter cited as *Treatise*.

41. Hume, *Treatise*, 542.

42. Hume, *Treatise*, 563.

43. Hume, *Treatise*, 541.

44. Hume, *Essays*, 468.

45. Hume does not, to my mind, come down clearly on these two sources of the rise of government, the second, about increased wealth, being mentioned in passing and the two being in one case tied together (Hume, *Treatise*, 540). But they share a single important feature: in each case insecurity exists.

46. Hume, *Essays*, 468–69.

47. See Hume, *Treatise*, 553-54 and Locke, *Two Treatises*, Book II, Sections 223ff.

48. Hume, *Treatise*, 550.

49. Note H. L. A. Hart's attack on John Austin's view that citizens have an obligation to obey the law because they come habitually to obey the sovereign. See H. L. A. Hart, *The Concept of Law* (Oxford: Clarendon Press, 1961) 55ff. One might object to Hume that he is assuming that citizens are obligated. One way to protect Locke's theory would be to argue that without a contract they could not be obligated— despite the appearance that they are. Hume's response sounds odd initially. What he says is that because people *say* they are obligated they *are* obligated. Thus he says that "there is a moral obligation to submit to government, because every one thinks so" (Hume, *Treatise*, 547). But he remarks that "the opinions of men, in this case, carry with them a peculiar authority, and are, in a great measure, infallible" (Hume, *Treatise*, 46). Judgments that one is obligated may thus be like judgments about what we say—just as native speakers are the best, and only, authority about whether they are obligated. If they say they are, they are. Of course, such sayings must presumably themselves have a certain character. They must express such a deep and generally

unspoken sense of commitment that a person in the street when asked whether he or she is obligated would be surprised at the question, why would anyone ask a question when the answer is so obvious? See, on this point, Ruth Benedict, *The Chrysanthemum and the Sword* (Boston: Houghton Mifflin, 1946) 16–17.

50. See Wade Robison, "Galileo on the Moons of Jupiter." *Annals of Science*, 31, no. 2 (1974): 165-69.

51. I do not mean to belittle such concerns, but to mark out a difference between such theoretical activities and practical ones. I do not mean to deny that theoretical activities have practical consequences: Locke's theory certainly changed the face of politics. But Hume's theory forces one to come to grips immediately with the practical problem of designing a government that provides security.

52. Hume, *Treatise*, 537.

53. *Ibid.*

54. See Gordon S. Wood, *The Creation of the American Republic* (New York: Norton and Co., 1969), esp. chap. X.

55. There are two security issues—how to protect a small set of sovereign states from being individually gobbled up by the European powers surrounding them, from Spain in Florida, to France on the Mississippi, to Great Britain in Canada and parts of the northwestern frontier, and—how to protect the individual states from themselves being divided by dissident groups, using, perhaps, principles derived from the Revolution, as those taking part in Shay's rebellion in Massachusetts did. For the former problem see *The Federalist Papers,* Numbers 3–8, and for the latter see, for example, Number 28. And note the Constitutional provisions in Article IV, Sections 3 and 4, the former against new states being formed within the jurisdictions of old states and the latter to "guarantee to every State in this Union a Republican Form of Government."

56. "Essays on Man," bk. 3, see Hume, *Essays,* 14, footnote 1.

57. "That Politics May Be Reduced To A Science," in Hume, *Essays,* 15.

58. Hume, *Essays,* 527 and 528, respectively.

59. See Douglass Adair, "'That Politics May Be Reduced to a Science': David Hume, James Madison, and the Tenth *Federalist*," in *Hume: A Re-evaluation,* eds. Donald W. Livingston and James T. King (New York: Fordham University Press, 1976), esp. 408.

60. Hume *Treatise,* 537.

61. See, for example, Madison, *The Federalist Papers,* Number 48.

62. Hume, *Essays,* 44.

63. Hume, *Essays,* 45.

64. Wills, ed., *The Federalist Papers,* 279.

65. See, for example, Catherine Drinker Bowen, *Miracle at Philadelphia* (Boston: Little, Brown and Co., 1986), 14.

66. See, in this regard, Jack N. Rakove, *The Beginnings of National Politics: An Interpretative History of the Continental Congress* (Baltimore: The John Hopkins University, 1979), esp. Chapter IX.

67. Those at the Convention even argued from their experience regarding county governments with states. See for example, Madison's remarks, in Adriene Koch, ed., *Notes of Debates in the Federal Convention of 1787 Reported by James Madison* (Athens, OH: Ohio University Press, 1966) 42-43.

68. Quoted in Wood, *Creation of the American Republic,* 565.

69. See Stephen Jay Gould, *Time's Arrow, Time's Cycle* (Cambridge, MA: Harvard University Press, 1987), esp. 63–66; and John C. Green, *The Death of Adam* (Ames, IA: The University of Iowa Press, 1959), 76ff.

70. See Gould, *Times Arrow* 104ff.

71. To be pushed out of center stage is not to be annihilated. The great compromise of the Constitutional Convention, in which citizens are represented in the House and states in the Senate, can be seen as taking place *within* the confines of Lockean contract theory, about which entities—states or persons—should be considered to be in an original state of nature. In justifying equal representation in the Senate, it was thus argued that "the minority in convention [the small states] reasoned on first principles, that, as all men, in a state of nature, are equal with respect to rights, so also are equal all separate and distinct states,—that, when individuals form a free government, they must all have equal suffrage, . . . ; so also, when several states unite, for common convenience, they must meet on terms of perfect equality. . . . " From Alexander Contee Hanson, *Remarks on the Proposed Plan of a Federal Constitution* (Annapolis: Printed by Frederick Green, no date, 5). Rather obviously, if one assumed that persons were in a state of nature, one would argue, as Madison and others did, that they were entitled to equal representation, which they would not get if each state had one vote. See, for example, George Mason's remarks in Koch, *Notes on Debates in the Federal Convention of 1787 Reported by James Madison*, 75. One cannot settle such disputes within Lockean contract theory and must appeal, I would argue, *if* one is to settle it on theoretical grounds, to Humean considerations about security. But, again, that is not to deny either the appeal of the power of Lockean contract arguments.

3

Montesquieu and Rousseau on Constitutional Theory

Guy Lafrance

Lafrance examines the writings on constitutionalism of two of the French Enlightenment's most distinguished philosophers, Baron de Montesquieu (1689-1755) and Jean Jacques Rousseau (1712-1778). The first section identifies the characteristic elements of Montesquieu's theory, particularly his original and enduring notion of the separation of powers. The second section deals with Rousseau's conceptions of the General Will and basic rights, with respect to the idea of a constitution. Lafrance highlights the broad significance of these philosophers' theories for modern constitutional thought. In his words, "we ignore their views at the risk of having to reinvent them."

GENERAL INTRODUCTION

Philosophers of the Enlightenment are usually seen as the principal conceivers of moders republics mainly because of the new ideals they proposed having to do with new constitutions, new forms of government, new conceptions of sovereignty, inspired originally by Locke and Spinoza. Enlightenment philosophers also promoted the idea of human rights and citizens' rights, projects for perpetual peace, and so on. In a word, they were the main architects of these political ideals, based on the principles of reason, liberty, justice, equality and tolerance.

Philosophers of the Enlightenment produced a deep historical and epistemological break with their predecessors, through their new approach to the study of man in his social and political life. It is in this very specific field of investigation that, long before Kant, the Copernican revolution was introduced into the human sciences, by Montesquieu and Rousseau, in particular. Montesquieu dealt with the concept of law, whereas Rousseau mainly worked at the level of political and anthropological theory. Both of them rejected the so-called "universal evidences" of the *Cogito,* in order better to understand the diversity of societies, civilizations, cultures, in a word, the diversity of the "worlds of men."

MONTESQUIEU—INTRODUCTION

Montesquieu's whole enterprise was an attempt to break up the universal conceptions of the self, of culture, civilization, morality and of legal and sociopolitical organizations. Montesquieu achieved this goal by introducing, at all these levels, the concept of "law-in-relation"; that is to say, the concept of law in its relation to empirical facts and to real history, history as lived by mankind. To use Montesquieu's ambitious expression, this is the concept of law in its relation to "all the institutions which are received among men."[1]

More immediately, Montesquieu broke away from the Natural Law school in refusing to continue the tradition of constructing theories of the essence of society and of law. His aim was to develop a better theory of real history, based on the observation of variable relations between the social institutions which shape each and every sociopolitical totality, revealing their laws and their spirit.

To achieve his goal, Montesquieu needed what Althusser has called a certain taste for "political exoticism"[2] in order to foresee this "other world" and to understand better the image of his own world. But there is much more than exoticism and originality in Montesquieu. There is fundamentally a concern for *scientificity,* a concern for positive knowledge which is constantly expressed in the desire to link up the law with sociohistorical data. One must understand by this not a mere equivalence of the law of empirical data nor a reduction of the law to the data, as this seems to have happened in Aristotle. What should rather be understood here is a true research program concerned with the foundations of law, as they are in correspondence with reality, with historical continuity, instead of foundations as a pure, idealistic vision of the mind or a simple confirmation of the facts.

Right at the very beginning of the Preface to *The Spirit of the Laws,* Montesquieu wrote: "I have not drawn my principles from my prejudice, but from the nature of things."[3] With the same care, he will defend himself against the charge of moralizing when he says: "I write not to censure anything established in any country whatsoever."[4] And after presenting his explanation on the circumstances favoring polygamy in different nations, he makes the following meaningful remark: "In all this I only give their reasons, but do not justify their customs."[5]

Already, it is possible to perceive, via these remarks, a new scientific spirit which is, at the same time, a new philosophical spirit. This is well demonstrated by Montesquieu, who has often been considered as the Newton of the social sciences, since he was really seeking a rational type of explanation of societal facts. "I have first of all considered mankind, says Montesquieu, and the result of my thoughts has been, that amidst such an infinite diversity of laws and manners, they were not solely conducted by the caprice of fancy. I have laid down the first principles, and have found that the particular cases follow naturally from them; that the histories of all nations are only consequences of them; and that every particular law is connected with another law, or depends on some other of a more general extent."[6]

It would be easy to present a longer list of examples taken from Montesquieu's work, which would demonstrate how he overthrew the traditional method of philosophers and how deeply he shocked the minds of his time. Instead of this, let us pay more attention to his concept of the law, which is a new and revolutionary conception of the law, ultimately connected with his ideas on political liberty and on constitutional theory.

MONTESQUIEU'S NEW CONCEPT OF THE LAW

In the beginning of *The Spirit of the Laws,* Montesquieu defined the laws as the "necessary relations" which regulate all beings. "Laws," he says, "in their most general signification, are the necessary relations arising from the nature of things. In this sense, all beings have their laws: the Deity His laws, the material world its laws, the intelligences superior to man their laws, the beasts their laws, man his laws."[7] Such a conception of the laws implies that the world is not the result of an accident, nor the consequence of blind fate. On the contrary, there is, behind the laws, a Reason which assures order and the constancy of the relations. "There is, then, a prime reason; and laws are the relations subsisting between it and different beings, and the relations of these to one another."[8] Such are the laws governing men and societies; they express rational and determined relations which can also be rationally interpreted.

One of the main achievements of Montesquieu is precisely this work of analysis and rational explanation of the laws regulating human behavior, in different nations. He has shown, in particular, how it is possible to determine a societal type, how it is possible to know and understand the laws and institutions of a specific society, and its form of government. This is done by establishing the relations between the volume of the society, the configuration of the soil, the nature of the climate, the fertility of the earth, and so forth.

Montesquieu did this work of rationalization through his concept of "law-in-relation." This law is not part of an ideal world, nor derived from a preconceived idea; it is rather the expression of an imminent relation between phenomena; it is directly derived from the phenomena. More precisely, it is derived from the observation of social reality, from research, from analysis and from comparison. It is closely related to hypotheses which could become principles or laws, through the verification of a series of facts. Montesquieu well described his scientific attitude at the end of his Preface to *The Spirit of the Laws* when he wrote: "I have followed my object without any fixed plan. I have known neither rules nor exceptions; I have found the truth, only to lose it again. But when I once discovered my first principles, everything I sought for appeared."[9]

The principles, to which Montesquieu is here referring, are discovered through the "law-in-relation," which is not a scientific law nor a juridicial law; it is more like an explanatory model for legal and political institutions or any other social institution such as religion, morality, customs and manners. The "law-in-relation" can establish the connection between different kinds of facts, such as morality, religion, type of government and even the climate. This means that moral laws, civil laws and political laws imply an antecedent order, that is, anterior relations to properly human institutions. "Particular intelligent beings may have laws of their own making," says Montesquieu, "but they have some likewise which they never made. Before there were intelligent beings, they were possible; they had therefore possible relations, and consequently possible laws. Before laws were made, there were relations of possible justice. To say that there is nothing just or unjust but what is commanded or forbidden by positive laws, is the same as saying that before the describing of a circle all the radii were not equal. We must therefore acknowledge relations of justice antecedent to the positive law by which they are established."[10]

Therefore, some laws existed prior to the laws established by men. And these latter laws were well connected to human and social conditions. They are called positive laws or, according to another of Althusser's expressions, they can be called "reminding laws," "laws against forgetfulness"; since they have their origin in the capacity of every man to disobey the order of nature. Such are, in particular, the "laws of morality" which are, for Montesquieu, under the authority of philosophers; and the "political and civil laws" which are under the authority of the legislators.[11]

These positive laws or "reminding laws" are not, for all that, arbitrary laws. They reconstruct an order; they express history and real dialectical relations of social life. But they are fundamentally "laws-in-relation"; which means that they are "in relation to the climate of each country, to the quality of its soil, to its site and size, to the principle occupation of the natives, whether husbandmen, huntsmen, or shepherds. They should relate to the degree of liberty which the constitution will bear; to the religion of the inhabitants, to their inclinations, wealth, number, commerce, manners, and customs. In sum, they are related to each other, as well as to their origins, to the intent of the legislator, and to the order of things on which they are established; in all of which different lights they ought to be considered."[12] All these relations constitute what Montesquieu called "the Spirit of Laws."[13]

We shall not investigate the details of these relations, which Montesquieu studied carefully and at length. We shall rather insist on the consequence of these relations for the political life of the citizens, that is to say, on the notion of political liberty, on the spirit and attitude of the legislator, on legitimate versus arbitrary power, and finally on the notion of the separation of powers and of fundamental laws or constitutions.

MONTESQUIEU ON POLITICAL LIBERTY

Political liberty, as presented by Montesquieu, has nothing to do with the philosophical, universal and nonhistorical concept of liberty which basically consists in the free exercise of the will. Political liberty is, on the contrary, deeply related to the soul of each people, with their customs and manners. Political liberty is related to the form of government selected by each people. Thus, says Montesquieu, "some have annexed this name to one form of government exclusive of others: those who had a republican taste applied it to this species of polity; those who liked monarchial state gave it to monarchy. Thus they have all applied the name of liberty to the government most suitable to their own customs and inclinations."[14]

Even though political liberty stands in relation to the customs and to the different forms of government, in order to be more stable and effective, it greatly needs a juridicial foundation which can be provided by the legislator and by the constitution. For this reason, political liberty, as Montesquieu says, "does not consist in an unlimited freedom. In a State, that is, in societies directed by laws, liberty can consist only in the power of doing what we ought to will, and in not being constrained to do what we ought not to will."[15] In a few words, the political liberty of the citizen is "the right of doing whatever the laws permit."[16] Consequently, the laws given by the legislator, should (in order to be efficient) stand in a close relation to the principle of government; since "the relation of laws to the principle strengthens the several springs of government."[17]

Montesquieu demonstrated well this relation of the laws to the different forms of governments in Book Five of *The Spirit of the Laws:* he also perceived the political Virtue of the citizens as residing in this close relation. It is precisely in that sense that he is referring to the laws which establish equality in a democracy and stimulate love of equality.[18] As in a monarchial government, laws should normally stimulate the feeling of honor.[19]

All this to say that laws which establish and regulate political liberty are not derived from an abstract idea; they are the most suitable laws for a concrete historical reality, for the mentality of the people, for the sociocultural elements, which shape the physiognomy of a nation. Montesquieu expressed this idea in referring to what he called "the spirit of the nation."[20]

THE ROLE OF THE LEGISLATOR

The intention of the whole of Book XIX of *The Spirit of the Laws* is to draw the attention of the wise legislator to the necessity to study and understand well the general spirit before proposing fundamental laws or a constitution. This is simply because one cannot be guided by absolute and universal principles in this matter. Laws and constitutions are considered to be valuable only in their relation "to the principles which form the general spirit, the morals, and customs of a nation," says Montesquieu.[21] In order better to support his thesis about the sociocultural implantation of the laws, which establish true political liberty, Montesquieu quotes Solon's reply to those who asked him if the laws he had given to the Athenians were the best: "I have given them the best they were able to bear." To this reply Montesquieu adds, "a fine expression that ought to be perfectly understood by all legislators!"[22]

Insisting further on the importance of the general spirit, Montesquieu shows how it is necessary that "people's minds should be prepared for the reception of the best laws," simply because "liberty itself has appeared intolerable to those nations who have not been accustomed to enjoy it."[23] At issue is the difficult, important and useful role of the wise legislator, whose main objective is to ensure political liberty and the happiness of the citizens. Constantly, Montesquieu reminds the legislator how much he "should be attentive lest the general Spirit of a Nation be changed," and that he ought not "to endeavour to restrain their manners by laws, unless he would lay a constraint on their virtues."[24] Montesquieu considers that this kind of respect for historical and sociocultural facts is a basic condition for the issuance of fundamental laws and constitutions, which cannot succeed by forcing the general spirit. Prudence and moderation are, for Montesquieu, the best ways by which political liberty can be reached. "It is the business of the Legislator to follow the spirit of the nation," says Montesquieu, "when it is not contrary to the principles of government; for we do nothing so well as when we act with freedom, and follow the bent of our natural genius."[25]

Prudence, moderation, careful obedience to history and to the sociocultural elements which determine the proper genius of a nation: these are Montesquieu's recommendations for anyone planning to write or modify the constitution of a country. Political liberty relies ultimately on the authority of the laws, of the constitution and of the legislator. For that very specific reason, Montesquieu enjoins the legislator from correcting everything, and from making laws which constrain sociability.[26]

One should not conclude from this that the role of the legislator, from Montesquieu's perspective, is confined to copying societal types, as if the function of the laws would be legally to reproduce the sociocultural reality. The legislator is much more the true maker of the laws by which he really shapes and structures the political society according to a model perfectly suitable for its societal type. In that sense, the legislator is really doing a job of rationalization. And the true political liberty of the citizen arises from the rational and dialectical process of law and reality. Change and progress are the results of this dialectical process. But in order to achieve this goal, the legislator must always be guided by prudence and moderation. This last point is considered by Montesquieu to be of such major importance that he deems it the main target of his research in *The Spirit of the Laws*. "I say it, and methinks I have undertaken this work with no other view than to prove it, the spirit of a legislator ought to be that of moderation; political, like moral good, lying always between two extremes."[27]

MONTESQUIEU: LEGITIMATE VERSUS ARBITRARY POWER

It is now possible to understand, from this idea of moderation, all of Montesquieu's contempt for arbitrary power and, at the same time, his profound admiration and sympathy for legitimate power. That is to say, political power which is well defined and constrained by a sage constitution which provides a check on the power itself. One can understand, by this, the meaning of the connection made by Montesquieu between political liberty and moderate government. But, since there is no specific type of state or political regime which can provide an absolute guarantee for liberty, it is necessary, then, to ensure that political power does not become oppressive or tyrannical. Of course, what Montesquieu says is that "political liberty is to be found only in moderate governments; and even in these it is not always found. It is there only when there is no abuse of power. But constant experience shows us that every man invested with power is apt to abuse it, and to carry his authority as far as it will go. Is it not strange, though true, to say that virtue itself has need of limits? To prevent this abuse, it is necessary from the very nature of things that power should be a check to power. A constitution may be such that no man shall be compelled to do things to which the law does not oblige him, nor forced to abstain from things which the law permits."[28]

As a consequence, it is clear that in Montesquieu's mind, true political liberty for the citizen can be assured in a moderate state as long as the constitution provides specific rules on the limitation of power. Because political liberty cannot remain a pure concept or an abstract ideal, it should be well perceived and felt by all citizens. As Montesquieu says: "The political liberty of the subject is a tranquility of mind arising from the opinion each person has of his safety. In order to have this liberty, it is requisite the government be so constituted as one man need not be afraid of another."[29] This assurance can be given only by specific rules in the constitution. Montesquieu explains these rules in his theory of the separation of powers, which has long been considered as the most original part of his constitutional theory.

MONTESQUIEU ON THE SEPARATION OF POWERS

This presentation and analysis of Montesquieu's constitutional theory would be incomplete without mentioning the originality of his theory on the separation of powers. This theory is based on the well-known division of power into three aspects; that is to say, legislative power, executive power and judicial power.[30] Political liberty is seriously threatened when the three powers are united in the same person. There is a necessity for a real separation between these powers, so that one power can serve as a check on the other. In order to implement this constitutional principle of separate powers, Montesquieu uses the principle of social forces or social groups; this states that the three powers should be distributed between three different persons, or groups of persons. Consequently, political liberty can be preserved in any moderate government, providing that this constitutional and sociological principle is satisfied.

Thus, the principle of the separation of powers is to be considered as an essential part of Montesquieu's constitutional theory. It is ultimately this principle which could better or more efficiently preserve political liberty. The principle of the separation of powers should not, however, be seen as a division of sovereignty; the three powers "are forced to move, but still in concert," writes Montesquieu.[31]

True sovereignty is to be found in a kind of harmony between these three powers. But sovereignty was not a major concern for Montesquieu, as it would be for Rousseau. Montesquieu's constitutional doctrine is mainly concerned with political liberty and with the restraint on power, rather than with the true foundation of power, which could improve social and political Justice. These concerns will become central issues in Rousseau's constitutional doctrines.

ROUSSEAU ON SOVEREIGNTY AND THE GENERAL WILL

Political liberty is a central issue also for Rousseau, as it was for Montesquieu, but it is intimately related to the notion of the sovereignty of the people. The notion of freedom for Rousseau becomes truly meaningful when it is associated with the collective freedom of the sovereign. Among philosophers of the Enlightenment, Rousseau is certainly the one who best crystallized the idea of collective freedom as the foundation of individual freedom. Consequently, political and legal liberty, for him, should be associated with the idea of sovereignty, as derived from the General Will. It is easy then to understand the precautionary measures taken by Rousseau in order to preserve fully this sovereignty, as derived from the General Will, and for which he claims absolute inviolability. For this reason, sovereignty cannot be divided, nor can it be "transmitted," nor "alienated." It cannot even be represented, save by itself. Rousseau writes, "The Sovereign, which is only a collective being, can be represented only by itself." He further adds the following detail, "Sovereignty cannot be represented for the same reason that it cannot be alienated; it consists essentially in the general will, and the will cannot be represented: it is itself, or it is something other; there is no middle ground."[32]

Sovereignty resides, according to Rousseau's expression, in this "moral and collective body," or what he also calls this "body politic."[33] Sovereignty, conceived in this way, is the sacred cornerstone of political rights and of citizen's liberties. Political rights, or individual rights if preferred, exist only through collective rights born from the sovereign, conceived as a whole. The ideal of political liberty can be achieved, according to Rousseau, only "if each Citizen is nothing, and can be nothing, except in combination with all others, and if the force acquired by the whole is equal or superior to the sum of the natural forces of all individuals"; only then can one "say that legislation has attained the highest possible point of perfection."[34]

ROUSSEAU ON THE CONSTITUTION AND ON THE ROLE OF THE LEGISLATOR

Without pursuing further the meaning of the concept of sovereignty in Rousseau, we shall show how he maintained extreme respect for sovereignty in the role of the legislator and of the fundamental laws as the only possible foundation for the legitimacy of the body politic, that is to say, of the constitution and the whole system of legislation.

In Rousseau's constitutional theory, the function of the law is to consolidate the body politic. Although it does not set up this body, properly speaking, it must, nevertheless, give it "movement and will."[35] In that sense, law is the exercise of the general will, and sovereignty is, properly speaking, the legislative power. For this reason, says Rousseau, "it is no longer necessary to ask who is responsible for making the laws, since they are acts of the general will; nor whether the Prince is above the laws, since he is a member of the State; nor if the law can be unjust, since no one is unjust to himself; nor how one is free and subject to the laws, since they are only registers of our wills."[36] Consequently, the object of the law is the "public interest" of the citizens, united in a body which consolidates, by a legal structure, their will to live together. That explains why Rousseau is saying that "laws are properly only the conditions of the civil and political association. The People, submitting to the laws, ought to be their author; it concerns only those who are associating together to regulate the conditions of the society."[37] Thus, the goal of fundamental laws or of a political constitution, or what Rousseau calls "the goal of every system of legislation" can be reduced to two principal items "*liberty* and *equality*."[38]

ROUSSEAU ON THE SOCIAL CONTRACT

The question which now arises is, how can this goal be achieved within Rousseau's constitutional theory? To answer this question, we must recall the general principles of the social contract, as conceived by Rousseau. As a guideline for the proper understanding of these principles, we should always keep in mind the subtitle of *The Social Contract*, which is "Principles of Political Right." The objective is thus clearly defined as being research on political rights. This objective is also affirmed by the first principle established by Rousseau, which is an a priori principle and a statement of value, "Man is born free." This value judgment is immediately set in opposition to a factual judgment, "everywhere he is in chains."[39]

But the value judgment, or the search for rights, is Rousseau's main concern. As he states at the beginning of *The Social Contract*, "I want to inquire whether, taking men as they are and laws as they can be, it is possible to have some legitimate and certain rule of administration in civil affairs."[40] This intention is probably stated more clearly in the first version of the *Social Contract*, commonly called the *Geneva Manuscript*, where Rousseau says, "I seek right and reason, and do not argue over facts." The search for "right and reason" is, for Rousseau, in direct relation to the principle of freedom; this is why the natural authority of the father, the right of the strongest, and the right of slavery are not real rights. They are in basic contradiction with the principle of freedom and consequently cannot be rationally justified.

The only true foundation for any political rights, then, is liberty; rights must be the result of free will. For that reason, the only conceivable form of legitimate political society should be based on free consent, a real pact of association which should in no way be a pact of submission. For Rousseau well recognized the necessity of some form of social and political life when he says, concerning the state of nature, that "this primitive condition can no longer subsist, and the human race would perish unless it changed its manner of being."[42] But, the problem consists in finding a legitimate grounding for the necessity of such a social life. That is to say, how can we make our social existence be governed by laws which can assure the good of all, in the respect of liberty and equality? This is the goal of Rousseau's social contract, which shall now be examined, both for its content and meaning.

The social pact, for Rousseau, should be established on the basis of a primary agreement or convention, which is a kind of sociological grounding for it. This is because, social existence, before being regulated by a system of laws, should rely on a will to live together. There is already an implicit pact as soon as people feel the necessity to live together and agree to live together. The voluntary and free adherence of individuals to their community is "the act by which a people is a people"; this act is also "the real foundation of the society."[43] Therefore, social and political life is not an artificial creation; it is, rather, deeply rooted in the collective consciousness. As Rousseau writes, "this act of association produces a moral and collective body, . . . which receives from this same act its unity, its common *self* (moi), its life, and its will."[44]

If social and political life is the consequence of a free and spontaneous agreement, we should then question the raison d'être of the clauses of the social contract, as stipulated by Rousseau. As a matter of fact, these clauses "although perhaps they have never been formally enunciated," says Rousseau, are intended to make explicit the conditions of both social life and political organization, which should be as perfect as possible, the most equitable possible, and fully respectful of liberty. These clauses, which can be compared to Kant's Regulative Ideas, define the ideal of a just society and the necessary conditions for such a society to preserve individual liberty and equality among people. These clauses, in a word, indicate how people can join together without being subjugated and without alienating their liberty. Rousseau stated this goal, or the intention behind the clauses of the social contract, "To find a form of association which defends and protects with the whole force of the community the person and goods of every associate, and by means of which each, uniting with all, nevertheless obeys only himself, and remains as free as before."[45]

ROUSSEAU ON THE GENERAL WILL

How do the clauses fulfil this goal? By proposing a total alienation or forgoing of each in favor of the whole community. As Rousseau says, "These clauses, rightly understood, are all reducible to one only, namely the total alienation of each associate, with all of his rights, to the whole community."[46] These are the artificial means by which to hold onto freedom by a form of alienation which is self-cancelling, so that "each, in giving himself to all, gives himself to nobody; and as there is not one associate over whom we do not acquire the same rights which we concede to him over ourselves, we gain the equivalent of all that we lose, and more power to preserve what we have."[47] Complete socialization, in that sene, is a guarantee of equality and liberty—guarantee of a renewed and well-assured freedom which is the outcome of the social contract.

According to the terms of the social contract, man gets more liberty and more autonomy through the contract, since his liberty is under the protection of the General Will, of which he is a member. Civil liberty within the contract is in fact liberty which the individual gives himself, with the support of the social body. Civil liberty expresses itself through the autonomy of the will, in relation to the General Will, of which the individual is both legislator and subject, governor and governed. Civil liberty is also guaranteed by the sovereignty of the people. Since the people do not delegate power nor rights, they have no other authority than themselves, and shall obey only their own commands. This is what Rousseau means when he says, "obedience to the law one prescribes to oneself is freedom."[48]

The sovereign people express their will through the General Will, which is the voice of reason, heard in the silence of passions and of individual interests. This is why laws of the General Will stand in relation to the common good and to reason. Thus, concludes Rousseau, "instead of destroying natural equality, the fundamental pact, on the contrary, substitutes a moral and legitimate equality for the physical inequality which nature imposed upon men, so that, although unequal in strength or talent, they all become equal by convention or legal right."[49] Social and political life is ultimately the kingdom of law, reason, common good, morality and justice, provided that they are the expression of the General Will.

The idea of the General Will is, without any doubt, one of the most difficult notions to grasp in Rousseau's constitutional theory. He himself considered that the General Will was not easily found by the people, who do not always discern the good, and cannot always keep passions silent to better hear the voice of reason. "How will a blind multitude, which often does not know what it wants because it rarely knows what is good for it, carry out an enterprise so great and as difficult as a system of legislation? By itself the people always want the good, but by itself does not always discern it. . . . Private individuals see the good they reject; the public wants the good it does not see. All have equal need of quides."[50] This is where we find, in Rousseau's theory, the discrete, ticklish and important role of the legislator, whose primary function is to serve as an enlightened guide.

ROUSSEAU ON THE FUNCTION OF THE LEGISLATOR

The legislator whom Rousseau has in mind is in no way a man of power; he is rather, as is Montesquieu's legislator, a man of knowledge and science, and even a genius, whose work is to set up what Rousseau calls "the science of legislation."[51] To achieve this goal, it is necessary for him to keep a certain distance from power; that is to say, in Rousseau's language, to stay away from Government, from Magistrates and from the Sovereign. This is because the legislator has to fulfill "a particular and superior function which has nothing in common with human dominion."[52] For this particular reason, as Rousseau says, "he who controls men should not have control over the law; he who has control over the laws should not control men; otherwise, the laws, as ministers of his passions, would often serve to perpetuate his acts of injustice; he would never be able to prevent his private views from corrupting the sacredness of his work." Such a difficult and important function explains why "the Legislator is in all respects an extraordinary man in the State."[53]

We can now understand, through this conception of the role of the legislator, the almost unlimited admiration Rousseau had for the wise and clever legislator that Lycurgus was; because, he says, "when Lycurgus gave laws to his fatherland, he began by abdicating the throne."[54] But we can also see, in his admiration, a constant concern, on the part of Rousseau, for the protection of the sovereignty of the people when dealing with fundamental legislation or the constitution. There is always a need for him to preserve the constitution against a possible violation on the part of government or even the legislator himself. In order to preserve the sovereignty of the people in constitutional matters, we have to ensure that "He who drafts the laws, then, does not have or should not have any legislative right, and even the people cannot, if it wishes, divest itself on this incommunicable right, because according to the fundamental pact, only the general will obligates individuals and one cannot be assured that a particular will has conformed to the general will until after it has been submitted to the free votes of the people."[55] Sovereignty is an absolute right which always resides in the hands of the people.

In a word, for Rousseau, the wise Legislator is the one who acts with extreme prudence and with moderation; he always keeps a certain distance from power in order to preserve his work, as much as possible, from the influence of passions, and in order to carry out his work inspired only by science and political virtue. These are the basic conditions foreseen by Rousseau, as necessary to establish principles of equality and political liberty in the constitution.

SUMMARY

As with Montesquieu, the form of government for Rousseau has no real importance in itself because any form of government which is respectful of the republican ideal is acceptable; and this flexibility can take into account the diversity of manners and cultures. But there are some external signs of a good government: these signs are connected to the ends of political association which are "the preservation and the prosperity of its members."[56]

In this brief study of Montesquieu and Rousseau, our intention has been to bring out some of the basic elements in each of their constitutional theories. We may say that these two philosophers of the Enlightenment were undoubtedly the best representatives of their times on constitutional matters. Their views on fundamental rights and political rights are still of great importance for our times. At the very least, they represent a constant and important point of reference on constitutional theory. At most, they may, between them, encapsulate, details apart, all there is to say on constitutional theory. On either view, we ignore their views at the risk of having to reinvent them.

Notes

1. Montesquieu, *Defense de l'Esprit des Lois,* (First Edition, 1773) in *Oeuvres completes,* vol. 2, (Bibliotheque de la Pleiade, NRF., Gallimard, Paris, 1966) 1137.

2. Althusser, Louis: *Montesquieu, la politique et l'histoire,* (Presses Universitaires de France, 1959) 14.

3. Montesquieu, *The Spirit of the Laws,* (First edition, 1773), translated by Thomas Nugent, with an introduction by Franz Neumann (New York: Hafner Publishing Co. 1949) XVII.

4. *Ibid.* XVIII.

5. *Ibid.,* bk. XVI, chap. 4, 253.

6. *Ibid.,* Preface, XVII.

7. *Ibid.,* bk. I, chap. 1, 1.

8. *Ibid.*

9. *Ibid.,* Preface, XIX.

10. *Ibid.,* bk. I, chap. 1, 2.

11. *Ibid.,* 3

12. *Ibid.,* bk. I, chap. 3, 6-7. [Translation amended.]

13. *Ibid.,* 7

14. *Ibid.,* bk. XI, chap 2, 149.

15. *Ibid.,* chap. 3, 150. [Translation slightly amended.]

16. *Ibid.*

17. *Ibid.,* bk. V, chap. 1, 40

18. *Ibid.,* bk. V, chap. 5.

19. *Ibid.,* bk. V, chap. 9.

20. *Ibid.,* bk. XIX, chap. 5, 294.

21. *Ibid.,* bk. XIX, title, 292.

22. *Ibid.,* bk. XIX, chap. 21, 305.

23. *Ibid.,* bk. XIX, chap. 2, 292.

24. *Ibid.,* bk. XIX, chap. 5, 294.

25. *Ibid.* [Amended translation.]

26. *Ibid.,* bk. XIX, chap. 6.

27. *Ibid.,* vol. Two, bk. XXIX, chap. 1, 156.

28. *Ibid.*, bk. XI, chap. 4, 150. [Translation revised and amended.]

29. *Ibid.*, bk. XI, chap. 6, 151.

30. This distinction is presented by Montesquieu in the following way: "In every government," he says, "there are three sorts of power: the legislative; the executive in respect to things dependent on the law of nations; and the executive in regard to matters that depend on the civil law." *Ibid.*, bk. XI, chap. 6, 151.

31. *Ibid.*, bk. XI, chap. 6, 160.

32. Rousseau, Jean-Jacques, *Of the Social Contract* (first edition, 1762), translation by Charles M. Sherover (New York: Harper & Row 1984), bk. III, chapter 15, paragraph no. (284), 90.

33. *Ibid.*, bk. I, chap. 6, paragraph no. (46), 15.

34. *Ibid.*, bk. II, chap. 7, (108), 37-38.

35. *Ibid.*, bk. II, chap. 6, (96), 33.

36. *Ibid.*, (102), 35.

37. *Ibid.*, (105), 35-36

38. *Ibid.*, bk. II. chap. 11, (135), 48.

39. *Ibid.*, bk. I, chap. 1, (5), 4.

40. *Ibid.*, (2), 3.

41. For the *Geneva Manuscript*, see the translation of Judith R. Masters in *On the Social Contract*, edited by Roger D. Masters, (New York: St. Martin Press, 1978) 169.

42. Rousseau, *Of the Social Contract*, trans. Sherover: bk. I, chap. 6, (37), 13.

43. *Ibid.*, bk. I, chap. 5, (35), 13.

44. *Ibid.*, bk. I, chap. 6, (46), 15.

45. *Ibid.*, bk. I, chap. 6, (40), 14.

46. *Ibid.*, bk. I, chap. 6, (42), 14.

47. *Ibid.*, bk. I, chap. 6, (44), 14.

48. *Ibid.*, bk. I, chap. 8, (57), 19.

49. *Ibid.*, bk. I, chap. 9, (65), 21–22.

50. *Ibid.*, bk. II, chap. 6, (105), 36.

51. *Geneva Manuscript*, ed. Masters: bk. II, chap. 1, 179.

52. Rousseau, *Of The Social Contract*, trans. Sherover: bk. II, chap. 7, (109), 38.

53. *Ibid.*

54. *Ibid.*, (110).

55. *Ibid.*, bk. II, chap. 7, (112), 39.

56. *Ibid.*, bk III, chap. 9, (248), 80.

4

Kant's Approach to Constitutionalism

Mary J. Gregor

Gregor presents an authoritative and meticulous outline of the approach to constitutionalism taken by the German Critical Idealist, Immanuel Kant (1724-1804). She examines the question about how Kant's idea of constitutionalism may be deducible from his fundamental notions of rational agency, human freedom, and self-determination. In doing so, Gregor stresses the importance of Kant's theory of property, that is, of rational entitlement, for his conception of a constitution. Another notable feature of her essay is its contribution to recent Kantian scholarship concerning the concept of basic rights, especially her identification of certain aspects of Kant's uncharacteristically incomplete analysis.

In the context of political theory, "constitutionalism" often signifies concern with the problem of how the institutions of a state are to be organized in order to secure the basic rights of men and citizens. Kant is clearly a constitutionalist in this sense. In a number of popular essays dealing with political matters,[1] he maintains that a constitution is conceptually republican and that an actual constitution ought to provide for republican government, that is, for separation of the legislative from the executive authority. This, he says, is how a state is organized in accordance with pure principles of rights. By such principles legislative authority belongs to the united will of the people, whose laws the executive is to carry out; for only "the original contract," which is "an act of the general will," can establish a civil constitution, by which a multitude of rational agents subjects itself to the authority of a legislator and becomes a people. Since legislative authority belongs to the collective will of the people, the concept of a constitution contains that of a separation of powers and excludes despotic government in which the legislator arbitrarily rules the state by laws he has himself made. Kant goes on to note that an actual constitution can approximate to its republican potentiality even if it provides for a form of government in which the ruling power is vested in an autocrat or a nobility, since these can represent the collective will of the people. He maintains, however, the actual constitution that best conforms to the concept of a constitution is one that vests legislative authority in representatives elected by all citizens.

As might be expected from the topical nature of these essays, what they contain is only a sketch of Kant's views on the organization of a state. More specifically, the driving force behind his theory is the concept of "the general will" and its "original contract"; but why legislative authority belongs to the general or collective or united will of the people is not adequately explained.[2] Whether Kant's formal treatment of the organization of a state in *The Doctrine of Right*[3] provides a coherent political philosophy is open to question. The concluding sentence in his Preface to his book[4] states that he has worked less thoroughly over some of its later sections (on public Right) than might be expected from the earlier ones (on private Right) (VI, 209). The scope of this remark is indefinite: the second major division of the work, "Public Right" includes not only "The Right of a State" but also "The Right of Nations" (or , better, of States) and "Cosmopolitan Right." Instead of speculating about what parts of "Public Right" Kant was dissatisfied with, I shall consider the positive implication of his remark, that is, that he has worked thoroughly over the first major division of the book, "Private Right"; for it is here that we learn why legislative authority in a state belongs to the general will of the people.

The first major division of *The Doctrine of Right*, "Private Right," contains the sum of those moral principles having to do with "external objects" that can be known by reason to hold, apart from any actual giving of positive law (VI, 210). In other words, having dealt in the "prolegomena" to the work with man's innate right to freedom, Kant discusses, in "Private Right," the contingent rights (for example, to things and the performance of actions promised) that can be acquired by acts of will in a state of nature (VI, 242). Considerations of what is lacking in a state of nature provide the transition from a state of nature to a "rightful condition," a civil society—that is, a state of distributive justice in which the rights that can be acquired in a state of nature are determined in accordance with laws by a judge or court whose decisions are effective. Finally, the later sections, on "Public Right," add nothing to the rights that it is the function of a civil society to secure but deal only with the form of a civil society, the second-order rights that a civil society must have in order to secure the primary rights of its members (for example, in the case of a state, the right to require that its citizens pay taxes to support institutions for securing their primary rights and perform military service to defend the state). Public Right is therefore the sum of laws that need to be publicized in order to produce a rightful condition, one in which individuals, nations and states can enjoy their rights (VI, 305-6, 311). As the transition from Private Right to Public Right indicates, the protection of private rights requires organization not only within a state but also among states and "citizens of the world." What is established in Private Right will provide the content for these further forms of rightful condition as well.[5]

One kind of right that can be acquired by an act of will is, Kant argues, a right to a thing, a property right. This kind of right involves a peculiar difficulty, since in asserting a right to a thing someone asserts that, as a result of his act of will, all others are under obligation not to do what they would otherwise be entitled to do, that is, use that thing. This is not the case with regard to the innate right to freedom of action which, Kant holds, all men have merely by virtue of their humanity. Any right on the part of one person limits another's freedom of action and, in the case of the innate right to freedom, all others' freedom of action. But since this right is not acquired by an act of will but belongs to everyone merely because of his status as a person, others can recognize that they are under obligation not to interfere with his freedom and give their rational consent to the corresponding limitation on theirs. Since people do not always do what they can recognize that they ought to do, civil society would be necessary to restrain them from interfering with one another's actions. But this is not the route Kant's argument to civil society takes. Rather, it concludes to the necessity of civil society from the impossibility of someone's "unilateral will" putting all others under a contingent obligation, and the need for an "omnilateral will" to impose the obligation correlative to rights to things. If Private Right establishes the possibility of having rights to things only under a general will, that is, within a civil society, and if the principles of private Right lead to the whole of Public Right, then the theory of property put forth in "Private Right" is crucial to the whole of Kant's political philosophy.

Although Kant suggests that he has worked thoroughly over Private Right, his care is not immediately apparent. The argument is cryptic even by his standards, and the main steps in it do not seem to follow in logical order (though this may have resulted from material that was misplaced or inserted by mistake in the published text).[6] To add to the difficulty, he seems as much concerned with epistemological as with moral problems. In the relatively few pages crucial to his theory of rights he attempts to accomplish everything at once. If this is the part he has worked over thoroughly, the reader may well wonder why he has presented the results in this manner.

A historical note may help to explain what has happened. *The Doctrine of Right* is a curious phenomenon in Kant scholarship. Having been virtually neglected for almost two centuries it has become, in the last decade, a subject of intense activity. This began shortly after Ritter's contention, in 1971, that *The Doctrine of Right* is a pre-Critical work onto which some Critical terminology has been grafted. With but scant attention to *The Doctrine of Right* itself, he maintained that Kant had arrived at its essential theses by about 1775.[7] What has emerged from more serious study of *The Doctrine of Right*, as well as the *Nachlass*, is that Kant apparently did not work out the crux of Private Right before 1794. In the unpublished *Bemerkungen* to his *Observations on the Feeling of the Beautiful and the Sublime* (1764), he put forward a labor theory of property which, like the *Observations* itself, was made obsolete by the *Inaugural Dissertation* of 1770. Between 1767 and 1788, Kant gave his course on *Naturrecht* at least twelve times, using as his text Achenwall's *Ius Naturae*. In 1793–94 he gave a course, "The Metaphysics of Morals," the lectures of which were transcribed by Vigilantius. Neither his annotations on Achenwall nor the Vigilantius lectures contain the theory of property that appears in his undated *Vorarbeiten* for *The Doctrine of Right*. In short, it was not earlier than three years before its publication that he worked out the theory of property that figures so prominently in *The Doctrine of Right*.[8] In view of his age and failing health, it is not surprising that he was in a hurry to publish it. These circumstances would account for its jagged style, Kant's concern to integrate it with the first two *Critiques*, and perhaps—because he was working on the second part of *The Metaphysics of Morals* when the first was published—his failure to correct the faulty text that appeared.

Kant scholars have only begun to deal with the *The Doctrine of Right*. In view of the importance of the work and the difficulties noted above, it is most unfortunate that about the only source that could throw light on it is the *Vorarbeiten*, in which he is obviously groping toward his theory, trying out one solution after another. Still, the main outline of his theory can be traced in a tentative way, and I shall attempt to do so even though its keystone, the principle Kant calls "practical reason's postulate with regard to rights," involves some basic tenets of his theory of knowledge.

"Private Right" has two sections: "How to Have Something External as One's Own" and "How to Acquire Something External." In the first section, Kant analyzes what it would mean to say that an external object rightfully belongs to someone, that someone has a right to it, and then gives a "deduction" or justification for using the concept of possession involved. The justification is the postulate referred to in the preceding paragraph. This, Kant derives from "the universal principle of Right", analysis of which yields the concept of a right. One would expect him to explain how this principle is derived from his supreme principle of morality, the categorical imperative. He seems in a hurry, however, to be done with the "prolegomena" and to get on to Private Right. Although he states repeatedly that this principle, or what can be developed analytically from it, is based on the categorical imperative (VI, 239, 252), he apparently expects the reader to supply what is missing. I shall attempt to outline briefly the considerations that seem relevant.

The Doctrine of Right and *The Doctrine of Virtue* are the two parts of *The Metaphysics of Morals,* for which the *Groundwork of the Metaphysics of Morals* laid the foundation. By analyzing the ordinary man's concept of a morally good action, one done from duty, the *Groundwork* established that the agent is thought to be willing his action on a subjective principle or maxim which could hold for all rational agents because he finds that his maxim has this form of universal law. If a rational agent's supposed capacity to will his actions on this principle, the categorical imperative, is what gives him unconditional worth or "dignity," and if this principle requires acting on maxims that could hold for all rational agents, then the agent is thought to be acting on a principle of treating rational agents never as mere means to his ends but also as ends in themselves.[9] After developing from the concept of a morally good action these (and other) formulations of the principle on which the agent is thought to be willing his action, Kant argues in the *Critique of Practical Reason* that consciousness of being under obligation or subject to a categorical imperative establishes for practical purposes that the agent is free, that is, capable of determining himself to act through a purely rational incentive, the thought of duty.[10] That a rational agent is free in this sense, and therefore has the status of a person, is apparently the ultimate basis of the universal principle of Right. As Kant notes," . . . we know our own freedom, from which all moral laws, and so all rights as well as duties proceed, only through the moral imperative . . . " (VI, 239). However, the principle presupposed from the *Groundwork* and the second *Critique* cannot function as a principle within *The Doctrine of Right.*

The basis on which Kant distinguishes *The Doctrine of Right* from ethics or *The Doctrine of Virtue* is the kind of lawgiving proper to each. Any giving of law, he notes, consists of two parts: a law and an incentive to obey it, which the lawgiver connects with the law. The only incentives that an external lawgiver can connect with a law are incentives drawn from the sensible nature of those subject to the law, their aversion from the consequences of breaking the law (VI, 219). Only the internal lawgiving of pure practical reason can connect with a law the incentive of duty. Since the kind of constraint available to an external lawgiver, coercion, can extend only to actions, duties prescribed by laws that can be given externally, external laws, can be only actions. Insofar as external laws are moral laws they are based on principles of pure practical reason, and those subject to them can always give such laws to themselves, that is, make it their principle to obey them because it is rational to do so.[11] But external laws can be laws only for actions.

That duties prescribed by external laws consist only in actions, however, tells us nothing about what sort of actions it is *morally* possible for external laws to prescribe or prohibit. At this point Kant, leaves the reader to fend for himself. However, when he begins to discuss the universal principle of Right, the concept of "outer freedom" is firmly in place, and in *The Doctrine of Virtue* he notes that the principle which distinguishes the two divisions of moral philosophy is that the concept of freedom, which is common to both, requires a division of duties into duties of outer freedom and duties of inner freedom, only the latter of which are ethical (VI, 406). Given the tenor of Kant's moral philosophy, it is clear that any moral law must be based on a rational agent's freedom, not on the inclinations belonging to his sensible nature. But the reader has not been adequately prepared for this concept of outer freedom, which apparently provides the link between the supreme principle of morality and the universal principle of Right.

The *Groundwork,* in discussing the principle of humanity as an "end" not in the sense of something that can be brought about by one's actions but in the sense of a limiting condition on them, noted that "the subject of all ends" is every rational agent as an end in itself (IV, 431: Paton, 98). On its negative side, and with regard to actions affecting the actions of others, this would suggest that others are at least not to be compelled to serve as mere tools to the ends someone else has set. In *The Metaphysics of Morals,* Kant characterizes "humanity" as the capacity to set an end for oneself, that is, to determine oneself to act through ends one has oneself adopted. This, he says, is what distinguishes a human being's acts of free choice from animal behavior. The end for which an animal acts is set for it by nature, and an animal is determined to act by its desire for that end. But "the capacity to set and end for oneself—any end whatsoever—is what characterizes humanity (as distinguished from animality)" (VI, 392). Although Kant holds that the capacity to determine oneself to act by adopting an end involves freedom as the capacity for morally good action,[12] and that this in turn involves the capacity and the duty to adopt ends without regard for one's inclinations (VI, 385, 395), such a duty can belong only to ethics. Laws that can be given externally cannot prescribe the adoption of ends, since one cannot be co-erced to adopt an end. One can, however, be coerced to refrain from actions that would interfere with others' actions toward whatever ends they have set for themselves. In short, what characterizes any free action is that the agent determines himself to act by setting his own end. It would, Kant holds, be inconsistent with the status of a free or rational agent to prevent him from acting toward his own ends, as long as his actions leave it open to all other rational agents to act toward their own ends.

Having distinguished the two parts of *The Metaphysics of Morals* through the kind of lawgiving proper to each and the aspects of freedom on which laws arising in one or the other kind of lawgiving are based, Kant proceeds to formulate his universal principle of Right. He begins by noting that, un-like a lawyer's empirical knowledge of "the law of the land," a metaphysi-cian's knowledge is the science of external *natural* laws, such as can be known a priori and provide the basis for any giving of positive laws (VI, 229). The sum or system of such laws (or, better, principles) comprises Right, and Kant first seeks the criterion by which one can determine whether any positive laws are compatible with Right. In three propositions, which seem to follow directly from the concept of external lawgiving for human agents, he circumscribes the concern of Right to actions by which someone directly or indirectly affects another's outer freedom (VI, 230). An action is right in accordance with external natural laws if what he chooses to do can coexist with everyone's freedom in accordance with a universal law of outer freedom. It is wrong if, by force, threats or deception, he compels others to perform actions that serve only his ends and not theirs, or prevents them from acting although their actions would be consistent with everyone's freedom. Right is, therefore, "the totality of the conditions under which what one chooses to do can be united with what another chooses to do in accordance with a universal law of freedom" (VI, 230), and its universal principle specifies that actions are right by virtue of their compatibility with the outer freedom of everyone.

From this principle, Kant then develops analytically the concept of a right,[13] a justification for using coercion. If my action or my condition is consistent with the outer freedom of everyone, anyone who interferes with it wrongs me. The compulsion he uses is a hindrance to freedom, and the coercion that checks such compulsion is consistent with and, indeed, a condition of outer freedom (VI, 231-32). Such coercion is therefore morally justified. Because it is exercised in accordance with principles of outer freedom it is external lawgiving, and to a right on the part of one there corresponds obligation on the part of others. The concept of a right, a capacity to put others under obligation, is identical with that of being entitled to use coercion.

By this analysis, Kant has established the condition under which someone can be said to have a right and, ultimately, the authority of a legislator to enact positive laws. The universal principle of Right is, of course, basic to Kant's subsequent derivation of rights, since these are to be derived not from the ends people may be assumed to have adopted in keeping with their natural inclinations (their happiness) but from the consistency of their actions with the freedom of all to act toward whatever ends they have set for themselves. But this principle sets forth only the formal condition under which someone has a right, namely that his action is compatible with the freedom of all others. It does not of itself specify what actions fulfill this condition and hence what rights people can have.

In formulating the universal principle of Right, Kant seems already to have used the concept of humanity as the end in itself. Hence he asserts briefly, in the Introduction to *The Doctrine of Right,* that all men, merely by virtue of their humanity, have the innate right to outer freedom, that is, to independence from compulsion by others insofar as their external exercise of freedom can coexist with the freedom of every other in accordance with a universal law (VI, 237-38). He is far more concerned, however, with the problem of how they can acquire rights by their acts of will. The innate right to freedom is only a right to freedom of action, to noninterference with one's person, insofar as one's action or one's condition accords with the universal principle of Right. If someone forcefully takes from me an object I am holding (for example, wrests an apple from my hand), he interferes with my person, my innate right to freedom which includes the right to noninterference with my physical possession of objects. But can I, by an act of will, acquire a right to an object I am not holding? This is the problem Kant addresses in "How to Have Something External as One's Own."

Kant begins by analyzing the concept of something external that is considered rightfully mine (VI, 245). To say that anything is rightfully mine is to say that I am so connected with it that another's use of it without my consent would wrong me, that is, I alone am entitled to use it. Because one must in some sense possess an object in order to use it, my innate right to freedom of action, put in terms of possessing something as a condition of using it, implies that I am in rightful possession of my person and hence of objects I am holding. To interfere with my freedom of action would be to wrong me "with regard to what is internally mine" (VI, 248). But to say that something *external* is rightfully mine would be to say that I am so connected with that object that I would be wronged by another's using it without my consent even though I am not holding it. To say, for example, that a book in my office is rightfully mine is to say that I would be wronged were someone to use it without my consent even though I am now at home, so that he does not affect my person. This may seem to be laboring the familiar concept of property. The analysis however, produces unexpected results.

In terms of empirical concepts, possession is holding an object, sensible or physical possession of it, and an external object is something distinct from me and located in a different region of space. To say that I could be wronged by another's use of an external object because, although he possesses it physically, I am in rightful possession of it would be to say that I possess it independently of its location in space or time. The concept would be merely that of something distinct from the agent that is an object of his will, something he can put to use for his ends (VI, 246). Kant intends, through practical reason's postulate, to establish that we are justified in using the concept of nonphysical possession. Ultimately, however, he intends to tell us "How to Have Something External as One's Own," namely, by living in civil society. In order to understand his procedure in this difficult chapter, we may note that to say I have something external as mine is to use the nonempirical concepts of "having," or being in control of, something distinct from myself regardless of its location. Unless we are entitled to use such concepts, Kant maintains, the only right anyone could have would be his innate right to freedom of action.

In saying that someone has something external as his own, the concept of an external object we are using is a purely intellectual concept (*Verstandesbegriff*), one that in itself contains nothing derived from sensibility, whether from its matter (sensation) or from its forms (space and time). It is merely the concept of something distinct from the subject that he has the physical capacity to use as a means to his ends. So too is the concept of "having" an object, which disregards holding it or being connected with it in space and time. Such concepts always require a "deduction," that is, it must be shown that we are entitled to use them. In theoretical philosophy, we would show that these concepts have objective reality by bringing them into relation with the forms of intuition and so limiting their applicability to conditions of physical possession. In the case at hand, however, what has to be justified is our using them without regard for conditions of space and time. If our use of them can be justified, we shall not be entitled to use them for theoretical purposes, as if they could extend our theoretical knowledge. We shall be justified in using them only for practical purposes, because practical reason wills that they hold (VI, 297).

The context in which these concepts arose was the question of whether someone can rightfully possess an object of will distinct from himself, that is, whether he can exclude others from it consistently with laws of outer freedom. Since the concept of merely rightful possession is a concept of freedom, it is a rational concept (*Vernunftbegriff*) that cannot be shown to have objective reality for theoretical purposes. However, Kant has argued, in the *Critique of Practical Reason*, that our consciousness of being bound in accordance with a categorical imperative reveals "the fact of reason," that pure reason can be practical, and establishes sufficiently, for practical purposes, that we are free. Hence he will have justified our use, for practical purposes, of the concept of merely rightful possession if he can show that it is presupposed by practical reason's postulate with regard to rights and if he can derive this postulate from his universal principle of Right, which is itself derived from the first principle of morality (VI, 252, 231, 239). He will then be able to use the intellectual concepts of "having" an "external object" to apply the concept of merely rightful possession to empirical objects without limiting possession of such objects to holding them.

Practical reason's postulate, in its first formulation, states in effect that it is possible for someone to possess merely rightfully any external object of will, that is, that "a maxim by which, if it were to become a law, an object of will would in itself (objectively) have to belong to no one (res nullius) is contrary to rights" (VI, 246). The intellectual concept of an external object of will is that of something distinct from an agent that he can put to use for whatever ends he has, something that someone has the physical capacity to make use of.[14] There is nothing in the concept of something usable that could put it beyond someone's using it, provided that he does so consistently with the outer freedom of everyone. To deny this would be to say that his external exercise of freedom is limited by something other than its own formal principle. It would be to say that practical reason gives a law of outer freedom which prohibits him from doing what he can rightfully do, and this is self-contradictory. A maxim in accordance with which an object of will absolutely could not be used by someone capable of using it could not hold as a universal law because it would be contrary to the universal principle of Right. Since possessing an object is a condition of using it, any object of will can be rightfully possessed by someone who has the capacity to use it. Hence the rational concept of merely rightful possession has objective reality, and Kant reformulates the postulate, "There is a duty of Right to act toward others so that what is external (usable) could become someone's" (VI, 252).

Needless to say, a good deal remains to be done by way of applying this concept of intelligible possession to objects of experience. As was noted above, it is to be applied to empirical possession not directly but through the intellectual concept of having.[15] By introducing the pure concept of having, Kant can use the categories of substance, causality and reciprocity to specify objects of will as things (objects of property rights), other person's acts of will (contractual rights), and other persons themselves (domestic rights) (VI, 247-48). Moreover, the concept of having adds something to the mere thought of an object of will; it adds that one is in control of what one has the physical capacity to use. To have an external object is to be in control of it independently of its location in space and time. The things, acts of will, and persons to which the concept of merely rightful possession applies must be in space and time. But to assert a right to them is to assert control over a field regardless of one's physical presence on it, over another's will regardless of the interval between making and fulfilling a contract, over one's children regardless of their being away from home. It is to assert that one would be wronged were someone to use the field without one's consent, to retract his promise before the time for fulfilling it had come, or to kidnap one's children on their way to school. We are entitled to make such assertions because we are entitled to use those intellectual concepts and hence to set aside or disregard conditions of space and time.

In discussing how one can acquire rights to objects we shall note briefly how Kant brings these concepts into relation to the choices and actions of human beings. Most of the details, as well as the problems involved, lie beyond the scope of this chapter. Of immediate concern, however, is what the concept of having adds to the thought of an object of will—being in control of an object through an act of will. In asserting a right to a thing, one asserts that all others have an obligation to refrain from using that thing. This is a contingent obligation, an obligation others would not have apart from one's act of will. The problem therefore arises, how can I, consistently with the universal principle of Right, put them under an obligation to refrain from doing what they would otherwise be entitled to do, that is, to use an object they have the physical capacity to put to use?

Since obligation can be imposed only in accordance with a universal law, my maxim must, first, qualify as a universal law, and this implies that I am myself bound to refrain from using what anyone else has taken under his control in accordance with such a maxim. Because no one can be bound to act or to refrain from acting except in accordance with a law binding on everyone, I cannot assert a right to a thing without acknowledging my duty to refrain from using what anyone else has willed to be his in accordance with a maxim that qualifies as a universal law. As Kant puts it, no unilateral will can put another under a contingent obligation (VI, 255-56). In the case of a right against a specific person, a contractual right, obligations arise from a bilateral will, that is, both parties to the contract agree to be bound by its terms. But a property right, a right to a thing, is a right against everyone else, and the obligation corresponding to it can arise only from an omnilateral will by which everyone, including the one asserting the right, is bound.

But a right is, secondly, a justification for using coercion. In asserting a right to a thing I assert that I am entitled to coerce all others to refrain from using it, and hence I acknowledge that they in turn are entitled to use coercion on me. Since in questions of rights it is neither expected nor required that anyone fulfill his obligations from a purely rational incentive, to acknowledge such obligations is to submit to a "collective, general [common] and powerful will" (VI, 256). In other words, it is to submit to an external lawgiver who unites the wills of all under its coercive laws, so that the rightful claims of each can hold against every other. Only so can each give every other the guarantee that his maxim could qualify as a universal law of outer freedom, so that the exercise of freedom possible in accordance with practical reason's postulate will be consistent with the universal principle of Right.

The conclusion Kant draws is that only in a "rightful condition," in civil society, can anyone's rights be conclusive, secured or guaranteed. In a state of nature there can be provisional rights, insofar as one's willing takes place in accordance with the Idea of a general will (VI, 256-57). That is to say, someone is entitled to use coercion to defend what he has, provided he is willing to enter civil society while others are not, and to bring them to submit together with him to an external lawgiver. Because one's rights are not created by acts of legislation but rather recognized in them, provisional rights must be possible in accordance with a priori principles of practical reason. What is lacking in a state of nature and can be provided only by civil society might seem, so far, to be the element of coercion in accordance with laws.

This is the more or less familiar part of Kant's theory of "the original contract" as an act of the general will by which a multitude forms itself into a civil society. What I have tried to stress is that in Kant's theory it seems to be property, rights against everyone, that requires such a contract as the basis for civil society. In order to do so it was necessary to consider his account of how it can be known that rights to objects of will in general and to things in particular are possible, and of how rights to things, correlative to obligations on the part of all others, lead to his theory of "the original contract." He does not, of course, regard such a contract as a historical fact; on the contrary, he notes that people's submission to an external lawgiver was probably accomplished by force (VI, 339). The original contract is rather an Idea of practical reason to which the laws of any civil society ought to approximate, since it is the concept of a condition in which everyone can enjoy the rights he can acquire.

But this account is obviously incomplete, as can be seen by two considerations. The first is that, although much has been said about rights to things, the laws of a civil society provide for transferring property by such means as buying and selling, legacies, and gifts (all of which can be treated as forms of contract). When such laws provide for settlers acquiring land that does not belong to an individual, they regard that land as public, belonging to the people as a whole, and therefore to be acquired contractually. What they cannot provide for is original acquisition of land that belongs to no one, because the land held by a civil society is already owned by the people taken either distributively or collectively.

The second consideration is the apparent discrepancy between Kant's account of the need for civil society just considered and the account that provides the "transition from the status of what is yours or mine in a state of nature to its status in a rightful condition generally." The difference in status is, again, that between provisional and conclusive acquisition; but here it is said that a rightful condition is necessary in order to *determine* and secure what has been acquired. In a state of nature, Kant tells us, individual men, peoples and states can acquire something in accordance with *their* concepts of rights, and have a right to do what *seems* right and good to them without being dependent on another's opinion about this (VI, 312). According to this account, what is lacking in a state of nature is not only the coercion in accordance with public laws that is necessary to secure one's rights but an impartial judge to determine what has been acquired. Moreover, it can be seen in retrospect that the "someone" who, Kant argued, can have something external as his own is not necessarily an individual person who enjoys his rights through the original contract that establishes a state. What states themselves have acquired must be determined in accordance with the Idea of an act of the general will. These two considerations are closely related. An adequate discussion of them would require a commentary on the entire *Doctrine of Right*. I shall attempt only to indicate how the problem of original acquisition leads to an unexpected extension of "the original contract."

As was noted above, the laws of a civil society regard rights to things as acquired by contracts. However, acquiring property by a contract presupposes that one of the parties already owns the thing that is to be transferred. As

Kant sees the problem, not all rights to things can be acquired by contracts or "derived from another." There must have been an original acquisition of things that was not contractual and hence did not take place through the agreement of others to the limitation of their freedom involved in someone's acquiring a right.

The object of original acquisition, Kant holds, must have been a specific piece of land. Although he argues this in terms of regarding land as substance and movables on it as modifications of substance (VI, 261-62), perhaps the point can be put more simply. Anyone who removes something from its location on land changes that land. To use what is on land is to use the land itself. In order to use anything on land one must therefore be in possession of the land on which the movable thing exists. Hence if one can acquire rights to things one must be able to acquire a right to a definite piece of land. The problem is how one could originally acquire land and so exclude others from using it.

Kant considers two theories of how this could happen: the theory that one can acquire land by laboring on it and Grotius' theory of a primitive common ownership of goods. Since Kant regards it as evident that laboring on land belonging to someone else gives one no title to that land, he considers whether laboring on land could account for acquiring it originally and concludes that it could not (VI, 268-69). Secular labor theories, as Kant views them, misconstrue the very concept of a right. Such theories would begin with someone's acquiring a right to a piece of land by laboring on it and then require the consent of others to his excluding them from using it. But this would be to think of a right as a direct relation of a person to a thing, which by definition cannot have obligations. Because the concept of a right involves that of a corresponding obligation, no such direct relation of a person to a thing is possible. Hence a labor theorist, obscurely aware of this correspondence of rights and obligations, has to personify things. He has to think of a piece of land as having been put under obligation to the person who labored on it, an obligation to serve only him and refuse itself to anyone else who wants to use it. Hence, he thinks of his right as a genie in the thing, and this is "an absurd way" of thinking of a right (VI, 260). A right cannot be a direct relation of a person to a thing. It must rather be a relation of wills with regard to a thing.

The second theory Kant considers, that of Grotius, does regard the first acquisition of private property as a relation of wills but conceives of it as taking place by a contract. According to Grotius,[16] the primitive state of the human race was that of common onwership of goods, a condition that could last only as long as men's needs remained simple and could be satisfied by what nature made available. But as men came to want a better life, work became necessary and with it a division of goods. This division took place by a contract through which everyone agreed either explicitly or tacitly to private ownership of land by whoever already occupied it. To this theory Kant objects, first, that it is not a theory of original acquisition and, second, that it is based on a fiction, an alleged historical fact for which there is no evidence (VI, 262, 251). Kant is quite willing to admit that a people could rightfully decide that there is to be no private ownership of land in the country it inhabits. It could declare the land "free" in the sense that all the land belongs to the entire people and each can therefore use any part of it (VI, 265-66). Such an arrangement would not conflict with practical reason's postulate; it would not make all things *res nullius* because anyone could own movables on the public land. However, such collective ownership would have to be instituted or established by a contract through which everyone renounced his right to the piece of land he had acquired. The problem of original acquisition has not been solved.

Like Grotius, Kant bases his theory of original acquisition of land on "original possession in common" of the habitable surface of the earth (its land) by the entire human race. Unlike Grotius, however, he regards this original possession in common not as a fact but as a concept of reason which alone yields a principle making it possible for individuals, families, nations or states to use land compatibly with principles of rights (VI, 262; XXIII, 317-18). Before arriving at this concept of original possession in common, however, Kant makes two points. The first is that all men have the innate right to be somewhere on the habitable surface of the earth, "wherever nature or chance has put them" (VI, 262). This is a condition of their existence (XXIII, 237), and their mere physical presence on the earth cannot wrong anyone since it is not even a deed, resulting from an act of will. They are therefore in rightful physical possession of some part of the land, which they have the intention and capacity to use (their capacity to use land is not, of course, limited to that on which they are physically present) and which they can bring under their control by defending it against others. In accordance with practical reason's postulate, they must be able, by a first act of taking possession of the land they occupy, to acquire a right to such land as they can use and bring under their control; otherwise the rational concept of merely rightful possession and the pure intellectual concepts of having an external object would be empty, without objective reality. Because it is original acquisition, it must take place by a unilateral act of taking possession (*facto*), not by a contract (*pacto*). But, as we have seen, it cannot take place by a unilateral will, because no unilateral will can put others under obligation to refrain from doing what they could otherwise rightfully do, that is, make use of that piece of land. Kant's second point is that, given the finite surface of the earth, their act of taking possession can affect all others whom it excludes from doing what they could otherwise rightfully do (VI, 262).

In saying that the habitable part of the earth's surface must be regarded as originally (prior to any act that would establish a right) possessed in common by the whole human race, Kant means that it must be regarded as in the possession of a general will, the wills of all united for the sake of giving universal law, because it is only in accordance with universal law that any-one can be put under obligation. Were it not for this Idea of original posses-sion in common, it would be impossible to move from the "empirical title" to a piece of land acquired by an act of taking first possession to the "rational title" to that piece of land, to the assertion of a right to it to which there cor-responds obligation on the part of every other (VI, 264.) In order to withdraw any part of land from the use of every other, men must acknowl-edge their reciprocal obligation not to use such parts of the land as others have withdrawn from common use, that is, they must enter a rightful condi-tion, civil society, in which distributive justice obtains. In a state of nature men can provisionally acquire the land they occupy (and with it, things on the land) in accordance with the Idea of a general will, that is, provided their maxim qualifies for being given as external law. But only when this Idea is realized in a physical person or persons, only when civil society comes into existence, can a part of the earth's land be acquired conclusively.

On a limited scale, the problem of what has been acquired originally has been solved through the original contract by which a multitude of in-dividuals forms itself into a state, with courts to settle disputes and deter-mine what has been acquired. But on a broader scale the problem has not yet been solved. In relation to one another, states are still in a state of nature, settling their disputes not by judicial proceedings but by war. Hence Kant concludes that until the original contract extends to the whole human race, all acquisition can be only provisional (VI, 266). Within a state, acquisition is, so to speak, relatively conclusive; but the constant threat of war makes it, at bottom, only provisional. As Kant remarks, in the transition, from Private Right to Public Right, there are three divisions of Public Right: the Right of a State, the Right of Nations, and Cosmopolitan Right; and the relation of these three forms of rightful condition is such that, if the principle of outer freedom limited by law is wanting in only one of them, the framework of all the others is inevitably undermined and must finally collapse (VI, 311). Hence the postulate of Public Right, which follows from practical reason's postulate, holds for states as well as individuals: You ought, with all others whom you cannot avoid being near, to leave the state of nature and enter a rightful condition, that is, one of distributive justice (VI, 256, 307).

With this we return to a more familiar part of Kant's political philosophy, his concern with the form that the association of individuals and states in a rightful condition, that is, their constitution, should have. The constitution of a state should be that which most closely approaches the Idea of a con-stitution; legislative authority should be vested in representatives elected by all the citizens who, having to pay the costs of a war, will not lightly declare war. As for the association of states in a rightful condition, the form their constitution takes can be only analogous to the constitution of a state. What they form is not to be a world-state but a federation of states—eventually, of all states—which will provide the means for settling disputes among them by judicial proceedings. These themes, familiar from "Perpetual Peace," reappear in *The Doctrine of Right.* The difference is that, in the latter work, they follow systematically from practical reason's postulate regarding rights.

As the title of this chapter suggested, its concern was not so much with the question of what form Kant thinks a constitution should take but rather with his approach to this question. His formal, and most mature, approach to the question is through the theory of property he developed shortly before writing his only systematic work on natural rights. As might be supposed, this theory is considerably more complex than could be indicated within the limits of this essay, which has only skimmed the surface. It is to be hoped that the recently awakened interest in *The Doctrine of Right* will resolve the many puzzles in it and explore its ramifications.[17]

Notes

1. Most notably, in "On the Common Saying: 'This May be True in Theory, but it does not Apply in Practice,'" Part II, and "Perpetual Peace." Both are included in Hans Reiss, ed.: *Kant's Political Writings* (Cambridge: Cambridge University Press, 1970), which contains a helpful introduction to Kant's political thought. Citations in this paper are to the volume and page of the Berlin Academy edition of *Kant's gesammelte Schriften.* Translations cited are Reiss, *Kant's Political Writings,* and H. J. Paton, *Groundwork of the Metaphysic of Morals* (New York and Evanston: Harper Torchbooks, 1964).

2. Kant does note that the legislator, from whom all rights are to proceed, must be incapable of wronging anyone and hence must include the will of all the people, since no one can be wronged by what he consents to (VIII, 294: Reiss, 77). This is repeated in *The Doctrine of Right* (VI, 213). In itself, however, it tells us nothing about what rights can be had or acquired. In "Theory and Practice" (VIII, 289: Reiss, 73), Kant enunciates his "universal principle of Right" (see page 73, this volume) and goes on to list the rights to freedom, equality and independence. This too is repeated in *The Doctrine of Right* (VI, 314–15). The third right, to independence as a citizen, includes the qualification of property and hence rights to things, the problem of which seems to lead to the general will as legislative. But only *The Doctrine of Right* deals with this problem.

3. There is unfortunately no common English word that would translate *Recht.* It is "the sum of laws for which external lawgiving is possible." Kant is not, however, concerned with any body of positive laws but with the system of "external natural laws," the moral principles on which positive laws are to be based (see page 73, this volume). By analyzing the concept of *Recht* he obtains the concept of *ein Recht,* an authorization to use coercion: actions prescribed by external laws are duties one can be coerced to fulfill consistently with one's freedom. In these introductory pages I shall move freely between *Recht* or *das Recht,* translated as "Right," and *ein Recht,* translated as "a right" or "rights."

4. *The Doctrine of Right* (the full title of which is *Metaphysical First Principles of the Doctrine of Right*) was first published separately in January 1797. *The Doctrine of Virtue* (*Metaphysical First Principles of the Treatise on Virtue*) was published in August of the same year. They are the two parts of *The Metaphysics of Morals*, which Kant had first mentioned in 1768. On the history of his long-delayed "Metaphysics of Morals," see Lewis W. Beck: *A Commentary on Kant's Critique of Practical Reason* (Chicago: University of Chicago Press, 1960), 5 ff.

5. In Bernd Ludwig's *Philosophische Bibliothek* edition of *The Doctrine of Right* (Hamburg: Meiner, 1986), Section(s) 41–44 form an introduction to Public Right, under the heading "Transition from the Status of What is Yours or Mine in a State of Nature to its Status in a Rightful Condition Generally." On this remarkable edition, see note 6.

6. In 1929, Buchda first suggested that paragraphs 4–8 do not belong in S6. On the history of this discovery, see Thomas Mautner, "Kant's Metaphysics of Morals: A Note on the Text," *Kant-Studien* 72 (1981) 356–59. In 1982, Bernd Ludwig argued that, were these paragraphs replaced by S2, "Practical Reason's Postulate with Regard to Rights," S6 would yield what its title, "Deduction of the Concept of Merely Rightful Possession of an External Object," promises. See "Der Platz des rechtlichen Postulats der praktischen Vernunft innerhalb der Paragraphen 1–6 der kantischen Rechtslehre," in Reinhard Brandt, ed., *Rechtsphilosophie der Aufklarung* (Berlin and New York: de Gruyter, 1982) 219–32. Ludwig's recent edition of the text (see note 5) is a reconstruction of the corrupt text of *The Doctrine of Right*, on the thesis that Kant's instructions regarding the arrangement of materials he had assembled were misunderstood (see Ludwig's Introduction, XXVII ff.), and that Kant (who was working on *The Doctrine of Virtue*) had little concern with the published text. The result was that some material was misplaced in the published text and some material from the *Vorarbeiten* was included. Ludwig's version of the text makes a good deal of sense. I look forward to his detailed defense of his reconstruction of the text in his forthcoming *Kant's Rechtslehre* (Hamburg, Meiner, 1988).

7. Christian Ritter: *Der Rechtsgedanke Kants nach den fruhen Quellen* (Frankfurt/ Main: Klostermann, 1971). His views are summarized on pages 339–41.

8. In addition to Ludwig's Introduction, see Reinhard Brandt: *Eigentumstheorien von Grotius bis Kant* (Stuttgart/Bad-Cannstatt: Fromann, 1974), 167. Brandt includes selections from the *Bemerkungen* and *The Doctrine of Right*, with valuable Introductions. The *Bemerkungen* are in Vol. XX of the *Akademie* edition, and the Vigilantius lectures in Vol. XXVII, 2. See also Wolfgang Kersting: *Wohlgeordnete Freiheit* (Berlin and New York: de Gruyter, 1984), 113 ff. In his Introduction, Ludwig quotes Schiller's letter to Erhard of October 26, 1794, to the effect that he has heard that something is to be expected, in the forthcoming *Metaphysics of Morals*, about the difficult problem of deriving the right to property, but that Kant is no longer satisfied with his ideas on the subject.

9. See H.B. Acton's gloss on IV, 427–430; Paton, *Groundwork* 95–98: "The Principle of Universal Law limits the actions of each individual to those which all men could do or will. In choosing his maxims, therefore, each individual ought to have a concern for the scope of choice of everyone else. No individual, therefore, can be left out from the range of those for which each ought to have a concern." *Kant's Moral Philosophy* (Macmillan, St. Martin's Press, 1970), 36.

10. See Beck, *A Commentary on Kant's Critique* 164 ff.

11. See VI, 223: "A *person* is a subject whose actions can be *imputed* to him. *Moral* personality is therefore nothing other than the freedom of a rational being under moral laws. Hence a person is subject to no other laws than those he gives himself (either alone or at least along with others)."

12. VI, 384–85: "An *end* is an *object* of free choice, the thought of which determines choice to an action by which the object is brought about. Every action, therefore, has its end; and since no one can have an end without *himself* making the object of choice into an end, it follows that the adoption of any end of action whatsoever is an act of *freedom* on the agent's part, not an operation of *nature*." In view of the distinction between *Willkur* and *Wille* that Kant drew in the second *Critique* and uses in *The Metaphysics of Morals* (see Beck, *A Commentary on Kant's Critique* 176 ff.), "choice" would seem, on the whole, the appropriate translation of *Willkur*. However, this distinction lies beyond the scope of this paper, and I have used "choice" and "the will" indiscriminately.

13. It may be noted in passing that the distinction between analytic and synthetic propositions in the *Doctrine of Right* is a serious problem. I take it that the concept of a right is developed analytically from the concept of Right or the condition of outer freedom (VI, 396). However, no analysis of a concept can establish that one is under obligation to act in accordance with the principle that yields that concept. Hence when Kant formulates the universal principle of Right as the imperative "so act externally that the free exercise of your will can coexist with the freedom of everyone in accordance with a universal law," he notes that reason "lays this down as a postulate which is incapable of further proof" (VI, 232). By a postulate in this context he apparently means "a practical imperative given a priori, for which no further proof can be given since its possibility cannot be explained" (VIII, 419 n.). However, it is apparently derived from the supreme principle of morality (VI, 239), which is a synthetic proposition. Whether practical reason's postulate with regard to rights is synthetic only because it is derived analytically from a synthetic proposition or whether further considerations are involved is a more complex question.

14. What we can use is not limited to things but also includes the wills of other persons and other persons themselves (VI, 247–48). Kant is here beginning to establish the basis for contractual and domestic rights, as well as rights to things. However, the text indicates that he is thinking primarily in terms of rights to things.

15. On the concept of "having," a predicable or derivative concept of the category of cause, see XXIII, 323. In the *Vorarbeiten* Kant was greatly concerned with categories and even schemata for applying these pure intellectual concepts to objects of experience. See Monika Sanger: *Die kategoriale Systematik in den "Metaphysischen Anfangsgrunden der Rechtslehre"* (Berlin and New York: de Gruyter, 1982). There is some use of modal categories in "How to Acquire Something External." But Kant's primary concern there is with the problem of moving from physical possession, possession in appearance, to merely rightful possession.

16. *De iure belli ac pacis libri tres*, II, 2, S 1–2. Brandt, in *Eigenstumstheorien von Grotius bis Kant*, provides a German translation of these sections.

17. For valuable suggestions regarding the content of this essay I am indebted to Reinhard Brandt for a letter regarding the translation of *Recht*; to Douglas Dryer for his comments on a paper, "Kant's Theory of Property," which I presented to the

North American Kant Society; to Betty Kiehl, whose thesis on Kant's antinomies includes the antinomy regarding the concept of possession; and to Leslie Mulholland for a letter regarding matters in his commentary on *The Doctrine of Right*, which I hope will soon be published. They are, of course, not responsible for the use I have made of their suggestions.

5

Hegel's Idea of Constitutionalism

Peter G. Stillman

The writings of G.W.F. Hegel (1770–1831) are commonly acknowledged as being among the most difficult and influential in philosophical literature. A major achievement of Stillman's essay is the clarity his approach brings to his analysis of the leading ideas in Hegel's constitutionalism. His study describes these ideas as largely originating in the ancient Greek philosophy of Aristotle but as redefined along the lines of eighteenth- and early nineteenth-century German Idealism. Finally, special attention is given Hegel's critique of important concepts in the liberal theories of Locke and Montesquieu, and its implications for contemporary constitutionalism. Stillman also includes a section about Marx's criticism of Hegel's constitutionalism which further elucidates Hegel's thought by outlining key differences between Hegel's and Marx's philosophy.

Hegel is self-consciously a modern political philosopher who sees himself as working within the philosophical tradition of Montesquieu, Rousseau, and Kant, as accepting the main values of the French Revolution, and as stressing freedom, that pervasive (and protean) modern political goal. At the same time, however, Hegel thinks that modern political thought and practice are not attentive enough to custom, community, and the social construction of the individual. So he looks outside the main strands of modern thought for insights into how political life should be structured.

When he discusses constitutions, he draws extensively on Aristotelian themes. Following Aristotle's lead, Hegel concentrates on existing practices and norms; he defines constitutions both narrowly (as governmental institutions and aims) and broadly (including also the values and goals of individuals and social structures within the state); and he looks at the interrelations of governmental and people, the interdependence of branches of government, and the need to make governments strong enough to govern as well as to maintain enforceable limits to their activities. As a result, Hegel's constitutional thought contains both ancient and modern influences; so Hegel has distinct, provocative, and frequently insightful views on many constitutional issues.

THE ARISTOTELIAN BACKGROUND OF HEGEL'S CONSTITUTIONALISM

Aristotle's theory of constitutions (*politeia*) stands as a major intellectual origin of Hegel's constitutional ideas. For Aristotle, the constitution of a city or state is essentially the ordering, functioning, and goal of its political institutions and practices. Partly because the boundaries of the "political" are uncertain, he uses two distinct definitions of constitution[1] In one definition, the one more familiar to modern thinking, he focuses on the government, the distribution of its offices and the arrangements for the determination of the ends to be realized by the polis (Pol. 1289a). In the other definition, best represented by Montesquieu's "spirit of the laws," Aristotle considers the totality of citizen activities and ends, the way of life of the citizen body (Pol. 1295a).

Aristotle's dual definition requires that his constitutional analysis have a dual concern. One concern involves a narrow focus on the arrangement of offices of the state and the goals they pursue. Some leading issues are the three different types of offices—deliberative, official, and judicial (Pol. 1297b); the different types of rule, such as democracy and oligarchy, as well as mixed government; and the different conceptions of justice operative in different cities (Pol. 1301a). These issues are Aristotle's equivalent of the institutional and normative concerns of much modern constitutional thought and, like many modern thinkers, he devotes much care to them.

As he considers these topics, however, his thinking drives him from concern with the purely governmental to a second and broader concern, the full range of all that citizens do and think. When he notes that many different kinds of constitutions exist—not only democracy and oligarchy but different degrees of democracies—he immediately looks to nongovernmental factors: "the reason for the plurality of constitutions lies in the plurality of parts in every state" (Pol. 1289b); "parts" such as households, families, and groupings based around the distribution of wealth, occupation, and arms (Pol. 1289b; see 1288b–1300b); "parts" that make up what in modern terminology might be labelled society or social organization. At the same time, just like Socrates' drawing parallels between regimes and character in the *Republic* (bks. 8 and 9), Aristotle looks at how the order and goals of the city and its "parts" influence and shape the values and virtues of its individual citizens (Pol. 1276b).

Conversely, when Aristotle examines his preferred mixed government, called polity (*politeia*), he directly notes the social and individual prerequisites of that form—most importantly, a strong middle class which produces social groups relatively free from sharp factions and divisions (Pol. 1296a), and individuals who tend to be moderate and not unjust (Pol. 1295b). In other words, when Aristotle considers constitutions in the narrow sense of governmental arrangements and goals, his logic impels him to consider also constitutions in the broad sense; and "constitution" in the broad sense connects into a unified whole the governmental arrangements ("constitution" in the narrow sense), the "parts" of the city (its social arrangements), and the values and virtues of individual citizens.

"Constitution," in Aristotle's twofold sense, carries other important meanings that reappear in Hegel's constitutionalism. Aristotle's twofold definition suggests that every city—except those ruled arbitrarily, without laws (Pol. 1292a)—has a constitution because it has a definite arrangement of governmental offices and a way of life; so almost every state has a constitution that can be described. Aristotle's discussions of constitutions include extensive descriptive analyses of how existing cities are ordered and how historically those orders developed. For Aristotle, constitutional thinking relies on description and history of government, "parts," and citizen virtue.[2]

At the same time, for Aristotle evaluation is always implicit in the study of constitutions: since both senses of the term include a city's understanding of justice, the good life, and its own goals, Aristotle judges these understandings and evaluates constitutions as good or bad, better or worse. Assessment allows prescription; and when Aristotle prescribes constitutions, he not only discusses how the government should be structured but also weighs heavily the qualities of the city's citizens and "parts." To try to reform a constitution requires diligent attention to what is possible in the current condition of citizen virtue and institutions. When Aristotle suggests the "best constitution and best life . . . for the majority of states and the majority of men" (Pol. 1295a), he proposes a mixed government called *politeia*, translated as "polity"—but it is the same word that in other contexts is translated as "constitution." I think Aristotle uses the same word because he regards polity as the practical—or most likely to be practicable—model constitution, that is, as the norm towards which existing constitutions ought to move, to the extent possible (Pol. 1296b–1297a). In other words, from his extensive and critical analysis of existing constitutions, ideas of justice, and understanding of the good life, Aristotle infers and develops a practical standard of a good constitution—polity. Sound and practicable standards are to be found in or developed from existing human practice.

Aristotle's constitutionalism is marked by a twofold definition of constitutions; a sense of the close relations among citizen, society, and state; and a concern with description, evaluation, and prescription. In a critical and appreciative manner, Hegel adopts and adapts these ideas. To use other terminology, in contrast to "modern constitutionalism," where constitutions are valued to the extent that they set limits on governmental power in order to protect individual rights, Hegel's thought is pervaded by "ancient constitutionalism."[3]

SOME MODERN INFLUENCES ON
HEGEL'S CONSTITUTIONALISM

The immediate background of Hegel's constitutional thought is formed by three factors. One factor is modern political philosophy. Hegel does not see his philosophy as a Copernican revolution that radically breaks from the past. Historically minded, he sees himself as building on, criticizing, and transforming previous philosophies. So, at the same time that he praises their accomplishments (3R),[4] he sees numerous shortcomings in modern constitutional thought. For instance, Hegel is uneasy with the sharp division, present in Machiavelli (*The Prince*, chap. XV), Locke, and Kant, between ethics and politics, between what ought to be and what is, between natural law and political science, or—in most general terms—between the theory that the state should be judged by and should aim to attain ethical or moral goals (such as classical natural law or the ideal Christian commonwealth) and the theory that the state should promote the earthly needs and interests of itself and its citizens, who use the government as a means to facilitate pursuit of their private goals (such as peace, order, and freedom). Hegel also thinks that his modern predecessors conceptualize the state too frequently in terms of oppositions either between citizen and government or among the governmental powers; that they view political institutions and laws too much in terms of limiting and restricting rights and freedoms (29); and that they conceive the free individual isolated from his fellows (258R) and thereby impoverished in capabilities and development.

The second immediate background factor of Hegel's constitutional thought is the German tradition of the *Rechtsstaat*, which flourished from at least 1750. Essentially this presents the state as a juridical association that declares, organizes, and defends the rights of citizens; these rights serve to limit and regularize the state's exercise of its power; and state action must respect the forms and limits of law. So a *Rechtsstaat* operates by settled, consistent, and predictable laws—it administers these laws fairly and abides by them itself.[5] From Hegel's point of view, a *Rechtsstaat* is a great accomplishment—it is "infinitely important" that the rights and duties of the state and the citizen be determined by law (258R, n.)—but he also sees a need to supplement the *Rechtsstaat* or juridical state to assure that the state enacts wise laws, is legitimate in the eyes of its citizens, and has vitality and unity.

The third influence on Hegel's constitutional thought is contemporary history. The influence of the French Revolution on Hegel's generation—he, like Beethoven and Wordsworth, was born in 1770—was so powerful, massive, and various as to be difficult to summarize. In terms of constitutional thought, Hegel saw the need to accept and institutionalize some key dimensions of the revolution, such as the rights of man, a legislative role for the Third Estate, and Napoleon's reforms of bureaucracy, rationalization of legal codes, and reshaping of the map of Europe. But how? The revolution also generated excesses—ideological thinking (WH, 91–92), extremist quests for absolute freedom, an intolerance of social differentiation (PhG, VI.B.iii), legislative supremacy, and a plethora of unstable and short-lived constitutions. Thus it left the immense problem of discerning and structuring a stable and free constitutional order, the political realization of freedom.[6]

HEGEL'S CONSTITUTIONALISM

Hegel's political philosophy responds to what he sees as the promise and failures of modern political and constitutional thought and practice. In terms of the dilemmas posed by the modern world in the aftermath of the French Revolution, Hegel wishes to embody in institutionalized practices the modern freedoms asserted by the Enlightenment, the new science of political economy, and the French Revolution, and at the same time to unify those potentially centrifugal freedoms within an ethical order (focused by a state), that assures political unity, community and cooperation, and spiritual and cultural development. In Hegelian terms, Hegel wishes to combine substance and subject—that is, the substantial order of a common political life and subjective freedom—or "the objective ethical order . . . made concrete by subjectivity" (144), the free subjective willing and acting of citizens.

In his political philosophy as expressed primarily in the *Philosophy of Right,* Hegel advocates and upholds liberal rights and personal morality; nuclear families based on love; a civil society marked by a generally free market economy (or "system of [the creation and satisfaction of] needs"); an open occupational and class system; a melange of groups and (Tocquevillean) "secondary associations" labelled Corporations; a liberal administration of justice and a "police" that also administers welfare measures and some price controls on staples; and a state, that unifies them all into an organic ethical community—a broad and self-conscious unity. Hegel thinks unification at the level of the state as a community is needed because he sees that, contrary to classical economic theory, a free economic order is not self-balancing (241–48). For Hegel, the constitution is the organization of the state (259, 271), this complex community composed of many parts. To conceptualize such a constitution, Hegel retrieves aspects of the Aristotelian approach to constitutions—that is, he insists on a double definition of constitution, includes goals or ends in his discussion of institutions and practices, and sees himself not as creating what ought to be but as discerning and describing the essential elements in the actual practices of contemporary Western European states.

Hegel's state, as a complex community, includes both the "strictly political state" (273) and the community taken with all of its parts. So the constitution, as the organization of this twofold state, is similarly twofold. Hegel's narrow definition of constitution—the "political constitution" (WH, 110)—treats, like Aristotle's, offices and ends. It is the "articulation and organization of state-power" which is "differentiated into particular agencies" and which pursues the goals of justice and liberty (Enc. 539; 272–73).

For Hegel, the modern and rational political constitution is a limited or constitutional monarchy. Institutionally—in terms of "offices"—the government is divided into three branches, the division of which is "of the highest importance" (272R). But it must be taken "in its true sense" (272R). Hegel's treatment of the division of powers is far from conventional. The three powers are the (legislative) power "to determine and establish the universal," the laws; the (executive) power "to subsume single cases and the spheres of particularity under the universal"; and the (authoritative) "power of subjectivity as the will with the power of ultimate decision" (273). The roughly corresponding branches of government are the legislature, the public authority or bureaucracy (labelled by Hegel the executive), and the constitutional monarch. For Hegel, the judiciary is not a major institutional branch; the separate branches share powers; and the three branches are conceptualized and structured so that they work together rather than oppose each other.

The power of ultimate decision is located primarily in the monarchial branch of government. The constitutional monarch is "absolute self-determination" (275), the final point of authorizing, the locus of subjectivity and individuality. The representation and culmination of the subjective freedom of the will of the modern world, the monarch works with the legislature by signing the laws and with the executive as its ultimate head. In a well-organized modern state, the monarch's discretionary power is limited: advised by a cabinet drawn from the legislature and from the executive, and working within a stable constitution, the "monarch's part is merely to set to the law the subjective 'I will'" (280A).

The executive power entails the application and execution of the general or universal statements of legislature, monarch, and constitution to specific cases, that is, it "subsumes the particular under the universal" (287). So the executive branch includes not only the usual cabinet-level officials but also the "powers of the judiciary and the police" or street-level public authorities, for example, the police, welfare officials, customs officers. Hegel characterizes the executive bureaucracy in terms similar to Weberian rational-legal bureaucratic structure, such as hierarchical accountability and appointments on the basis of merit.[7] Hegel also insists that civil servants receive a classical, humanistic, and political "education in thought and ethical conduct." (296; HPW, 257); be drawn from the "politically conscious" middle class (297); and so act with a "dispassionate, upright, and polite demeanour" (296) and have deep and "comprehensive insight into the state's organization and requirements" (301R).

The third power of government is the legislative, whose primary concerns are the further development and refinement of the laws and attention to home affairs generally (298). The legislature, the Estates, is divided into two houses, reflecting the agricultural and business estates or classes of civil society (312). One house is similar to a House of Lords. According to Hegel, members of the landowning class have "independent" wills (306A): their wills are self-determining because, like the monarch's, they rest only on nature, on birth and inheritance; and, even though they engage in the system of wants in civil society, they are independent of the "uncertainty of business, the quest for profits, and any sort of fluctuation in possession" (306), secure in their inherited status and entailed landholdings.

The "second section of the Estates comprises the fluctuating element in civil society" (308), that is, the workers and owners who make up the business class. They elect representatives, who are chosen—and here is a point on which Hegel insists frequently—by the society "as a society, articulated into associations, communities, and Corporations" (308) in order to assure both the representation of the "essential spheres of society and its large-scale interests" (311) in the Estates and, conversely, the political significance of the major associations of civil society and therefore the political education of their members. These representatives are chosen by voters on "the strength of confidence felt in them" that they have "a better understanding" of public affairs (309). The assembly itself is "a living body in which all members deliberate in common and reciprocally instruct and convince each other" (309), in which specific interests of associations and their members are "made good in an assembly whose concern is with the public interest" (309A),[8] and in which all debates are public.

At the same time that Hegel insists on the division of powers and characterizes each branch of government primarily in terms of one governmental power, he insists that the separate branches share powers. The legislative power, for instance, is shared by the Estates, who vote on legislation according to their common sense of the needs and shared interests of civil society; the monarch, who has the ultimate decision on all legislation, to sign or not; and the executive, who serve as an advisory body to monarch and Estates because of their extensive political knowledge.

That the branches share powers means that each branch depends on the others. In describing this interdependence of the branches, Hegel in his constitutional thought rejects the idea of the independent self-subsistence of any branch or power; the claim of primacy of any branch; and the prevalent theory that the branches are essentially opposed to, mutually restricting of, or mutually checking each other by a process of "power opposing power" or "ambition counteracting ambition."[9] Hegel's comprehension of the division of powers produces what he calls an organic unity. In an organic unity, divisions must be sharp and clear so that each part is not independent but relies on the whole. In Aristotle's analogy, the human body is an organic unity because the parts of the body all have clearly distinguished functions, each part by itself (for example, a hand cut off from the body) cannot act, and every part in order to perform relies on the whole and its unity with the whole.

So each branch is in itself only a partial actor, able to perform merely a portion of what the state requires: only by mutual conjunction are they made whole, able to legislate, authorize, and execute the laws the state requires. "A living interrelationship exists only in an articulated whole whose parts themselves form particular subordinated spheres" (HPW,263); the political constitution is the living, articulated whole, divided into parts that are separate spheres and whose partiality is eliminated and made whole only by their mutual cooperation with the other parts. With both powers and branches of government, what is crucial in terms of an "organic unity" is the mutual dependence of each on the other, their insufficiency on their own, and the need for mutual cooperation to sustain the whole (and thus themselves as parts of the whole). "In the rational organism of the state, each member, by maintaining itself in its own position, *eo ipso* maintains the others in theirs" (286; WH, 123).

Because of Hegel's interpretation of the division of powers, he sees that the "constitution is essentially a series of mediations" (302A) (and not, for instance, as a series of oppositions where each branch is fortified against the others). The political constitution and the nation as a whole are complex unities made up of many parts. In order that the parts in potential opposition to each other do not fall into actual opposition, other parts must "mediate" their relations—which may mean to arrange a compromise but more likely means to convey information and arguments, to provide a different perspective that may be decisive, or to agree with one party and persuade the other to go along. Because the first and most extreme constitutional division is between rulers and ruled, a most important mediation is between government and people, and is performed by the Estates.

Through that branch of the government, the people—articulated into their associations by their representatives in the Estates—have a voice for their concerns to the government in general and the government has a route by which to express and legitimate its goals.

Further mediations permeate the political constitution and relate the strictly political institutions to civil society and the broader constitution in general. Both bureaucracy and Estates mediate between private persons (again, as organized into their associations) and the monarch, to keep the monarch from becoming isolated from popular opinion and particular concerns and to keep the people informed about the intentions underlying authoritative governmental actions. When necessary, the upper house of the Estates mediates between the lower house and the monarch, since the members of the upper house are like both those represented in the lower house, because they all participate in civil society, and the monarch, because they attain their status and their self-determining volition by birth.

The mediations necessary between the people and the government with its branches indicate that the political or narrow constitution necessarily relates to what Aristotle and Hegel see as the broad constitution. The broad constitution encompasses political institutions, social structures, and individual culture; it is the way of life of the citizens or "the character and development of [their] self-consciousness" (274)—including especially their education, will, and rights, their social institutions, the political constitution, and their goals (264–65). So the broad constitution consists of the political constitution as well as the operative ideologies of liberal rights and personal morality and the institutionalized interactions of family, civil society, and state, that is, the full content of the *Philosophy of Right*. The broad constitution structures a variegated and differentiated community with a plurality of attitudes and practices, in which individual freedom and *Bildung* (education and cultivation) occur; in which public order, law, and community prevail; and in which the demands of *Geist* or spirit are realized because the society has attained self-conscious knowledge actualized in institutions. The political constitution is the internal structure of the state; the broad constitution is the way of life and the spirit of the citizens and the state as a whole.

Following Aristotle in distinguishing political and broad constitutions, Hegel if anything puts more emphasis than Aristotle on the descriptive element in constitutional thinking. Although he transforms reality into the philosophical terms of his own categories, Hegel nonetheless sees himself as presenting the essential elements in the actual practices of existing Western European states (and constitutions). The *Philosophy of Right*, "as a work of philosophy . . . must be poles apart from an attempt to construct the state as it ought to be. The instruction which it may contain cannot consist in teaching the state what it ought to be; it can only show how the state, the ethical universe, is to be understood" (Preface, 11).

At the same time, Hegel's descriptive method, like Aristotle's, leads to evaluation, "the essential determination of the constitution amidst all the various aspects of political life can be expressed in the following proposition: the best state is that in which the greatest degree of freedom prevails" (WH, 119). Since the *Philosophy of Right* describes what attitudes and practices are required to attain "the greatest degree of freedom," Hegel is not averse to criticizing explicitly the misguided French and English policies on Corporations (290A; 245R), English common law (211A; 225R), and the impotence of the English monarch (HPW, 330). Any reader who knows the institutions of contemporary German states (such as Prussia) knows how far each falls short of the institutions of true freedom Hegel presents.[10]

Hegel's description and evaluation also lead to prescription: within the limits of what is possible, state officers and citizens should try to reform their institutions and ideas to more closely resemble those presented in the *Philosophy of Right*. So the general direction for reform is stated, even if the specifics, as always, are a matter for political prudence not philosophical speculation, and even if the limits of what is possible can be quite severe for Hegel's state as for Aristotle's city. Both require an extensive middle class, and Hegel's state requires certain attitudes and ideas—like liberal rights and personal morality—that cannot be simply manipulated into existence, as may sometimes be the case with institutional reforms.

Like Aristotle, Hegel's constitutional thought includes not only institutions and attitudes but also goals. The goals of the political constitution are the maintenance and reproduction of the structure of the state and the actualizing and guaranteeing of the "modern principles of right" (Enc. 544R), such as personal liberty, liberty of property, the freedoms of civil society, and the like, all of which make possible the full development of individual freedom. The goals of the broad constitution are to maintain and reproduce the society as a whole in all its "moments" or parts and to actualize and guarantee personal liberties ethical communities, openness, and hierarchy, all of which encourage and facilitate the full development of individual freedom and the rationality of the state.

THE RATIONAL CONSTITUTION: LOGIC AND FREEDOM

For Hegel, the state and constitution described in the *Philosophy of Right* are rational because they express and manifest the highest development and actualization of human potentialities yet seen. The constitution does so in essentially two interconnected ways. First, it embodies Hegel's logic, which especially tries to explain differentiation and diversity as well as the relations and unities among diverse elements (272). Any fully developed concept contains deeply developed differentiations. In the case of the concept of the constitution, "the nature of the concept" demands the establishment of differentiations or "moments" that are based in logic (individuality, particularity, and universality), in governmental powers (authorizing or deciding, executive, and legislative), and in governmental branches (monarch, public bureaucracy, and Estates).

In Hegel's logic, divisions must be distinct and developed for unity to come into being; his logic asserts the ultimate fluidity of sharp differentiation—so that each factor or moment takes on the essential characteristics of each other, continues to relate to each of them, and thereby maintains the unity of the whole (Enc. 189). In terms of one governmental branch, for instance, the monarch, the individual who decides and authorizes, also considers particular matters in his position as the ultimate head of the executive and plays a role in stating or changing the laws. Sharing powers, the monarch must also interact with the other branches (for example, the monarch could not sign a law unless the Estates had passed it). The result is that the three governmental branches are mediated and unified into a purposive whole (273; WH, 123). The organic unity of the branches also exists for the powers of government and the moments of the concept. So "the [political] constitution is rational in so far as the state inwardly differentiates and determines its activity in accordance with the nature of the concept." (272).

The constitution is also rational to the extent that it expresses concretely—that is, in articulated institutional form—the will of the people and their freedom, specifically, their self-knowledge of themselves as self-determining self-conscious actors who choose and accept structures and practices in which they can develop and cultivate their capacities for family life, free (and legal) use of their property and talents in the system of needs, memberships in civil society, and citizenship. In short, the rational constitution must express the free will of the people, their values, rights, interests, customs, and purposes. "The will is free, so that freedom is both the substance of right and its goal, while the system of right is the realm of freedom made actual" (4), the constitution being the framework of that system of right. Or, in another Hegelian phraseology, "an existent of any sort embodying the free will, that is what right is" (29). For Hegel, every major institution discussed in the *Philosophy of Right* is "an existent . . . embodying the free will" because it expresses freedom and assists the development of freedom; the broad constitution and the political constitution are the organization of those free institutions. Since both constitutions mediate oppositions and have parts that work organically together for freedom and other goals, both broad and narrow constitutions not only express but also maintain or re-create the ordering of the institutions of the *Philosophy of Right* and its state as well as the freedom of the citizens.

Indeed, for Hegel, the two dimensions of the rationality of the constitution—logic and freedom— are two sides of the same coin or, more precisely, two different ways of stating the same matter. Hegel sees his logic as a logic of development, generated internally by insufficiency or incompleteness, to greater knowledge; Hegel sees freedom as development, generated internally by dissatisfaction with the underdevelopment of individuals and institutions, to greater self-knowledge. The rational political constitution reflects that fully developed logic and manifests that fully developed freedom in its organization of state power; the rational broad constitution does the same for all the major practices and attitudes of the lives of the citizens.

HEGEL'S RESPONSES TO MODERN CONSTITUTIONAL THOUGHT

Hegel's constitutional theory addresses many dilemmas that he saw in previous constitutional thought and practice. He wishes to criticize the *Rechtsstaat*, retain it, and subsume it into a larger whole. His criticism is acute. Too frequently, its advocates engage in a naive constitutional thinking "in which the state is portrayed from top to bottom as an abstraction which is supposed to rule and command" (273R), with no attention to how the governors and government officials act and interact or to how citizens regard the state. Equally, and as Marcuse has pungently argued,[11] when Hegel connects the rule of law and the protection of property, he sees the limits of the rule of law. "The function of judicial administration is only to actualize to necessity the abstract side of personal liberty in civil society" (Enc. 532), that is, to assure individuals' rights of life, liberty, and property. But the administering of the rule of law cannot be, for Hegel, a final point of integration of a society, because the rights of the person are only one dimension of the full individual. Thus, any rights-based community would be only a partial community (or a partial universality), because the inequalities and conflicts that attend property relations in the administration of justice prevent any civil society from attaining a full community among all its members (241–48), and because the rule of law can be administered without individuals' attaining consciousness of its universality, validity, and legitimacy (Enc. 532). So, for Hegel, the *Rechtsstaat* alone is an inadequate and insufficient vision of a lawful political order.

At the same time, the *Philosophy of Right* presents a constitution which retains the valuable features of the *Rechtsstaat*. Hegel insists repeatedly on the importance of law to define and make known the rights and duties of the state and the citizens (258R n.). For Hegel, the government operates by set legal procedures (Enc. 543) and acts "in subordination of the laws" (Enc. 544R); and citizens live under a public and systematic legal code of positive law (215) that reflects the abstract or liberal rights (of life, liberty, and property) of the person (211–12).

Hegel also goes beyond the juridical state that rules through law. Since he insists that citizens be "knowing subjects" who recognize and consciously will their relation to the law (WH, 101), his constitutional state has popular and public dimensions; since its laws are concretized rights, it is based on rights and is philosophically justifiable; with its systematic laws, it contributes to the rationality of the state and the *Bildung* of the citizen. So the juridical state reaches into and becomes a subordinate element in Hegel's broad constitution. As subordinate, it is superseded: it is not enough that citizens obey the laws; the laws must be good laws that warrant obedience. For Hegel, right laws can only be determined by the members of the political constitution, who know that they must legislate in accord with the broad constitution, if the laws are to be effective and regarded as legitimate, and who do legislate only after consulting public opinion and debating in the Estates. In all these activities the legislation must consider not only individual rights but also social institutions (such as family, associations, and Corporations) operated by the broad constitution. In Hegel's constitution, in other words, power and influence flow in all directions, not only from the top down; the law takes into account not only narrow jurisprudential or rights-based logic but also the complex of essential social institutions; political institutions and sociopolitical mediations attempt to ensure that the laws are good and right; and obedience derives from popular knowledge of the laws and how they were made.

The French Revolution and its aftermath posed a different set of dilemmas. Responding to the problem of political ordering in constitutional terms, Hegel insists that "a constitution is not just something manufactured"; it depends on society and citizens[12] and so "is the work of centuries" (274A). He thinks that (political) constitutions must be in accord "with the national spirit at a given stage of its development" (WH, 123) and are "not a matter of free choice" (WH, 117–18). Consequently, a constitution cannot be made, maufactured, or created a priori and given to a country.

In order for a state to have a rational political constitution, that state must contain the social structures, that is, the broad constitution (spelled out in the *Philosophy of Right*) such as the nuclear family and corporations (255R) and citizens who will act politically and in congruence with the constitution; the best or rational constitution cannot be successfully installed anywhere. In general, political constitutions are not matters of choice; they follow from the broad constitution of a country, and therefore they should be seen as the political expression of the consciousness and way of life of the citizens— "every nation has the constitution appropriate to it and suitable for it" (274R). As long as the political consciousness and social organization of a people remain roughly stable, the range of possible effective political constitutions remains very restricted.[13]

Hegel argues, in effect, that every nation should accept and respect its constitution. If the constitution is regarded as expendable, Hegel fears the return of the revolutions and political chaos of 1789–1815 (HPW, 330) with

the attendant lack of secure rights, real freedom, and individual development (153R). Where the constitution is accepted, then people will think in
terms of reforming (rather than discarding or ignoring) it, and can use the
Philosophy of Right as a model for reform. Unlike those conservatives who
advocate venerating the constitution in the hopes of preventing change, and
unlike those revolutionaries who advocate replacing a constitution whenever it does not work very well, Hegel tries to strike an intermediate ground
that both upholds the constitution and leads to its reform.

For Hegel, the contemporary crisis of constitutional order lies partly in
the dislocation of people's sense of history, a dislocation caused by the
massive impacts of the French Revolution and symbolized by ideologies of
left versus right, by a traditional conservatism embracing all of the past except the recent history of twenty-five years of European revolution (HPW,
282), and by a radicalism appealing to the tradition of the French Revolution. Rather than see the tradition and revolution as dichotomies or op-
posites, Hegel wishes to see history as both: tradition is retained and
revolutionized, revolution becomes part of tradition. So Hegel presents a
tradition that encompasses revolution, takes over its significant achievements, and casts aside its (more radical) failures. At the same time, the
revolution has transformed many customs and traditions: personal rights,
bureaucratic rule, and systematic rationalized law have replaced positive
privileges, irregular execution of laws by noblemen and tax farmers, and un-
codified law.[14] Hegel insists on emphasizing both tradition and revolution
in order to enable constitutional order and action in a present that has been
formed by both.

From Hegel's point of view, some other erroneous views displayed during
the French Revolution are closely connected with ideas of previous constitutional theorists. Hegel's interpretation of the division of powers differs
importantly from Montesquieu's. In opposition to Locke and many actors
of 1789–95, Hegel argues against the predominance of the legislative power,
fearing that only disorder and tyrannies can come from popular rule when it
is not ordered and made rational by the two houses, monarch and executive.
Along similar lines, he argues against universal participatory democracy
(308R) and unlimited free speech (319R); for Hegel, all are equally abstract
(or ideological) ideas that ignore the rich articulated context of society and
the need for differentiated organization of government. He also objects to
theories that oppose the people against the government, or the government
against the constitution; linked as they are in the broad constitution, their
relations and mediations must be sought. Likewise, he thinks that constitutions are not simply means to allow citizens to further their own private
ends, or neutral procedures that let citizens then do as they wish; rather,
constitutions shape—and are shaped by—the people, their actions, and
their goals.

Hegel thinks that constitutions and constitutional law should be seen not as limiting rights and freedoms (nor, indeed, as creating them, as bills of rights may seem to do), but as stating, defining, and expressing the rights and freedoms that citizens have. Three separate points are at issue here. One is that Hegel disagrees with those (social contract) theorists who start from the single individual with rights and then have him limit his freedom with a social contract (258R); for Hegel, the individual with rights is (and should be recognized as) a product of a long sociohistorical development, not a product of nature (52R; Enc. 502), and his rights inhere in him as an individual who is a member of a specific modern state and constitution. The second is that constitutions neither limit nor create freedoms; rather, they express the level of freedom that has attained in a state. But, third it is important that the expression be explicit: for freedom requires an organized and articulated society and government, and the constitution, by making explicit and clear that organization, regularizes and ratifies those freedoms (258R; PhG, VI.B.iii).

Finally, Hegel addresses and tries to resolve the dilemma of the split between what political life ought to be and what it is, or between ethics and politics. Hegel's constitutional thought encompasses and unites both sides of the opposition. Hegel's broad constitution embodies norms and values about how governments ought to act (or, to use other terminology, norms and values that the government must respect if it is to be a true government); the broad constitution encompasses the citizens' political consciousness (for example, their sense of their rights), their associations with their (partial) goals, proper and just relations among these associations, and the *telos* of the political constitution. In more Hegelian terms, *Geist* or spirit—the historically developing intersubjective community of all human beings—has attained a stage of maturation (in the actualized institutions and culture of political, social, and individual life described in the *Philosophy of Right*) that is the highest that human beings can at present attain; so to attain and maintain that level is the goal for existing states.

At the same time that constitutions reflect the norms of a mature *Geist*, constitutions (both political and broad) exist as the assurance of law, peace, and order. The political constitution must, of course, be effective at maintaining the peace; but for Hegel "law and order" stem not so much from the central government as from the consciousness of the citizens, that is, from the broad constitution. "Commonplace thinking often has the impression that force holds the state together, but in fact its only bond is the fundamental sense of order which everybody possesses" (268A). For Hegel, keeping order is the minimal requisite and defining characteristic of a constitution, and one that fails is inefficacious and unreal, a constitution in name only, not in fact. So, for Hegel, the constitution contains both ethical ends and political order, and thus unites the two divergent philosophical traditions; as in the book's alternate title, *Naturrecht* and *Staatswissenschaft* join in the *Philosophy of Right*.

Hegel's *Philosophy of Right* is thus also an attempt to refute—and eliminate from contemporary political impact—all arguments advocating a higher ideal or standard for political and social life. Hegel does not wish external standards, whether they be substantive goals like ancient natural law or procedural requirements like popular sovereignty, to be operative. For Hegel, these ideals upset the current order with its values and mitigate against its reform. They do not make persons virtuous or free, which only actual constitutions can do; they are advocated by ideologues (HPW, 263) who think abstractly and ignore the complexity and variety of human earthly life; and they lack philosophical grounding (and usually turn out to be the subjective or personal utopia of their author). Hegel wishes to replace the appeal to higher standards with standards and goals that are already existent and discernible in the actions and institutions of the society (Preface, 10–13); to displace energy from creating utopias to political activity that actualizes existing social potential; to undercut the ideologue and justify the liberally educated and politically practiced individual; and to transform political and constitutional thought from the pursuit of higher, external ideals to the interpretation and comprehension of contemporary actuality.

THE GUARANTEES OF CONSTITUTIONAL RULE

In the *Philosophy of Right*, the philosophical comprehension of the modern state, Hegel presents the political constitution as functioning smoothly. But he is acutely aware that constitutional arrangements need to be assured and guaranteed; the benevolent promises of those in power or the elegantly written documents of statesmen or philososphers do not suffice to maintain constitutional rule. So Hegel discerns and discusses many factors that assure that, though the state be powerful enough to rule, neither the state nor any of its parts attain disproportionate or despotic might. Hegel looks to the legal and settled structure of the government, the mediations and organic relations among its branches, intermediate social organs, and the spirit of the nation.

Like Aristotle, Hegel thinks constitutionally in terms of the institutions and the patterns through which power is exercised; like Aristotle (and unlike much "modern constitutionalism"), Hegel therefore describes "an intricate sociopolitical system in which the arbitrariness" and despotic tendencies that plague authority are "diminished, not by independent control from above or below, but by the institutional and legal instruments through which that authority itself is executed,"[15] by the relations among those authoritative institutions, and by the interaction between those institutions and the people.

One important guarantee of constitutional rule exists when the political constitution is legally established and determinate (258R n.); "it is precisely the fact that everything in the state is fixed and secure which is the bulwark against caprice and dogmatic opinion" (270A). In other words, Hegel sees constitutional stability in the rule of law of the *Rechtsstaat,* unheld by both ruler and ruled.

A related guarantee of constitutional rule exists in the mediations and organic interconnections of the branches of government (276, 286). Because the constitution is a highly complex series of relations and lines of communications, all branches depend upon each other for their efficacy, influence, and power; they are interdependent. Because that interdependence is organic, no branch can act despotically, Hegel thinks, because any governmental action—undertaken by any of the powers of government—requires and permits for its completion that all branches of government agree. Legislation is but the most obvious example. Or, to put the same guarantee in different terms, no branch of government can legislate, authorize, and execute a policy without the concurrence of the others.

Hegel also discusses structural constraints specific to each branch of government, and the discipline and education imposed by the structure on those in power and on the way in which they can exercise their will. For instance, despite his absolute self-determination, the monarch is guided by his counsellors (279A), cabinet ministers, who should be members of the legislature (300A), and the objective order of the constitution (279A, 280A). The executive is also structured to try to minimize the possibility of bureaucratic despotism (296, 297, Enc. 544R). But Hegel is especially concerned with the Estates, who proved so powerful and so disruptive during the French Revolution; who exercise too much power in England, Hegel thinks, and prevent much rationalization of the laws, rights, and bureaucracy (Enc. 544); and who, in the age of democratic revolution generally, seem to have a claim to exceptional legitimacy and primacy as the representatives of "the people," a claim that threatens what Hegel values in a constitution—the division of powers, mediations, and articulation of governmental branches and of society in general. So Hegel explicitly gives the other branches important roles in legislation—the monarch must sign (or veto) all legislation and the executive both decides how to apply the law and advises the Estates about possible reforms (304). Moreover, Hegel asserts that, in a smoothly working constitution, the most the legislature has to do is to modify, clarify, and add subsections to existing laws (Enc. 544R). He does not allow Parliament the power of the purse, at least to the extent that the government must always have funds enough to function (Enc. 544R). He maintains an upper, agriculturally based house. He insists that the lower house reflect and uphold the articulations already found in civil society, and not be a purely popular body—based on representation in geographically defined electoral districts.

Those associations and Corporations are important in guaranteeing both the political and the broad constitutions. With both houses of the Estates, Corporations serve as intermediate organs between monarch and people. They give an orderly, legal, and structured form to the vox populi, allow it legitimate expression and effective power when valid (290A), and educate the citizens into political activity and thoughtful opinions. So they allow structured thought and power to ascend and to descend, prevent governmental despotism and popular discontent, and prove absolutely vital to the proper working of the constitution.

The final type of guarantee of constitutional rule rests with the citizens. Hegel looks to "the collective spirit of the nation—especially in the specific way in which it is itself conscious of its reason" (Enc. 540) and its liberty. For Hegel thinks he sees a powerful insistence on liberty common to citizens of the major Western European states: the "will to liberty is no longer an impulse which demands satisfaction, but the permanent character—the spiritual consciousness grown into a non-impulsive nature" (Enc. 482R)—of the modern Western world. Free citizens, Hegel thinks, will not stand to be subjected to despotic rule; constitutional rule can rest on the spirit of these free citizens.

HEGEL'S CONSTITUTIONALISM AND MARX'S THOUGHT

While Hegel attempts to reestablish constitutions and constitutionalism in the face of the problems of the modern world, Marx criticizes Hegel's constitutional thinking.[16] Marx sees his criticism as extending beyond Hegel's thought to the bases of the modern state, because Hegel's political philosophy presents that state in thought, "Hegel is not to be blamed for depicting the nature of the modern state as it is, but rather for presenting what is as the essence of the state" (CHPR, 64). So Marx's critique of Hegel's thought generates, Marx thinks, a radical critique of the modern bourgeois constitutional state.

Marx finds neither logic nor freedom in Hegel's modern constitutional state. That state cannot be justified as logical because Hegel does not derive its logical structure from its own components and relations (CHPR, 92). Rather, Hegel assumes the logic of his *Science of Logic* and then applies it to politics, looking for institutions that actualize the *Logic's* categories. Faced with a category from his *Logic*, Hegel "picks anyone of the empirical existences of the Prussian or Modern state (just as it is), which among other things actualizes this category even though this category does not express its specific nature" (CHPR, 48). As Marx puts the point polemically, "thought is not conformed to the nature of the state, but the state to a readymade system of thought" (CHPR), 19).

Similarly, although "in the state Hegel wants everywhere the realization of free will" (CHPR, 57), at crucial points he undercuts freedom. For instance, the gradual evolution of the constitution (298A) is, for Marx, "not a conscious law of the state, but is mediated through chance and ratified *contrary* to consciousness" (CHPR, 57). The monarch, the symbol of self-determination, holds in the right to pardon criminals (282) "the ultimate expression of contingent and arbitrary choice" (CHPR, 36), not rational freedom. The aristocracy's independence from both monarch and civil society (306–307) "in reality is the crudest dependence on the soil" (CHPR, 104). The lower house of the legislature is built on the mystery that the members of civil society, who have no "political significance and efficacy" in civil society, undergo a complete "transubstantiation" into political beings when they discuss political matters and vote (CHPR, 71, 76–78). In such a constitution, the individual must "undertake an essential schism [into bourgeois and citizen] within himself" (CHPR, 77) and consequently must experience politics as alien and alienating (CHPR, 78, 80, 116).

Marx perceives that the freedom lacking in Hegel's constitutional vision is equally lacking in the constitutions of existing states. Freedom in any existing constitution is limited because the usual rights of man—life, liberty, and property—preclude certain relations and encourage others. Significant community is impossible when men relate only through contract or self-interest, when "the only bond between men is natural necessity, need and private interest, the preservation of their property and their egoistic persons" (JQ, 43). Individual development is circumscribed when others are "not the realization, but rather the limitation" of one's own liberty (JQ, 42). Indeed, the individual's rights themselves are sharply limited by the others' rights and the state's need for security and order (JQ, 43, 44). Political life itself is alien because sharply separated from the everyday life of individuals (JQ, 33–34) and biased by class conflict (ICHPR, 62–65).

Lacking the justifications of logic and freedom, Hegel's constitution—and current states' constitutions—also lacks efficacious guarantees of constitutional rule, according to Marx. Structural constraints built into constitutions are for Marx sorely inadequate. The bureaucracy can effectively control the state in Hegel's political philosophy (CHPR, 42–45, 52–55) as in France in 1851 (18thB, 121–122). The monarch rules arbitrarily (CHPR, 29–32, 35–37), as does Napoleon III (18thB, 120–21, 131–35). Mediations fail, sometimes existing only as allegory or illusion (CHPR, 94; 18thB, 31–33), sometimes degenerating into conflict (CHPR, 53; 18thB, 48–51 and *passim*) or into a "mutual reconciliation society" (CHPR, 88; 18thB, 25, 133–35).

Marx rejects other structural constraints—such as the rule of law and the influence of the corporations—on grounds that are central to his critique of Hegel: the state (with its political constitution) is not a universal but rather a particular institution, because the state is separate from civil society, opposed to it, not standing over it, and so on its level (CHPR, 76), not overarching and universal, but one institution among many struggling for power. Consequently, the laws of a *Rechtsstaat*, executed by the bureaucracy—(Hegel's "universal class" (205)—have particular ends, such as increasing bureaucratic influence (CHPR, 46–48; 18thB, 30–32). At best the interaction between corporation and bureaucracy is a relation between two particulars, not a corporate body with the universal class (CHPR, 53; 18thB, 61–62).

Indeed, Marx rejects the legitimacy of structural constraints in general. Where Hegel devotes much effort to articulating a complex, structured, and dynamically balanced constitutional monarchy, Marx accuses Hegel of falling into the logic fetishism (CHPR, 83–84) of confusing subject and predicate, actor and result. For Marx, "the state is an abstraction; the people alone is the concrete" (CHPR, 28). So Marx insists that the people do "have the right to give itself a new constitution" (CHPR, 58), wishes that the constitution be "the free product of men" (CHPR, 30), and rejects all nondemocratic forms of constitutions. "In monarchy the whole, the people, is subsumed under one of its modes of existence, the political constitution; in democracy the constitution itself appears only as one determination, and indeed as the self-determination of the people. . . . Democracy is the resolved mystery of all constitutions" (CHPR, 29–30), may well be the route to communism in advanced countries, and takes the form of workers' control in the future society (ICHPR, 64–65). Marx takes his critique one crucial step further. He argues that the asserted universality of the modern state, declared explicitly by Hegel and implicitly in modern constitutions (JQ, 33–34; 18thB, 30–31), conflicts with the state's particularity in its opposition to civil society; so the modern state, as a particular, is an illusory universality and, equally, an illusory political community (CHPR, 64; JQ, 31–33). Of course, once the state's universality is shown by Marx to be an illusion, then its ability to constrain, channel, and educate the passions and interests of men in civil society is also an illusion, and the system of needs, production, and exchange becomes dominant in forming society, politics, and the lives of individuals (JQ, 47–52).

In short, Marx breaks with almost every dimension of Hegel's constitutional thought. But Marx does retain Hegel's Aristotelian idea of the broad constitution: the way of life of the citizens (Pol. 1295a), their character and self-consciousness (274). As a consequence, Marx is able easily to move from economics—production, labor, commodities, and exchange—to politics in his analysis of bourgeois society, because Hegel's sense of the broad constitution easily integrates economic activity into constitutional (and political) thinking. Moreover, Marx is able easily to see that his future society will have a constitution, because it will have a way of life of its members (in Aristotle's terms) or because it will have been constituted and can be reconstituted by self-determining individuals (in Marx's terms). Ironically, perhaps, Hegel's idea of a broad constitution is retained by Marx at two crucial nodes of his thought: the relation between economics and politics, and the ordering of the future society.

HEGEL'S CONSTITUTIONALISM—ITS IMPLICATIONS FOR CONTEMPORARY CONSTITUTIONAL THOUGHT

Although embedded in his philosophical system and in his comprehension of his world, and despite extensive criticism from Marx and his followers, Hegel's constitutional thought does have some important resonances and implications for the late twentieth century. Our discussion of the Guarantees of Constitutional Rule suggests that assuring constitutional rule is one resonance. Hegel tries to spin a web that is varied and complex enough to be able to maintain the political constitution no matter what flies into it, even if some strands weaken. This chapter is not the place to analyze and evaluate different approaches to guaranteeing constitutions, but a few comments are in order. Hegel's approach indicates at least the extraordinary difficulty of the task: any single institutional proposal (or other single idea, such as that of equally ambitious individuals) seems unlikely to be sufficient, even though each one may be necessary.[17] Hegel's multiplicity of guarantees, even in the rational and free state, suggests the extraordinary perplexities that surround political power and the attempt to render it constitutional: the government must be so framed—and its officers so brought up and educated—that it is strong enough to be able to act, that in its strong actions it act justly and in accord with the goals of the people, and that in its just and teleological laws and policies it finds that it cannot act unjustly, contrary to the spirit of the state, tyrannically, or destructively.

Another important set of implications of Hegel's thought revolves around the political constitution. Hegel criticizes the idea of the division of powers as a system of oppositions, of "checks and balances" in the American shibboleth. Hegel's criticism seems reasonable: a government in which each branch is opposed to and constantly checking the others is likely to become bogged down in impotence—as has been the case in the United States during Watergate and the Iran-Contra scandal; when it works, a system of checks and balances can prevent tyranny, but the government—its branches stymied into motionless equilibrium—cannot govern. In contrast, Hegel emphasizes cooperation (or organic unity) and mediation among powers.

For him, the government must always be able to govern, and no active and balanced government can exist without the cooperation of the separate branches, nor claim breadth of consultation and legitimacy without mediation among the branches. Hegel's conceptualization allows analysis of governments in various conditions of order and disorder, not only the situation where one branch threatens tyranny. When the constitutional order functions smoothly, then personal particularities (of opinion or ambition) find little scope for any significant effects. When one branch of government—an imperial president, to take a current example—tries to become tyrannical, the other branches can work to restrain him, through their shared powers, through their mediations with each other and the people,

and because of everyone's knowledge that governing requires the cooperation of all. When one branch—a strong president, for instance—exercises
creative and wise rule, the other branches can work with him and can
legitimate his ideas to the people. When one branch—a weak president, for
instance—does little, the other branches can govern competently.[18]

Hegel's treatment of the executive shows prescience, both in his emphasis
that modern civil servants need a liberal and humanistic education and in
his assertion that the executive is the third branch of government. Certainly
the development of the state since Hegel's time has borne out his understanding of the importance of the state bureaucracy. The Iran-Contra
scandal in the United States has shown the deeply ambiguous position of
the bureaucracy under the American constitution—whether it be responsible to Congress, beholden solely to the President, independent to pursue its
own policies and goals, or involved in some other set of powers and
relations.

At the same time, Hegel's treatment suggests looking critically at the idea
of the judiciary as the third branch. Even in the United States, the judiciary
seems different from the other branches. The differences may stem from the
institutional position of the court itself: except in unusual instances, it does
not share the power to interpret constitutionality; except for legal arguments, it is insulated from regularized channels of influence and opinion;
and it has no ability to initiate, enforce, or advise. In Hegel's terms, then, the
judiciary as a branch of government is anomalous: it does not share powers;
it is not mediated with and by other branches; and it is passive and dependent (not interdependent). So it is not part of an organic unity, but rather a
body largely disconnected from the rest of the government; and Hegel dis-
trusts such disconnection. Because the judiciary's function of subsuming
the particular under the universal is the same function as that of other parts
of the civil service, Hegel makes the judiciary a part—differentiated, to be
sure, from the others—of the executive. Because the Supreme Court's function of deciding constitutionality is critical to a constitution, Hegel spreads
that concern throughout the branches of government (and throughout the
broad constitution). The legislative, authorizing, and executing branches—
as well as the people in their corporations and public opinion—all must be
concerned that governmental laws and policies be constitutional and respect the rights of citizens.

Hegel's concern with the broad constitution suggests the importance of
the political education of the citizens for the proper working of the constitution and the state. Therefore, the student of the constitution must look not
only to the legal side of constitutional issues but also to the sociological; the
study of social institutions and citizen character is integral to constitutionalism. The politician must realize that political education requires
social and economic institutions which encourage the development of
citizen values, virtues, and goals that will uphold the state—as well as each

citizen and (for Hegel) the demands of *Geist*. Because political education is a long-term project that depends on socioeconomic institutions, it is difficult to change, and reforms must be both basic and slow. Governmental action cannot create or generate meaning; short-term attempts to manipulate education or the symbols of the system are almost certain to be transitory unless underlying substantive change also occurs.

Finally, from Hegel's perspective the constitution is an expression of the spirit of the people. So constitutions, even those drawn up by committees of learned individuals, must express that spirit, and not, for instance, try to arrange every country's constitution on the American or British model. Equally, constitutions must not overreach in trying to hold people and politicians to standards too far beyond their current condition of political education. At the same time, for a country to have an explicitly known constitution is essential, because the constitution is the register and precis of a country's rights and order,[19] knowledge of which is the right and duty of every citizen as well as the basis of the stability, vitality, and orderly legitimacy of the state.

Notes

1. Aristotle's *Politics* is cited according the page numbers, found in the margins in most translations, of I. Bekker's 1831 Berlin edition; citations are in parentheses in the text, preceded by "Pol." I use T.A. Sinclair's translation (Revised edition; Harmondsworth: Penguin, 1981), checked against Carnes Lord's excellent translation (Chicago: Univeristy of Chicago Press, 1984). At Pol. 1278b, Aristotle defines constitution only in terms of offices and their relative authority, with no mention of goals; although not important for the argument of this chapter, I take Pol. 1278b to be a preliminary definition, subsumed under that of Pol. 1289a, rather than a third and most narrow definition.

2. Walter Bagehot's *The English Constitution* (London: Fontana, 1963) exhibits an Aristotelian approach to the narrow constitution: he describes and analyzes current practices and how they developed, and does not stress the explicit words of laws nor worry whether a single written document called a constitution exists.

3. The terms come from the important study by Charles McIlwain, *Constitutionalism: Ancient and Modern* (Ithaca, NY: Cornell University Press, 1947).

4. G.W.F. Hegel, *The Philosophy of Right*, trans. with notes by T.M. Knox (Oxford: Oxford University Press, 1942). References to *The Philosophy of Right* are placed in parentheses in the text and, except for Hegel's preface, are according to section (not page) number; where the material cited is from the main text of the section, the section number alone is given; where it is from the "remarks" Hegel added to the text, the section number is followed by "R"; where it is from the "additions" which later editors appended to posthumous editions by collating student lecture notes, the section number is followed by "A." The material in *The Philosophy of Right* is presented in briefer compass in G.W.F. Hegel, *Philosophy of Mind*, trans. William Wallace and A.V. Miller (Oxford: Clarendon Press, 1971); it and G.W.F. Hegel, *The Logic of Hegel*, trans. William Wallace (Oxford: Oxford University Press, 1892) are cited in paren-

theses in the text, with the section number preceded by the abbreviation "Enc." Other works by Hegel are also cited in the text. G.W.F. Hegel, *Hegel's Political Writings*, trans. T.M. Knox (Oxford : Oxford University Press, 1964), is abbreviated as "HPW" and cited to page number. G.W.F. Hegel, *Lectures on the Philosophy of World History: Introduction*, trans. H.B. Nisbet (Cambridge: Cambridge University Press, 1975), is abbreviated as "WH" and cited to page number. G.W.F. Hegel, *The Phenomenology of Spirit* (1807), is abbreviated as "PhG" and cited by chapter and section.

5. On the *Rechtsstaat*, (given the book's praise of the German *Rechtsstaat*, its date of original publication, 1925, and the author's sincere liberalism) see especially Guido de Ruggiero, *The History of European Liberalism*, trans. R.G. Collingwood (Boston: Beacon, 1959), 251–62; also Mack Walker, "Rights and Functions: The Social Categories of Eighteenth-Century German Jurists and Cameralists," *Journal of Modern History* 50 (June 1978); 234–51.

6. See PhG. VI.B.iii; also Joachim Ritter, *Hegel and the French Revolution* (Cambridge, MA: The M.I.T. Press, 1982), esp. chap. 1, 47.

7. See H.H. Gerth and C. Wright Mills, eds., *From Max Weber: Essays in Sociology* (New York: Oxford University Press, 1946), 196–237; see also 241–43, where Weber contrasts the "cultivated man," which Hegel wishes the civil servant to be, with the "specialist." For a contemporary version of this contrast, see Jurgen Habermas, *Legitimation Crisis* (Boston: Beacon, 1975), last sentence.

8. On these points, Hegel suggests Hannah Arendt's notion of political debate *On Revolution* (New York: Viking, 1963) 128.

9. See, for example, *Federalist Paper* No. 51.

10. See T.M. Knox, "Hegel and Prussianism," *Philosophy* XV, no. 1 (January 1940): sec. II.

11. Herbert Marcuse, *Reason and Revolution* (Boston: Beacon Press, 1960 [1941]), 210.

12. See also Arendt, *On Revolution*, 174.

13. Conversely, of course, effective change of the political or the broad constitution necessitates not only governmental reform but also a social dimension: constitutional improvement involves and requires improving the social organization and political consciousness of the people.

14. True to the French Revolution, Hegel favored the systematic codification or "scientific remodelling of law," in which "statute books and political institutions have been framed on general principles" (HPW, 300); he opposed English common law and constitutional practices as "this inherently disconnected aggregate of positive provisions" (HPW, 299–300)—where by "positive provisions" or "positivity" Hegel means "particular rights, freedoms, privileges conferred, sold, presented by or extorted from kings and Parliament on special occasions" to specific individuals or groups, rights and privileges whose form is that of private rights and whose content depends partly on the accidental circumstances of their origin (HPW, 299).

15. Nannerl O. Keohane, "Claude de Seyssel and Sixteenth-Century Constitutionalism in France," in J. Roland Pennock and John W. Chapman, eds., *Constitutionalsim: Nomos XX,* (New York: New York University Press, 1979) 76.

16. As with Aristotle's and Hegel's, Marx's works are cited in parentheses in the text. Karl Marx, *Critique of Hegel's Philosophy of Right*, trans. Joseph O'Malley (Cambridge: Cambridge University Press, 1970), is abbreviated as "CHPR" and cited to

page number. Karl Marx, *The Eighteenth Brumaire of Louis Napoleon* (New York: International Publishers, 1963), is abbreviated as "18thB" and cited to page number. Karl Marx, "On the Jewish Question," abbreviated as "JQ," and "Introduction to the Critique of Hegel's Philosophy of Right," abbreviated as "ICHPR," are cited to page number in Robert C. Tucker, ed., *The Marx-Engels Reader,* 2d ed., (New York: Norton, 1978). This section relies on Marx's very early (1843) writings and his occasional writings; had the section been based on Marx's major published works (such as the *Communist Manifesto* or *Capital,* vol. I) or on his major unpublished works (such as *The German Ideology* or the *Grundrisse*), quotations and emphases would have been different, but the substance of the argument would have remained the same.

17. That ambition be made to counteract ambition is recommended in *Federalist Paper* no. 51. Even a bill of rights or a supreme court serves as a good example of the limits of any single guarantee: for an exacting analysis of doubts about the value of a bill of rights, see Wilfrid Rumble, "James Madison on the Value of Bills of Rights," in Pennock and Chapman, eds., *Constitutionalism;* for an extensive study of the insufficiency of the court, see Robert A. Dahl, "Decision-Making in a Democracy: The Role of the Supreme Court as a National Policy-Maker," *Journal of Public Law*, 6, no. 2 (Fall 1957).

18. See Keohane, "Claude de Scyssel," 70. Ultimately it may be the case that "modern constitutionalism," with its concern to limit government to protect individual rights, needs to be joined with Aristotle's, Hegel's, or Seyssel's versions of "ancient constitutionalism" (and, perhaps, a political theory of constitutional leadership) to produce a full constitutional theory.

19. Despite the praise accorded its unwritten constitution, Britains's need for an explicit constitution, including a statement of those rights validly and successfully claimed by British citizens, was highlighted by the government's injunctions, affirmed by the Law Lords on 30 July 1987, against three British newspapers prohibiting them from publishing excerpts or summaries of Peter Wright's *Spycatcher,* as well as the government's banning sale of the book in Britain and limiting what newspapers can divulge of the book's contents in their reporting on the ruckus.

6

Philosophy in the Debates at the United States Constitutional Convention of 1787

Andrew Reck

Reck presents a brief comparative analysis of the various plans which were considered in the framing of the United States Constitution. His focus is on the set of philosophical ideas which most influenced the Great Compromise *at the Constitutional Convention (1787) and, specifically, on the innovative American political principle of divisible or "shared" sovereignty.*

FOUR PLANS

Records of the debates at the United States Constitutional Convention of 1787 provide the contemporary student a truly excellent opportunity to witness the clash of political philosophies as the founding fathers formulated the document that remains today as the core of the Constitution of the United States. Our sources are the several reports of the Constitutional Convention recorded in the papers of the participants. Of these the most complete, informative and insightful record is *The Debates in the Federal Convention of 1787*, as reported by James Madison.[1] Four plans for the Constitution were presented during the Convention: (1) the Virginia plan by Edmund Randolph, (2) the plan by Charles Pinckney of South Carolina, (3) the New Jersey plan by William Paterson, and (4) the model of government unveiled in a speech by Alexander Hamilton. I will try to sketch briefly the political philosophies implicit and explicit in these plans and in the minds of their proposers.

As regards the use and mention of the philosophers during the debates, the student will be struck by the paucity of references, especially by comparison with the citations of the philosophers in the pamphlet literature of the American revolutionary era from 1763 to 1776. Montesquieu is mentioned twice by Madison: first, in respect to the Lycian confederacy, which was based on the proportional representation of its members (130); and second, on the separation of powers (397). He is also cited by Edmund Randolph on the topic of suffrage (354). In the notes taken by Robert Yates, a delegate from New York, Montesquieu is invoked by Pierce Butler of South Carolina to caution on the corruption that results from entrusting persons with too much power and without checks.[2] The contents and direction of the debates confirm the commonplace of scholarship that Montesquieu was the main philosopher who influenced the thinking of the American statesmen and politicians of the era.

Unfortunately for the reputation of philosophy in matters of practical politics, however, the delegate who most indulged in explicit philosophizing was Luther Martin of Maryland. In behalf of the rights of States and their equal representation in the Legislature, Martin paraded many of the political theorists—Locke, Vattel, Priestly—who had inspired the pamphleteers of the American Revolution;[3] his exhortation to the convention on June 27 lasted "more than three hours" (289). Exhausted, he requested permission to continue his speech the next day and he did so, "with much diffuseness and considerable vehemence" (290). Of Martin, William Pierce, a delegate from Georgia, surmised, "This Gentleman possesses a good deal of information, but he has a very bad delivery, and so extremely prolix, that he never speaks without tiring the patience of all who hear him."[4]

THE VIRGINIA PLAN—RANDOLPH

The revolutionary character of the Convention of 1787 in its departure from the Articles of Confederation, the first and at that time the prevailing constitution for the American states, is manifest in the first plan presented, the Virginia plan introduced on May 2 by Edmund Randolph. Although the first resolution of the Virginia plan proposes, perhaps with guile, to correct and enlarge the Articles of Confederation, the remaining resolutions unveil a totally different frame of government—a national government resting not on the states but rather directly on the people.

The government outlined in the Virginia plan would be both national and radically republican. The idea of a republic, originating in ancient philosophy and practice and modified by modern thinkers and states, had inspired the majority of the framers. It was a complex idea embracing five component principles: (1) that liberty be the cardinal feature of political society; (2) that government be a government of laws and not of men; (3) that political society be a commonwealth in which private and public property are protected; (4) that government be popular, at least representing the people; and (5) that the system of government be constituted of checks and balances which reflect the classes of men in society as well as the divisions of political powers and functions.[5]

In the Committee of the Whole into which the Convention entered after Randolph had submitted his plan, he followed the suggestion of Gouverneur Morris that, before debating the particulars, two other propositions be argued. The first affirmed "that a Union of the States merely federal will not accomplish the objects proposed by the Articles of Confederation, namely common defense, security of liberty, and general welfare," and the second held "that a *national* Government ought to be established consisting of a *supreme* Legislative, Executive, and Judiciary" (120). These two propositions underscored the major theme of Randolph's plan—that it was a plan for a national government supreme in sovereignty over the states.

While the republican and nationalist features of the Virginia plan were retained in the United States Constitution of 1787, revisions arose during the debates that significantly altered the nature of the plan and the way the various branches would function. When the adjective "supreme" was struck out as descriptive of the government proposed, and the term "federal" substituted, the issue of the sovereignty of the individual states was propounded in a way that jeopardized the sovereignty of the new government. The issue was additionally complicated when the States were granted equality of representation in the Senate. A peerage of States, alien to Randolph's nationalism and his republicanism, was entrenched. Further, when the Executive was defined as a single person eligible for reelection by electors chosen by the States, he decried the resultant presidency as (to use a phrase from one of his sentences which a sympathetic 19th century biographer has claimed became "proverbs in the Convention"[6]) "the foetus of monarchy" (132). As he condemned the construction of the Senate based on the peerage of States for being a stroke for aristocracy, so he viewed with dismay the single Executive as a blow for monarchy, and he feared that the popular republicanism which he espoused would be trampled under these other undesirable forms of government.

THE SOUTH CAROLINA PLAN—PINCKNEY

Charles Pinckney of South Carolina, although only 24 years of age, presented the second plan for a general government at the Convention on the same day that Randolph had offered his. This plan did not survive in any of the records of the Convention, although an abstract of it has been found among the papers and in the handwriting of James Wilson, a delegate from Pennsylvania. In Wilson's outline of Pinckney's plan,[7] it is proposed that the "confederation between the free and independent States" be strengthened under "one general superintending Government," the main organ of which was to be a bicameral Legislature. After Pinckney presented his plan, he confessed, according to the notes of Robert Yates, delegate from New York, that "it was grounded on the same principle as the . . . resolutions" of Randolph.[8] Although Pinckney's plan was submitted along with the Virginia plan to the Committee of the Whole, it was never debated either in the Committee or the Convention. Yet some concepts—the three-fifths rule for blacks in measuring population on which representation in the lower chamber of the Legislature was to be calculated, and the title of the Executive—survived and became part of the Constitution that was drafted in 1787.

THE NEW JERSEY PLAN—PATERSON

William Paterson of New Jersey led the opposition against the supremely national government proposed in the Virginia plan. At the theoretical level the controversy pivoted on the nature of sovereignty, whether the national government would be sovereign or the individual states would retain their sovereignty, while at the practical level it sprang from the apprehension of the small states that they would be swallowed up by the large states. Paterson, like the delegates from Virginia, also wanted a stronger federal government than the one existing under the Articles of Confederation. Yet in the proposal that the representation of the states in both houses of the legislature be proportional rather than equal, Paterson perceived the undermining of the sovereignty of the individual states, especially detrimental to the interest of such small states as his own. In his own notes on the Convention, Paterson's sole objection to Randolph's plan was written below the provision for proportional representation, "Sovereignty is an integral thing."[9] His opening salvo against the Virginia plan, as reported by Madison, was triggered by his perception that proportional representation struck at the existence of the small states. He adverted to a consideration of the nature, structure, and power of the Convention, and insisted that the people of America would not follow the Convention in establishing a national government that would swallow up the states. On June 9, Paterson argued:

> The idea of a national Govt. as contradistinguished from a federal one, never entered into the mind of any of them (the States), and to the public mind we must accommodate ourselves. We have no power to go beyond the federal scheme, and if we had the people are not ripe for any other. We must follow the people; the people will not follow us.—The *proposition* could not be main-

tained whether considered in reference to us as a nation, or as a confederacy. A confederacy supposes sovereignty in the members composing it and sovereignty supposes equality (181–182).

When the Virginia plan emerged from the Committee of the Whole, the proponents of proportional representation of the states in both chambers of the legislature had won the day. But Paterson did not give up the fight. He requested that he be permitted to present a plan "purely federal, and contradistinguished from the reported plan" (203). On June 14, Paterson introduced the New Jersey plan.

The New Jersey plan merely offered, in its first proposition, to revise, correct and enlarge the Articles of Confederation in order "to render the federal Constitution adequate to the exigencies of Government, and the preservation of the Union" (204). Since the New Jersey plan was not proposed as a constitution supplanting the Articles of Confederation, the structure of the confederacy remained in place in two essential respects: first, as provided in the Articles of Confederation, II; "Each state retains its sovereignty, freedom, and independence, and every Power, Jurisdiction, and Right, which is not by this confederation expressly delegated to the United States in Congress assembled,"[10] and secondly, in the Congress, which remained unicameral, as provided in Article V: "each shall have one vote."[11]

With the presentation of the New Jersey plan, those who wished to retain the sovereignty of the states were pitted against those who favored a national plan that subordinated the states to the federal government. Declared Paterson, "If the sovereignty of the States is to be maintained, the Representatives must be drawn immediately from the States, not from the people: and we have no power to vary the ideal of equal sovereignty. The only expedient that will cure the difficulty, is that of throwing the states into Hotchpot" (209). Randolph responded, "The true question is whether we shall adhere to the federal plan, or introduce the national plan. The insufficiency of the former has been fully displayed by the trial already made ... We must resort therefore to a National *Legislation over individuals,* for which Congs. (under the Articles of confederation) are unfit" (214). The only solution to the difficulties confronting the states in 1787 was, he contended, to be found in the erection of a national government, and "he begged it be considered that the present is the last moment for establishing one. After this select experiment, the people will yield in despair" (215).

HAMILTON'S PLAN

On the next day, June 18, with the convention still in the Committee of the Whole, Alexander Hamilton, a delegate from New York, rose to express his dissatisfaction with both the Virginia plan and the New Jersey plan. In a speech which lasted five or six hours, and which reflected the influence of the Scottish Enlightenment, especially the work of David Hume as philosopher and as historian,[12] Hamilton examined the defects of both plans and sketched and justified his own model of sound government.

As early as 1780, Hamilton had suggested a Constitutional Convention to strengthen the central government.[13] He was therefore adamantly opposed to the New Jersey plan. According to Madison, Hamilton was

> convinced, that no amendment of the confederation, leaving the states in possession of their Sovereignty could possibly answer the purpose. On the other hand he was much discouraged by the amazing extent of country in expecting the desired blessings from any general sovereignty that could be substitued (215).

In the 18th century, it was an axiom of conventional political theory backed by the authority of Montesquieu that the republican form of government could work only in a state of small geographical size—a state like the ancient cities of Athens and Rome or the modern cities of Venice and Florence.[14]

Nevertheless, in opposition both to Paterson's remarks on the limitations placed on the Convention by the states and also to the New Jersey plan, Hamilton posed several pointed objections. Paterson's judgment that the convention could not propose a national plan of government because it had been assembled for the purpose of rectifying the defects in the existing Confederation, according to Hamilton, stemmed from "distinctions and reasonings too subtle" concerning the nature of a federal government. Hamilton defined a federal government as "an association of different communities into one" (216), and he observed that, since the powers of such a government differed with the different associations in history, "great latitude therefore must be given to the signification of the term" (216). As to the New Jersey plan it, too, proposed to rest on individuals as well as states. As to the powers of the Convention, Hamilton remarked that, since the Convention had been called to meet a crisis and "provide for the exigencies of the union," it would be inappropriate "to propose any plan not adequate to these exigencies," although he conceded that the states "in which no constitutional authority exists in the Legislatures" may be legally bound, as in the case of New York, to refer the plan "to the people at large" for its ratification (216).

Before demonstrating the defects in both the Virginia and the New Jersey plans, Hamilton went on to list the five "great essential principles necessary for support of Government:"

(1) (A)n active & constant interest in supporting it . . .
(2) The love of power . . .

(3)   An habitual attachment of the people . . .

(4)   *Force* by which may be understood a *coertion of laws* or *coertion of arms*

(5)   (I)nfluence . . . not . . . corruption, but a dispensation of those regular honors & emoluments, which produce an attachment to the Govt. (216–217).

Observing that "almost all the weight of these" principles falls on the side of the states and away from the general government, Hamilton considered that the only remedy would be to grant the general government such complete sovereignty as to turn the great principles and passions mentioned above in its direction. The New Jersey plan failed miserably in this regard; it merely reinforced the sovereignty of the states. As Paterson on behalf of states rights had believed that "sovereignty is an integral thing," so Hamilton in pursuit of a vigorous national government proclaimed, "Two Sovereignties can not co-exist within the same limits" (219).

Hamilton was dismayed by the prospects for a republican form of government over a country the size of the United States. The sheer expense of such an establishment, drawing its members from remote places, could be borne only if the expenses of the state governments could be reduced. Costly inducements, moreover, would be necessary to lure "representatives from the extremes to the center of the community" (220). In effect, he suggested the consolidation of the states under the general government, although he recognized the need for subordinate authorities. Because he did not wish to shock public opinion, he refrained from actually proposing the abolition of the states.

Hence, Hamilton esteemed the British constitution as the best model of government. As Madison reported, Hamilton exalted the British constitution "as the best in the world: and . . . he doubted much whether anything short of it would do in America" (220). The British government, he continued,

> . . . unites public strength with individual security . . . Their house of Lords is a most noble institution. Having nothing to hope for by a change, and a sufficient interest by means of their property, in being faithful to the national interest, they form a permanent barrier against every pernicious innovation, whether attempted on the part of the Crown or of the Commons . . . As to the Executive, . . . [he questioned whether there can be] a good Govt. without a good Executive. The English model was the only good one on this subject. The Hereditary interest of the King was so interwoven with that of the nation, and his personal emoluments so great, that he was placed above the danger of being corrupted from abroad—and at the same time was both sufficiently independent and sufficiently controuled, to answer the purpose of the institution at home (221–222).

Hamilton appreciated the mixed polity of Great Britain for keeping at bay corrupting foreign influences and for holding in balance the internal interests that always threaten political instability and civil strife. He explained:

> In every community where industry is encouraged, there will be a division of it into the few and the many. Hence separate interests will arise. There will be debtors & creditors & c. Give all power to the many, they will oppress the few. Give all power to the few, they will oppress the many. Both therefore ought to have power, that each may defend itself against the other . . . To the proper adjustment of it the British owe the excellence of their Constitution (221).

Of course, Hamilton knew that the American people would not accept any government except one based on republican principles. Consequently, he proposed a government republican in character, but one in which the principle of democracy, which requires the direct participation of the people or their equal representation as people in the political process, would be curtailed. According to Madison, Hamilton observed, "The members most tenacious of republicanism . . . were as loud as any in declaiming against the vices of democracy" (220). So, from his reflections on the British Constitution, Hamilton recommended that "we ought to go as far in order to attain stability and permanency, as republican principles will admit" (222).

The model of government Hamilton sketched contained a bicameral legislature, an executive and a judiciary. In outlining this model of government, Hamilton was aware that the lifetime terms he advocated for the Senators, the Governor, and the Judges smacked of antirepublicanism. He was apparently most sensitive to the probable objection that the Executive he delineated "will be an *elective Monarch,* and will give birth to the tumults which characterize the form of Government" (222). Hamilton evaluated the question whether Senators and a Governor who would serve for life could be principal institutions in a government that would properly be denominated republican. He concluded that such a government would, indeed, be republican "if all the magistrates are appointed, and vacancies are filled by the people, or a process of election originating with the people" (222).

Nevertheless, Hamilton was cognizant that his plan "went beyond the ideas of most members" of the Convention, and that it was unlikely to be adopted by the people "out of doors" (223). In the critical situation of 1787, with the union dissolving, Hamilton threw his support behind the Virginia plan, because for all its weaknesses the people would now incline toward it and were not at the moment ready for the superior plan he delineated. Consequently, Hamilton, as Madison reported, "did not mean to offer the paper he had sketched as a proposition to the Committee. It was meant only to give a more correct view of his ideas, and to suggest the amendments which he should probably propose to the plan of Mr. R. [the Virginia plan as it came out of the Committee of the Whole] in the proper stages of its future discussion" (223).

VIRGINIA PLAN RECONSIDERED

As the debate resumed in the Convention, it revolved around the Virginia plan. A delegate who expressed a social and political philosophy in opposition to Hamilton's was Charles Pinckney, whose own plan had fallen stillborn. In his speech of June 25, Pinckney cited the American situation as manifesting "a greater equality, than is to be found among the people of any other country," and he reflected that this equality would continue because of the immensity of the uncultivated lands and the opportunities for industry (267). Although he esteemed the Constitution of Great Britain "to be the best Constitution in existence," he did not think that it could or should be introduced into our system. The British system rested on a division of classes, ranks, or orders of men, and balances Crown, Nobility, and People. By contrast the United States, with its pervasive equality, does not have three orders, ranks, or classes; it has but one. As Pinckney exclaimed, "this is the order of Commons" (273). So it would be folly to fashion a government with three organs, like the British government, designed to represent three orders or ranks of people, for in America "two . . . [of these organs—Kings and Lords] have nothing to represent" (273). Pinckney did, of course, distinguish classes among the American people, but his distinctions were based on function rather than on birth or wealth. The three classes he differentiated are the professional class, the commercial class, and the landed interest. Hailing from South Carolina, Pinckney naturally favored the landed interest. This group, he said, consists of "the owners and cultivators of the soil, who are and ought ever to be the governing spring in the system" (272). Pinckney continued:

> These three classes, however distinct in their pursuits, are individually equal in the political scale, and may be easily proved to have but one interest. The dependence of each on the other is mutual. The merchant depends on the planter. Both must in private as well as public affairs be connected with the professional men; who in their turn must in some measure depend upon them. Hence it is clear from this manifest connection & the equality which I before stated exists, and must for the reasons then assigned, continue, that after all there is one, but one great and equal body of citizens composing the inhabitants of this Country among whom there are no distinctions of rank, and very few or none of fortune (272).

THE ISSUE OF SOVEREIGNTY—LARGE VERSUS SMALL STATES

The ongoing debate turned away from the rival portraits of society as Hamilton and Pinckney had depicted them and organized along the battlelines which Paterson had drawn, battlelines that separated large states and small states—namely, the issue of sovereignty. It is difficult to find a more metaphysical notion than the idea of sovereignty. As F.H. Hinsley had said in his classic study of the topic, the idea of sovereignty in the beginning "was the idea that there is a final and absolute political authority in the community; and everything that needs to be added to complete the definition is added if this statement is continued in the following words: *'and no final and absolute authority exists elsewhere.'*"[15] In the American situation of 1787, while the delegates who agreed with Hamilton or who supported the Virginia plan were nationalists and intended that sovereignty in this sense reside in the national government, others favored the segmentation of sovereignty among the several states.

As the debate over sovereignty raged, the focus shifted to the principle of representation in the Senate. Paterson and his allies had invoked the fears of the small states, while Hamilton even suggested the abolition of all the states and their consolidation within the national scheme. Madison retreated from so extreme a nationalist position. Denying that a real political division existed between large states and small states, Madison cited the record of history to show that large states, instead of combining against small ones, tend to compete with and wage war against one another. Still the issue would not disappear, and the Convention almost broke down, provoking the intervention of Benjamin Franklin of which I will say more later. In the ensuing debate Madison, who acknowledged the validity of the concept of the mixed polity, nonetheless lamented that too much stress was placed on "the rank of the States as political societies" (299). He feared that equality of representation of the states would "infuse mortality into a Constitution which we wished to last forever" (300).

One June 29, Oliver Ellsworth, a delegate from Connecticut, had moved that the rule of suffrage in the Senate should be the same as that in the Articles of Confederation—in short the states would share an equality of representation in the Senate. As Madison reported Ellsworth:

> it would become a ground of compromise with regard to the second branch. We were partly national; partly federal. The proportional representation in the first branch was conformable to the national principle and would secure the large States against the small. An equality of voices was conformable to the federal principle and was necessary to secure the Small States against the large. He trusted that on this middle ground a compromise would take place. He did not see that it could on any other. And if no compromise should take place, our meeting would not only be in vain but worse than in vain (304).

THE GREAT COMPROMISE—FRANKLIN

The Great Compromise was not immediately grasped, nor easily achieved. Major credit for its formulation belongs to Benjamin Franklin, then 81 years old. In a deferential society, such as even revolutionary America in the 18th century had been for the most part, Franklin's presence would have sufficed to impart a modicum of acceptability to the proceedings. But the indefatigable Franklin was more than a passive spectator. On June 30, Franklin, the leading proponent of unicameralism in the American states, threw his influential support behind Ellsworth's plan of June 29; he moved the principle of the Great Compromise—namely, equality of representation of the states in the upper chamber, with proportional representation remaining for the lower chamber. Franklin introduced his motion by means of the following remarks which are as clear and succinct a statement of the theory of compromise in ethics and politics as is to be found in all the writings of all the philosophers.

> The diversity of opinion turns on two points. If a proportional representation takes place, the small States contend that their liberties will be in danger. If an equality of votes is to be put in its place, the large States say their money will be in danger. When a broad table is to be made, and the edges of planks do not fit, the artist takes a little from both, and makes a good joint. In like manner here both sides must part with some of their demands, in order that they may join in some accommodating proposition (313).

Whatever the validity of the arguments against the equality of representation of the states in the Senate—whether it be based on the moral principle of democracy that maintains one man, one vote, or whether it be grounded on a realistic appraisal that the interests which divide people are not drawn along the lines of the size of states—the Great Compromise prevailed at the Convention. It is, indeed, an innovation of political thought, discarding once for all the axiom that sovereignty is indivisible and cannot be shared. This axiom had guided the thinking of the opposing extremists—Paterson and Hamilton. Defying this axiom, the Great Compromise introduced the new principle of shared sovereignty—a genuinely novel doctrine of a sovereign federal republic embracing within its fold a number of sovereign state republics. It also illustrates how the doctrinaire abstraction of sovereignty as "integral" and absolute, central to 18th century political philosophy, fell before the innovative thinking of men who, engaged in an historic struggle, surpassed themselves and their philosophical predecessors with the invention of a new political principle.

Notes

1. In this paper I will use the edition of Madison's notes published in *Documents Illustrative of the Formation of the Union of the American States* (Washington: Government Printing Office, 1927). Citations to Madison's notes will be inserted in the text by means of page numbers to this edition in parentheses or brackets.
2. "Secret proceedings and debates of the convention assembled at Philadelphia,

in the year 1787, for the purpose of forming the Constitution of the United States of America." [From the notes taken by the late Robert Yates Esq., Chief Justice of New York (Albany, 1821), in *Documents*, (800)].

3. See my paper, Andrew Reck, "The Philosophical Background of the American Revolution," *Southwestern Journal of Philosophy*, V (1974), 179–202.

4. "Notes of Major William Pierce [Georgia] in the Federal Convention of 1787," *Documents*, (103).

5. See my paper, Andrew Reck, "The Republican Ideology" in *Ideology and the American Experience*, edited by John Roth and Robert C. Whittemore (Washington, D.C.: The Washington Institute, 1986).

6. Moncure Daniel Conway, *Omitted Chapters of History Disclosed in the Life and Letters of Edmund Randolph* (New York: G.P. Putnam's Sons, 1888), 90.

7. "The plan of Charles Pinckney [South Carolina], presented to the Federal Convention, May 29, 1787," in *Documents*, (964–966).

8. "Secret proceedings . . . ," in *Documents*, (748).

9. "Notes of William Paterson in the Federal Convention of 1787," in *Documents* (879).

10. The Articles of Confederation, II, in *Documents*, (27).

11. *Ibid.*, (29)

12. See my paper, Andrew Reck "Moral Philosophy and the Framing of the Constitution," to be published in the proceedings of the Bowling Green State University Conference on the U.S. Constitution and Economic Rights, held October, 1986.

13. Henry Cabot Lodge, *Alexander Hamilton* (Boston: Houghton, Mifflin and Co., 1899), 28.

14. This axiom Hamilton apparently abandoned in Federalist Paper No. 9, in which he cited Montesquieu as an authority in support of the contention that the very size of the American Union would be a bulwark of security without the liberty within. See *The Federalist Papers*, edited by Clinton Rossiter (New York: New American Library, 1961). The quotation in this note is from Rossiter's analytical table of contents, page xx.

15. F.H. Hinsley, *Sovereignty*. 2d ed. (Cambridge: Cambridge University Press, 1986), 26. Hinsley, however, missed the contribution of the Americans to the doctrine of sovereignty. Neglecting the contrivance of shared sovereignty between the states and the national government, Hinsley condemned the Americans for following a confused theory when they borrowed the separation of powers doctrine from Montesquieu, *Ibid.*, 152.

PART II

Contemporary Philosophical Perspectives on Constitutionalism

7

The Constitution, Rights, and the Conditions of Legitimacy

Jeffrey Reiman

Reiman asumes that a legitimate government is necessarily nonoppressive. His analysis of the essential conditions of political legitimacy also features a carefully fashioned defense of American constitutional democracy on both "human rights" and "social contract" grounds. Reiman's argument includes an answer to the perennial question, why is a minority obligated to obey laws expressive of the will of a majority? He concludes his paper with a rebuttal of a "critical legal studies" approach to the Constitution and to constitutional interpretation as he understands it, namely, that the indeterminacy of judicial decision-making defeats the enterprise of legitimate governance.

I am not an advocate for frequent changes in laws and constitutions, but laws and institutions must go hand in hand with the progress of the human mind. As that becomes more developed, more enlightened, as new discoveries are made, new truths discovered and manners and opinions change, with the change of circumstances, institutions must advance also to keep pace with the times.

Thomas Jefferson*

*Letter to Samuel Kercheval (Monticello, 7/12/1816). From *The Portable Thomas Jefferson*, ed. Merrill Peterson, (New York: Viking, 1975).

MUST WE CHOOSE BETWEEN PROTECTING RIGHTS AND KEEPING GOVERNMENT LEGITIMATE?

For much of the twentieth century, the United States Supreme Court has functioned as a forum for determining the fundamental rights possessed by American citizens, and as a court of last resort for the protection of those rights. The Court has, as courts generally have, claimed to *find* these fundamental rights in the law, in particular in the provisions of the Constitution. But this claim is dubious. The Court's recent "findings" have emerged in two waves of constitutional interpretations which are, to say the least, *creative.* The first wave, beginning in 1925 with *Gitlow v. New York,* was characterized by increasing application to state governments of the provisions of the Bill of Rights by interpreting the Fourteenth Amendment to require such application. This first wave was the basis for the second: Beginning in 1954 with *Brown v. Board of Education,* the Supreme Court has more or less openly read new meanings into the terms of the Constitution and issued rulings desegregating public facilities, shoring up the rights of criminal suspects, enhancing the protection of free expression, and carving out a constitutional right to privacy with important implications for contraception, abortion and unconventional sexual practices.

Even among those who believe that these rulings recognize rights we do have morally and should have legally, a troubling question has been raised. It seems undeniable that virtually none of these decisions can be thought to be part of what the framers of the Constitution thought they were doing when they designed the articles and amendments upon which the Court has relied in making those decisions. If this is so, then it follows that the Court has effectively revised the Constitution to reach its decisions, and it is far from clear that they have any right to do that. Writes Michael Perry:

> In the modern period of American constitutional law—which began in 1954, with *Brown v. Board of Education*—the United States Supreme Court has played a major and unprecedented role in the formulation of human rights. Most first amendment doctrine regarding political and religious liberty; most equal protection doctrine regarding racial, sexual, and other forms of discrimination; all due process doctrine concerning rights pertaining to contraception, abortion, and sexual behavior . . . reflect not value judgments . . . made and embodied in the Constitution by the framers, but value judgments made and enforced by the Court against other, electorally accountable branches of government. Thus, in America the status of constitutional human rights is almost wholly a function, not of constitutional interpretation, but of constitutional policy-making by the Supreme Court.[1]

In response to this, continues Perry, there has emerged "a major debate in contemporary constitutional theory. Many theorists contend that constitutional policymaking by the Supreme Court is illegitimate . . . on the ground that it is fundamentally inconsistent with our societal commitment to democracy."[2] Later, we shall have occasion to consider Perry's own defense of the Court's constitutional policymaking. For the moment, it is important to get clear on what the problem is.

At issue here is not the Court's authority to invalidate laws on the basis of their incompatibility with the Constitution. That authority, though not without its detractors, is arguably implicit in Article III which establishes the Constitution as the "supreme law of the land." A law can be the supreme law of the land only if it supersedes all other laws of the land. And for one law to supersede another law means that when the two laws conflict, the superseded law is rendered nugatory—literally *over*ruled—by the superseding one. If we make the plausible assumption that the Constitution should be read as establishing the institutions necessary to achieve its stated goals, then we can read it as establishing an institution capable of determining when a law is overruled by the Constitution. Since determining which law is valid when two conflict is the traditional business of courts, and since the other two institutions of government—the legislature and the executive—are directly involved in the making of laws, the Supreme Court is the natural candidate for the job of determining the constitutionality of the laws made subsequent to it.[3] But this does not show that the Court has the right to make the kind of constitutional decisions it has made of late.

The reason is that the argument just sketched justifies no more than the right of the Court to determine the compatibility or incompatibility of laws with the Constitution. And that, in common sense terms, implies "the Constitution *as it was understood by its framers.*" By "common sense terms," I mean that if you and I understand ourselves bound by a contract we drew up and signed fifty years ago, we will normally think that we are bound now to what we thought we were binding ourselves to then *and not to what the language in our contract might mean today that it did not mean then.* And in the same way, determining what the Constitution requires will normally be understood as determining what is required when it was written and ratified—that is, "as it was understood by its framers." To be sure, since the Constitution includes twenty-six amendments, it was not written and ratified at a single time. Moreover, not only is the understanding of the authors relevant, that of the ratifiers is as well. Thus, by "framers" I mean those who wrote the original Constitution and those who wrote the subsequent amendments, and those who participated, even from the sidelines, in debating and eventually ratifying the original Constitution and then each amendment that eventually became part of the Constitution. The problem of the Court's decisions since *Gitlow* and *Brown* is that these decisions clearly read the Constitution in terms that go beyond the understanding of the framers.

There is wide agreement among scholars that the authors and ratifiers of the Fourteenth Amendment did not understand it to apply the Bill of Rights to the states. Moreover, the framers surely would not have understood the

Constitution to outlaw racially segregated schooling, since the authors and ratifiers of the original document explicitly countenanced much worse (namely, slavery), and the generation that adopted the Fourteenth Amendment was quite content with "separate but equal" public facilities for the races.[4] Nor can the framers be thought to have understood the Constitution to include a right to privacy that would prohibit the state from interfering with a married couple's right to use contraceptives or with a pregnant woman's right to have an abortion, since the framers lived at a time when such matters were taken as legitimately subject to legal regulation.[5] In short, the problem is not whether the Court has the authority to judge the constitutionality of legislation. The problem is whether, in doing so, the Court may legitimately go beyond the understanding of the framers in determining what the Constitution mandates.

Following Perry, let us say that when the Court tests the constitutionality of a law in light of an interpretation of the framer's understanding of the Constitution, the Court engages in "interpretive review," and when it tests the constitutionality of a law by going beyond the framers' understanding, the Court engages in "noninterpretive review."[6] For reasons already indicated, I assume that interpretive review is acceptable. It is noninterpretive review that raises the problem.

Those who object to noninterpretive review are not simply knee-jerk antiquarians who want to bind our current fate to the wishes and understandings of the people who set up our form of government two centuries ago. The issue is rather that a constitution is supposed to be a set of limits on the exercise of state power, such that power exercised within these limits is legitimate and power exercised outside these limits is not. If the Constitution is supposed to limit the exercise of state power, then the limits in the Constitution must exist in advance of the exercise of state power. This implies that the nature of the limits must be thought of as established when the Constitution was written and ratified—and the same for the content of the limits that are spelled out in the amendments subsequently adopted. And this implies that where the plain language of the document is unclear, ambiguities must be cleared up by reference to the understanding of its authors and their contemporaries. If, instead, the intentions of the framers are left behind and the Constitution freely renovated by the Court, then, since the Court is an organ of the state, the Constitution becomes the product of the exercise of state power, rather than limits on the exercise of state power.

This is all the more troubling since the Court lacks the other feature that is widely accepted as rendering the exercise of power legitimate, namely, accountability to the electorate. The Court is not electorally accountable in the way that the executive and legislative branches are. Indeed, the Court is intentionally designed to be insulated from electoral politics. The worry about the Court's right to go beyond the framers' understandings is then based on the notion that there are two ways in which an institution can exercise legitimate power. It can either do what the Constitution *as it was written* says it can do, or it can do what the electorate directly empowers it to do.[7] Since neither will justify decisions of the sort made since *Brown*, we appear to face a dilemma: We seem forced to choose *either* holding to the understandings and intentions of the framers at the cost of forgoing valuable recent (and potential future) decisions that expand and more effectively secure our rights, *or* setting the Constitution free from those origins at the risk of losing the very fixity and independence that enables a constitution to protect us from the exercise of illegitimate power. "The stakes," as Perry notes, "are very high indeed."[8] Must we choose between securing our rights and keeping our government legitimate?

In what follows, I shall argue that this "dilemma" is a false one. The appearance of a real dilemma comes from assuming that the conditions of legitimacy are given once and for all. Then government either holds to those conditions or does not, and where those conditions do not already provide for all our rights, we shall have to choose between rights and legitimacy. I shall argue that, since legitimacy is a moral notion, we cannot take for granted that any existing formulation of its conditions is complete. Consequently, to be legitimate a government must do more than merely keep within some identified set of conditions—it must be continually monitoring the conditions of its legitimacy and effectively correcting existing formulations of these conditions as needed. Thus, I shall contend that a legitimate government is not simply one that keeps to a pre-established recipe for legitimacy but one that has built into it an institutional mechanism for continually reflecting on the conditions of its legitimacy and for effectively translating the results of that reflection into law. I maintain that a Supreme Court able to engage in noninterpretive constitutional review is *part* of such a mechanism.

Further, I contend that chief among the conditions of legitimate government is respect for and protection of the fundamental rights possessed by human beings. If a legitimate government is one that is continually and effectively monitoring the conditions of its legitimacy, then it is one that is continually reflecting on the question of what rights people truly possess and building its answers to this question into its practice. If this is so, then the Supreme Court's "discovery" of new rights in the Constitution may be a condition of the continuing legitimacy of our government rather than a violation of it. Moreover, I maintain that while this leaves much to the judgment of the justices of the Court, it does not give them *carte blanche* to revise the Constitution according to their personal moral views. The reason for this is that the question of the conditions of legitimacy is a particular question with a particular shape that constrains the kinds of arguments that can be made for answers and thus ultimately constrains the kinds of answers that can be persuasive. I contend that the question of the conditions of legitimacy is essentially the question at the heart of the social contract theory, namely: What basic rights would rational human beings with differing or potentially differing moral beliefs insist upon as a condition of subjecting themselves to governmental power that may enforce rules with which they do not agree?

The argument I shall present for these propositions is far from complete. The area is large and the issues complex and controversial. Spelling out the details of the entire argument would require space far beyond that available to me here. Faced with the alternatives of setting forth the details of a part of the argument and sketching out roughly the shape of the whole, I have opted for the latter.

THE CONSTITUTION AS PAPER, PRACTICE, AND PROMISE

Justices (and commentators) who hold that we should interpret the Constitution in terms of the framers' understandings and intentions have been called "strict constructionists," and those who hold that the Constitution should be interpreted in terms of evolving moral and social conceptions have been called "loose constructionists." For simplicity sake, I shall use these labels, but only with the caution that they are misleading. The fact is that it is not possible to choose either alternative without having some theory of what the Constitution *is*, what its point is, what its source of obligatoriness is, and so on. To the so-called "loose constructionist" justices who think that the Constitution is an organic, living thing, waiting to be reinterpreted by each generation, their rulings that go beyond the intentions of the framers result from strict interpretations of the Constitution *given what they think the Constitution is*. And the so-called "strict constructionist" justices who hold that the Constitution must be interpreted in light of the original intentions, should not be thought of as taking the Constitution *as it is*. Rather, they read it in light of their own theory of what the Constitution is, namely, that it is a document recording a particular agreement about how power should be exercised that was hammered out two hundred years ago in Philadelphia. At heart, the disagreement between the so-called strict and loose constructionists is not a disagreement between strictness and looseness, but between two theories of what the Constitution is. To understand the conflict between strict and loose constructionists then, we must pose the question, what *is* the Constitution?

At first glance, the answer is easy. The Constitution is a bunch of words on a few sheets of paper (originally parchment, of course), set down in 1787 and ratified a couple of years later. Let's call this the Constitution as *paper*. But this is not enough, since a constitution that exists only as paper is not a real constitution, in the sense that it fails to do any constituting. For that, the paper constitution must play an important role within the system of behaviors that constitutes government. And, strictly speaking, that role is not correctly described as "limiting those behaviors," since words on paper alone cannot limit anything. Rather, there must be a social practice in which reference to those words is generally effective in getting governmental behavior limited to the range permitted by those words. Let's call this the Constitution as *social practice*, or, for short, the Constitution as *practice*. It should be clear from the case of Great Britain that one can have a constitution as practice without a constitution as paper, and I suspect equally clear from the case of the Soviet Union that one can have the paper without the practice.

It is not satisfactory to leave matters here. The reason is that neither as paper nor as practice nor as both, does the Constitution do what we expect of constitutions. As I said earlier, a constitution is supposed to be a set of limits such that power exercised within those limits is legitimate. We can understand the proposition "power exercised within constitutional limits is legitimate," in two ways, either as a tautology or as a synthetic statement. As a tautology, power exercised within constitutional limits is legitimate because legitimacy means no more than "within constitutional limits." But tautologies are empty, as can be seen from the fact that, so understood, a constitution that said no more than "Do whatever the dictator orders" would render the dictator's power just as legitimate as governmental power hemmed into the space between people's rights by a constitution such as ours. Since I take it that we mean more by legitimate than this, the proposition "power exercised within constitutional limits is legitimate" must be synthetic. The term "legitimate" must add something that is not already present in the notion of constitutional limits. What it adds is (at least) the notion of moral obligatoriness. Legitimate power means (at least) power with which we are morally obligated to comply. This obligation need not be thought of as binding us absolutely or as supplanting our own judgment about how to behave.[9] Rather, that an exercise of power is legitimate is something that a rational individual should recognize as a moral consideration weighing heavily in favor of compliance—possibly, but not easily, outweighed by conflicting moral considerations.

Governmental power, then, is not legitimate only because kept within *just any* set of constitutional limits. Rather, the limits must be good enough to make power exercised within them legitimate. Put otherwise: That power is limited is a factual claim, but that the power so limited is legitimate is a moral claim. And if legitimacy entails moral obligatoriness, then a constitution only does what we expect of a constitution to the extent that its limits are those that render power exercised within them morally obligatory.

Since the obligation at issue in legitimacy is a moral one, it follows that neither the fact that the Constitution exists on paper nor that it governs an ongoing practice can supply this obligation-creating function. For that, the Constitution's limits must promise something of a moral nature, something that is sufficient to establish an obligation owed in return. Thus the Constitution is something else besides paper and practice. Let's call this the Constitution as *moral promise,* or for short, the Constitution as *promise.* Now, since this promise is a moral one, we cannot take for granted that any given set of constitutional limits succeeds in making good on the promise. And this, as we shall see, has far-reaching implications for our understanding of the conditions of legitimate power and thus of the role of the Supreme Court.

THE MORAL PROMISE AND THE CONDITIONS
OF LEGITIMATE POWER

As we have seen, those who question the legitimacy of noninterpretive review by the Supreme Court assume generally that there are two ways in which exercises of governmental power are legitimate, namely, either the exercises are subject to the electoral process or they are provided for in the Constitution. But this view is inadequate on several grounds.

First of all, there is nothing inherently legitimating about the electoral process. If anything, the electoral process is the problem, not the solution. Thinkers like John Locke, who so profoundly influenced the formation of our governmental system, were deeply concerned to show how the electoral process could be legitimate. The point is this. The problem of the legitimacy of governmental power arises most strikingly with respect to those against whose views or actions that power is exercised. Subjecting power to the electoral process means allowing the voting public to determine whether or not a particular exercise of power is acceptable. This renders governmental power legitimate by subjecting it to the choices of those who are governed by it, since people are normally bound by what they agree to and not oppressed by what they choose. However, since there will rarely be unanimity, the outcome of the electoral process will normally reflect the choices of the majority. But this entails that the policies that emerge from the electoral process will be imposed on the dissenting minority against its wishes. And then, rather than answering the question of legitimacy, this will raise the question with respect to those dissenters. Why are the exercises of power approved by the majority against the wishes of (and potentially prohibiting the desired actions of) the minority obligatory with respect to the minority? Why are such exercises of power not simply a matter of the majority tyrannizing the minority?

These questions not only point up the error of taking electoral accountability as an independent source of legitimacy, they also suggest that it is mistaken to think of electoral accountability and constitutional provision as alternative sources of legitimacy. Rather, the Constitution *with its provisions limiting the majority's ability to exercise power* is the answer to the question of why decisions voted by a majority are binding on the minority who disagree. We shall look more closely at the details of this answer shortly. For the moment, it suffices to note that, insofar as the Constitution hedges majority rule in a way that establishes the obligation of the minority to go along with the majority, the Constitution makes good on the moral promise and keeps the exercises of governmental power legitimate. But, and this is crucial, this works only to the extent that the Constitution really does keep the promise and really does limit power in ways that establish the obligatoriness of governmental power for all citizens. It must be an open question whether our Constitution actually succeeds.

Here then we see the deeper inadequacy of the notion that legitimacy is provided by either electoral accountability or constitutional provision. Electoral accountability renders power legitimate only within a constitutional framework. And that works only if the constitutional framework is the right framework, that is, if it contains limits on majority power that are good enough to render that power obligatory on all citizens. Rather than legitimacy being a matter of meeting one of two existing conditions, legitimacy is a matter of whether the Constitution actually makes good on the moral promise. Let us then consider how a constitution keeps the moral promise.

There are two ways in which a constitution might keep this promise, which we can call respectively "formal" and "substantive." *Formally,* the limits set forth in a constitution will establish obligations on us *if we have agreed to be governed by power exercised within those limits.* This is "formal" because it does not depend on the content of the limits: Any limits to which we agree will be thought binding on us. And consequently, any exercise of power within limits to which we have agreed will be binding on us and thus legitimate. *Substantively,* the limits in a constitution will establish obligations on us if those limits conform to a valid moral conception of the rightful exercise of governmental power. This is "substantive" because it depends exclusively on the content or substance of the limits: If they conform to a valid moral conception of the rightful exercise of governmental power, they—and power exercised within them—will bind us morally whether or not we have agreed to them. I shall say more about this in a moment, once we see why the formal approach won't work for us.

The Formal Approach

The formal approach won't work for our Constitution for the simple and obvious reason that we didn't agree to it. We weren't there at the time, and by no stretch of the imagination could those who were there have had the right to agree for us. And further, only a fraction of those who were there were even eligible to vote—women, blacks, and many of the poor having been excluded. And among those who did vote—as the debates between the Federalists and the Antis testify—not everyone agreed. The majorities by which it was approved in the state ratifying conventions were often quite slim—a mere 10 votes in Virginia, and only 3 votes in New York![10] The bald fact is that the number of people who actually agreed to the Constitution is surely no more than a fraction of a percent of all the Americans who have lived at any point between 1787 and now, all of whom are thought morally bound by the system the Constitution establishes. And there is no plausible way to claim that the agreement of that fraction of a percent represents the agreement of us all.

Nor will it do to claim that, by choosing to stay here and enjoy the benefits of the Constitution, we tacitly agree to the conditions of those benefits and thus to the Constitution itself. Tacit agreements are real enough, but their existence depends on a number of conditions. First of all, it must be plausible to construe our being here as choosing to stay here. And for that, we must have the real possibility of leaving (which requires not only the legal freedom to leave, but the financial means) and the real possibility of getting in somewhere else—possibilities that not everyone here does have. And, even for those of us who have these possibilities, it must be that we stay here for reasons that are distinct from those that would hold even if we had a different constitution or none at all (such as personal attachments or habit or inertia or familiarity or fear of the unknown or a level of prosperity due to natural abundance). Suffice it to say, it is far from obvious that the reasons that some or all or most of us are here are reasons distinct from these.

Moreover, even if we are here because we choose to stay, and even if we choose to stay because of benefits linked to our Constitution, problems still remain. The tacit agreement argument works by the notion that in accepting some benefit X, we accept the conditions necessary to make X possible. But that means that in accepting the benefits linked to our Constitution we accept only those aspects of the Constitution that are actually necessary to produce those benefits. And then, it remains an open question how much of the existing Constitution we are tacitly agreeing to. Further, if the benefits produced by our Constitution could be improved by altering the Constitution, then accepting the existing benefits doesn't amount to accepting the existing Constitution, since, if given a real choice, we would opt for other benefits under another constitution. In short, even after we meet the requirements for construing being here as choosing to stay here because of benefits linked to the Constitution, we can make the tacit agreement argument work only if the benefits are optimal and the existing Constitution the necessary condition of those optimal benefits. And this means that the tacit agreement argument forces us to consider the substance of the Constitution's limits.

The Substantive Approach

We turn then to the substantive way in which the Constitution might establish legitimate exercises of governmental power. To this question our own system gives an answer which stems from John Locke. In outline it is the following: If some form of government can be thought of as something that it would be rational for human beings to choose over other forms or over no government at all, then such government cannot be thought of as tyrannical or oppressive. Moreover, since that form of government will provide benefits (the ones that make it rational to choose it) only on the condition that people generally comply with its laws, rational human beings must recognize that they are obligated to comply with its laws as the necessary price of obtaining and enjoying the benefits. What are the benefits? The Lockean answer is that (over and above the increased productivity and security against foreign invasion that cooperation brings) the decisive benefits are the rights that government protects for citizens. Since these rights are to be protected generally, they must be protected against the government itself, and consequently they provide the boundaries within which government is properly limited. Thus, if the government is limited in ways which respect everyone's rights sufficiently to make it rational for everyone to choose this form of government over others or none at all, then government is legitimate in the sense of obligatory upon everyone. A constitution that limits government in ways that ensure sufficient protection of everyone's rights keeps the moral promise.

Within this set of limits, the outcomes of majority decisions will be binding on everyone and thus on the minority who dissent. This is so because even the most legitimate government will have to reach decisions when citizens disagree about which decision is best. In such cases, it is unavoidable that some will be disappointed, since even "not deciding" will effectively amount to deciding upon some policy that some citizens will like and others will not. The question is how best to arrive at decisions in such cases. It is here that majority rule is recommended, not because majorities are more likely to be right than minorities, but because what a majority approves of has fewer dissenters than what a minority approves of. Remember that electoral accountability renders government power legitimate by subjecting it to the wishes of the governed. The real virtue of majority rule is simply that it is not minority rule. And this is clearest with simple majority rule, since requiring two-thirds allows a minority of one-third-plus-one to decide for the rest, and requiring unanimity allows one person to decide for all. If governmental activity is limited in a way that leaves it unable to tread upon the basic rights of all citizens, then, when the government rules in ways from which some dissent, the dissenting minority can recognize that this is just an inevitable feature of group decision-making rather than something that subjugates them to the will of others. Government so limited is legitimate. If this is true (and I shall assume henceforth that it is), it follows that government is legitimate to the extent that it protects people's basic rights *sufficiently* to defeat the suspicion that those who dissent from governmental actions are subjugated by those actions.

I have emphasized the term "sufficiently" in the last sentence because much hinges on this. Simply paying lip service to people's basic rights won't defeat the suspicion of subjugation. Nor will it do to protect some basic rights and allow others to be trampled. Moreover, and this is crucial to my entire argument, *we cannot be satisified that any actual inventory of basic rights is sufficient since any such actual inventory that fallible and limited human beings come up with may miss some basic right which is essential for protection against subjugation.* To be sure, we can identify some of the basic rights with considerable certainty. For instance, protection against subjugation seems surely to require that people have freedom of movement and of expression and of religion, as well as rights to *habeas corpus* and representative republican government, all of which our Constitution currently places safely beyond the reach of the majority. I for one believe that it requires generally that government not become an engine for the imposition of some people's moral views on others. Thus, I believe that the commitment to keep exercises of power nonsubjugating goes beyond at least what the current Supreme Court believes the Constitution to require, since this commitment would, for example, require prohibiting laws against homosexual sodomy even if there were no right to privacy in the Constitution at all.[11] But, whatever we can determine right now to be required, the fact is that we cannot say once and for all what are the subjugating exercises of governmental power. The simple fact is that we are forever learning that arrangements once taken as natural and neutral are actually oppressive. And this fact has enormous implications for the reality of the Constitution as promise.

Merely subjecting government to some supreme law of the land won't guarantee fulfillment of this promise, since law itself can be a means to subjugation. Not even establishing a supreme law that appears fair will suffice, since appearances can deceive. It is always possible that some existing set of laws, generally thought fair, amounts to no more than a level of subjugation to which we are inured so that we don't notice it. Laws that establish property qualifications on holding office, or that limited the vote to men, are examples. But this means that while the reality of the Constitution as paper can be found reading the text, and the reality of the Constitution as practice can be found by studying the actual workings of the government, the reality of the Constitution as moral promise can be found only by the process of moral argument rooted in an ongoing reflection on the conditions of nonsubjugating governance.

This implies that, rather than thinking of legitimate government as government operating within given limits, we need to think of legitimate government more dynamically, that is, as government that continually and effectively monitors its own legitimacy. This amounts to thinking of legitimate government as government that continually and effectively monitors the adequacy of its recognition of basic rights. And insofar as doing this amounts to making good on the Constitution as moral promise, a legitimate government is one that includes an institutional arrangement by means of which the Constitution is treated as a living thing, to be reinterpreted in light of our best understanding of the rights to which people are entitled as this understanding evolves.

To be sure, this monitoring need not necessarily be done by the Supreme Court. Perhaps the amendment process set forth in the Constitution is enough to do the job, as the strict constructionists generally maintain. The conflict between the strict and loose constructionists is not a conflict between those who think of the Constitution as paper and those who think of it as moral promise. Rather, since both sides think that the Constitution is obligatory and sufficient to establish the legitimacy of power exercised within its terms, the two alternatives are better seen as two theories of the Constitution as moral promise. The so-called strict constructionists emphasize the fact that to make good on the moral promise, the Constitution must provide relatively rigid limits on power fixed in advance and thus not be open to revision by reinterpretation. And the nearest we can come to reading the Constitution as containing limits fixed in advance is by trying to read it as it was understood by those who wrote it. For the strict constructionists, the amendment process that the framers spelled out must suffice for correcting the conditions of legitimacy.

The problem with this proposal, however, is that the amendment process leaves it to the very holders of power (and the majority behind them) to determine the conditions of the legitimacy of their own power—when it is precisely the Constitution that is supposed to do that for them. The amendment process cannot suffice for the Constitution as promise, since the promise is precisely that the laws which represent the will of the majority not subjugate the minority whose will is otherwise. The moral promise can be kept only if the Constitution keeps the majority from acting in ways that subjugate the minority. The amendment process cannot satisfy this since it leaves to the same majority that passes laws that are potentially subjugating the determination of whether they are subjugating. And this is a problem not because of the venality of the majority, but because the very strength of conviction that leads the majority to think some law is necessary will lead them as well to think that that law is the very opposite of subjugation. This naturally turns us toward the Supreme Court as the appropriate place for the debate about how the Constitution should be interpreted so as to fulfill its moral promise.

THE SUPREME COURT, THE CONSTITUTION, AND THE SOCIAL CONTRACT

Once we see that the Constitution does its job only to the extent that it sets forth the conditions of nonsubjugating governance, and once we see that this in turn requires respect for basic rights *sufficient* to defeat the suspicion of subjugation, there is no alternative but to allow the Constitution to be interpreted in light of our developing understanding of the basic rights that must be protected. And if allowing this interpreting means that to some extent the Constitution inevitably becomes the product of governmental power rather than the limit on it, there is much to recommend putting this unavoidable task of interpretation in the hands of the Supreme Court. This is because, as Hamilton recognized in *Federalist #78,* since the Supreme Court controls neither the purse nor the sword, it is the "least dangerous" branch.[12] To be sure, my argument to this point supports the views of the loose constructionists. However, I think that it is necessary to understand the implications of the argument in a way that does justice to the wisdom of the strict constructionist position.

In my view, the so-called loose constructionist judges who produced the revolutionary decisions of the past three decades were making good on the Constitution as moral promise. They were spelling out the conditions that we currently understand as necessary to make the power of government nonsubjugating. More aware than the framers about the social-psychological effects of institutional arrangements, we can see how separate but equal public facilities relegate part of society to diminished power over their fates compared to the rest; more aware of the pressures on and disabilities of suspects of crimes, we can see how ignorance of rights can undermine the power of suspects to play their proper role in defending themselves against the power of the state; more aware of the pervasive influence of self-righteous moral vigilantes, we can see how lack of a firm boundary around private life can render individuals unable to control the terms of their intimate life and reproduction.

But, it will be objected, doesn't this defense of the loose constructionist view amount to an open invitation to the justices of the Supreme Court to read their personal moral views into the Constitution? I think not, for two reasons. The first is that the question of legitimacy is a distinct one, and it shapes the kinds of arguments that can be put forth in defense of constitutional rulings. Those arguments must show that a given right is a necessary condition of nonsubjugating government. And for this, I believe, the Court is forced back onto the *contractarian* foundations of the Lockean rights doctrine discussed in Chapter 7. In order to ask the question of the conditions of legitimacy, once we are no longer content to rest with any previously given answer, we must ask, what rights would rational men and women with differing or potentially differing moral beliefs insist on as a condition of putting their fates in the hands of government that may make and enforce rules against their wishes?

My point here is easily misunderstood. I am not saying that the Court is entitled to interpret the Constitution in terms of "social contract" theory because this was the theory subscribed to by the framers and implicitly built into the Constitution by them. Nor am I saying that the Court should opt for "social contract" theory because it is the best, or currently the most satisfactory, moral theory. I think both these claims are largely true, but besides the point. My claim is that once government undertakes to monitor the conditions of its own legitimacy understood as the conditions under which governmental power is obligatory,there is effectively no satisfactory way to engage in this monitoring, other than by posing the question that social contractarians pose.

The reason (all too briefly put) is that what it would be rational for human beings to agree with does not subjugate them. With existing answers to moral questions no longer taken for granted, we cannot find what does not subjugate by asking for what people actually agree to. People are shaped by existing moral beliefs and therefore may agree to arrangements which in fact do subjugate them. What remains then is to look for nonsubjugating governance by asking what it would be rational for people to agree with. Moreover, since we seek the conditions of legitimate governance among people whose moral views do (or may) differ, we cannot simply assume the truth of any controversial moral view in answering the question of legitimacy—even if it is the moral view of the majority. To do so may in effect license the subjugation of the minority who hold a different moral view. Consequently, if we understand the question of legitimacy as that of finding the conditions of nonsubjugating governance among people who do or may differ in their moral views, the general shape of that question is: What rights would rational men and women with differing or potentially differing moral beliefs insist on as a condition of putting their fates in the hands of a government that may make and enforce rules against their wishes? And this question will limit the kinds of evidence and arguments that can count toward an answer, for example, by ruling out appeal to disputed moral beliefs.

It is likely to be countered that the social contract is only one among many moral visions and thus my proposal amounts to enshrining one moral belief at the expense of others. This objection is a welcome one, because it points to the real virtue of the social contract. The social contract is a way of determining what form of government is nonsubjugating among people who have (or may have) differing moral visions. To be sure, the outcome of asking what people with (possibly) differing moral visions would agree to will be different from what people with one moral vision will agree to. Thus, one can say that the social contract is also one moral vision among others. So be it. It remains the case that what is unique about this vision is that it aims to eliminate subjugation among the holders of disparate visions, and this feature, I contend, uniquely recommends treating the social contract as *the* moral vision embodied in our Constitution—once the Constitution is understood as moral promise. After all, the moral promise is offered to one and all, irrespective of their moral vision.

The second reason, that allowing the Court to make good on the Constitution as moral promise doesn't invite the justices to read their own moral

views into the Constitution, brings us to the wisdom in the strict constructionist view. The strict constructionists are generally right in thinking that at
least one of the ways in which the moral promise is kept is by providing a
kind of fixity to the rules which make up the Constitution. Their mistake as
far as I can see is that they see no alternative between adherence to the
original intentions and chaos. My own view is that requiring justices to defend their decisions publicly as interpretations of the Constitution limits the
range of outcomes they can reach and the sorts of arguments they can present for those outcomes. And this too is part of the answer to the social contractarian question stated earlier because, among the things on which it
would be rational for people to agree regarding their government, is the requirement that there be some structure that constrains the range of answers
that can be given about the conditions of legitimacy.

The "dilemma" of rights versus legitimacy we met at the outset is a false
one. The real dilemma that we face is that the conditions of legitimacy are in
conflict. Both the loose and the strict constructionists have wisdom on their
side. Government is kept legitimate by continually monitoring the conditions of legitimacy *and* government is kept legitimate by holding it within
conditions that cannot easily be overturned or revised. Requiring justices to
show that their interpretations are continuous with the written Constitution
serves to constrain their decisions within the terms in which the reflection
on the conditions of legitimacy has slowly evolved over the course of our
history. Among other things, this has the effect of spreading the discussion
of the conditions of legitimacy out over time. Instead of allowing the Court
to come up with its specific answers *ex nihilo,* this requires that they fit their
answers into the discussion as it evolves over the history of the Court.
Rather than a mere fiction, the convention of requiring the justices to link
their decisions to the Constitution as it has been interpreted by the Court
before them serves to limit the possible novelty of the decisions of any particular Court by requiring that they at least plausibly fit into the Constitutional culture that has evolved to that point.

The Constitution may be interpretable in many ways, but not in just any
way one wants. It cannot plausibly be interpreted in ways that deny that
citizens have important rights against government, or that deny that elected
officials must be effectively accountable to the public, or that assert the existence of rights wholly discontinuous with the rights enumerated in the Bill
of Rights. We are sometimes so struck by our disagreements that we think
that all we have are disagreements. But our disagreements over the Constitution are shaped by and contained within the moral vocabulary of the
Constitution, and thus they are disagreements about those things on which
we have agreed to disagree. Disagreements over whether the Constitution
requires desegregated public facilities or Miranda warnings or noninterference with a pregnant woman's decision to abort are disputes that are *all
in the family,* as the Constitutional family has matured since its birth. They
are worlds apart from disputes over whether we should censor the press or

own slaves or outlaw unpopular religions or abolish private property. The Constitution projects a moral culture, and this itself, even if it doesn't constrain us to one single outcome, constrains us nevertheless and thus does the work of limiting governmental power—even the Supreme Court's power as it reinterprets the Constitution.

Before proceeding, it will be worth pausing to consider Michael Perry's defense of noninterpretive review by the Supreme Court in human rights cases, since his position may easily be confused with the one I have put forth here. Recall that noninterpretive review means that, when testing the constitutionality of a law, the court reaches beyond the framers' understanding of what the Constitution prescribes. Perry claims that, while there is no constitutional justification for the practice of noninterpretive review (and of course no justification in terms of electoral accountability), there is a *functional* justification. Noninterpretive review serves a function good and important enough to our polity to justify its continuance. Perry writes:

> The basic function of that practice is to deal with those political issues that are also fundamental moral problems in a way that *is* faithful to the notion of moral evolution (and, therefore, to our collective religious self-understanding)—not simply by invoking established moral conventions (as electorally accountable institutions are prone to do) but by seizing such issues as opportunities for moral reevaluation and possible moral growth.[13]

In short, Perry claims that we as a people are committed (on quasireligious grounds) to the notion that there are right answers to moral questions, and thus that any existing answer provided by accepted moral conventions may be wrong. Consequently, he holds that we are committed to the search for answers that are better than those currently accepted. Electorally accountable officials, however, are loath to stray from accepted conventions because this may end up costing at the polls. The Supreme Court, precisely because it is insulated from electoral politics, serves the function of enabling us as a people to make good on the commitment to search for better answers to moral problems than those provided by existing moral conventions.

Now, I agree with Perry that the fallibility of existing moral beliefs is part of the justification for noninterpretive review. Where we differ is that Perry takes the Supreme Court as a kind of general agent of moral growth, reviewing—and, where necessary, revising—our moral conventions. My view is that the Court's assignment is narrower and more focussed. I take it not as a general agent of moral growth, nor as a general reviser of moral conventions, but as an institution aimed at providing answers to a specific moral question, namely: What are the conditions of legitimate exercises of power? Which question, I have argued, is equivalent to: What basic rights would rational human beings insist upon as a condition of agreeing to government that may enforce rulings against their wishes? For example, I take it that, on abortion, Perry would have the Supreme Court serve as a forum for the general assessment of existing moral beliefs about abortion. On my view, the Court would address the narrower question of whether it would be rational for people with differing moral beliefs about abortion to subject themselves to a government with the power to prohibit the pregnant women among them from having abortions.

Though there is much to recommend Perry's view, I think the view I have defended has three important advantages over his. First of all, by narrowing the focus of the moral question we take the Court to be answering, my proposal has the virtue of making the Court's actions more structured, less open-ended, and to that extent reducing the danger of the Court itself becoming an engine of oppression. By contrast, Perry's view leads him to have to admit that the source of the decisions in noninterpretive review will be "the judge's own moral vision."[14] Second, since my proposal is based on satisfying the conditions of legitimate government, it has its source in the very value that those who question noninterpretive review explicitly endorse. By contrast, Perry's view requires believing the rather speculative claim that we Americans are somehow committed to moral reevaluation to such an extent that we must assign this job to some institution of government.

Third, Perry's view does not, as far as I can see, explain why the outcome of the Court's moral reevaluation should be legally binding on the legislature and the citizenry. Why wouldn't it suffice for the Court to issue its judgments on an advisory basis? (We are, after all, also committed to the notion that there are true answers to scientific questions and thus that there may be better answers than those provided by existing scientific beliefs. Nonetheless, we do not ask some scientific institution to make binding decisions about what scientists may believe.) If we are, as Perry claims, truly committed to moral growth and the search for better answers than those given by our existing moral conventions, it would seem that nonbinding judgments on such matters issued by the highest court of the land would have considerable influence on legislators and voters *without raising the specter of the Court exercising power beyond Constitutional or electoral mandate.* On my view, the Court's decisions must be legally binding precisely because they are decisions about the conditions of legitimate governance by the other branches, conditions whose determination cannot be left up to those branches. Unless the Court's decisions are legally binding, a necessary condition of legitimacy, namely, a built-in mechanism for not only monitoring but effectively correcting the conditions of legitimacy, is lacking. I think, by the way, that it is because Congress at least dimly perceives that its own legitimacy is bound up with the effectiveness of the Supreme Court's reflection on the conditions of legitimacy, that so little use has been made by Congress of the enormous power granted to it over the Court by Article III of the Constitution.

INSTITUTIONS, ARGUMENTS AND
THE MORAL CONVERSATION

Recently, a group of legal writers identified broadly as "The Critical Legal Studies Movement" has reinvigorated the notion—propounded earlier in this century by the "legal realist" school—that law is made by judges. Renewing the critique of the picture of judges deciding cases by "finding" the appropriate statute and "deducing" its implications for the case at hand, the CLSMers have argued that our law is incurably indeterminate with respect to particular outcomes in particular cases, such that judges invariably have to make political-moral choices in deciding any case. One target of this argument is the claim that either the Constitution itself or any widely acceptable theory of constitutional interpretation sets forth our fundamental rights with sufficient specificity to determine judicial decisions about our rights.[15] The implication is that such decisions will also reflect judges' political-moral choices.

Needless to say, this poses a substantial challenge to the proposal which I have tried to defend here. I have argued that a legitimate state is one that includes an institutional mechanism for monitoring and correcting the conditions of legitimacy, and that the Supreme Court engaging in noninterpretive review is *part* of that mechanism. I have argued further that this does not simply leave matters to the personal moral views of the judges, because the question of the conditions of legitimacy—the question of the basic rights that must be safeguarded if governmental power is to be nonsubjugating—is a determinate question. It has the shape of the contractarian test of rational agreement, and this constrains the types of arguments that can be adduced for rights and thus the range of outcomes. At the same time, the outcomes are constrained from the other side by the practice of requiring judges to defend their decisions as interpretations of the Constitution. If, however, after all is said and done, constitutional decisions about basic rights come down to political-moral choices by judges, this seems to leave the project of monitoring and correcting the conditions of legitimacy to the whimsy of the sitting justices—and this would appear to deprive our rights of precisely that fixity and independence necessary for them to function as real limits on governmental action.

I shall close this essay by defending my proposal against this critique. In general, my view is that while the CLSMers are right in maintaining that there is a range of indeterminacy in Supreme Court judgments about basic rights, they are wrong about the implications of that indeterminacy. They are wrong because they fail to see that human institutions cannot have the kind of determinacy that, say, good arguments possess regarding their outcomes. Accordingly, the CLSM critique applies a standard of determinacy that no institutional framework could, or should, match. The result is that the CLSMers fail to see that the institutional ways in which Supreme Court decisions are constrained suffice to provide as much determinacy as is needed.[16]

Some of the indeterminacy to which the CLSMers point is the inevitable product of the fact that laws are expressed in general terms which must be interpreted when applied to individual cases, at least in any cases controversial enough to be brought as far as the high court. And some of the indeterminacy to which they point is the product of the fact that our own society is not of one mind about the ultimate values that the law ought to embody. The first type of indeterminacy is the sort that haunts familiar constitutional phrases such as "due process," "cruel and unusual punishment," "equal protection," and of course such legal perennials as "harm" and "reasonable." The second type reflects the fact that we want the law to respect free choice *and* to serve the general welfare, to protect people from unwanted interference *and* support the value of community, to respect precedent *and* to adapt to new circumstances, to be knowable in advance *and* flexible enough to be tailored to individual circumstances, and, of course, to do justice *and* be merciful—and all of these are pairs of tendencies that are not only conflicting but on which we are unable to agree about the final priorities when they come into conflict. Accordingly, any actual judicial decision will necessarily have to stake out positions on the meanings of the tricky legal phrases and cut a course across opposing moral tendencies in the law, in ways that are inherently disputable and about which reasonable men and women will disagree.

However, rather than defeating the project of legitimate governance, it seems to me that these kinds of indeterminacy are unavoidable aspects of real institutions, operated by real people. Institutions are not arguments. They do not start from self-evident premises and proceed syllogistically to inescapable conclusions. They are actual deployments of real human beings who are required to use judgment in evaluating evidence and arguments, and to make and defend decisions that cannot wait until every conceivable objection has been heard and assessed. We cannot ask of such institutions that they proceed according to some algorithm that would yield a single unique answer to every problem. Consequently, while the CLSMers (and the legal realists before them) are right about the indeterminacy of the legal system, the implications of this is not that legal decisions are simply up for grabs. Once we see that indeterminacy is an inescapable feature of real institutions, we see as well that it can only be controlled institutionally—that is, we need institutional arrangements that narrow the range of possible outcomes to an acceptable range, and that subject indeterminate judgments to broad challenge and review. The general point is that legal indeterminacy cannot be eliminated theoretically—but it can be tamed institutionally. The line between the indeterminate and the arbitrary cannot realistically be drawn in advance. Rather, that line has to be actively policed. As we already knew, eternal vigilance is the price of free institutions.

Here we would do well to remember the multiplicity of institutional arrangements that circumscribe the activities of the Supreme Court. Legally, there is the amendment process (by means of which a sufficient majority of citizens can literally remake the Constitution as they see fit), there is the power of Congress to determine the jurisdiction of the Supreme Court (by means of which a majority in Congress can set virtually any controversial issue off limits to the Court), the power of the President and Congress to appoint the justices of the Court (which effectively limits the Court membership to judges whose views are within the range broadly acceptable to the electorate), and of course there is the power of impeachment (whose infrequent use is, in my view, less a testimony to the difficulty of carrying it off than to how well-behaved the Court has generally been). But beyond this, there are the press and the professional community of lawyers and law professors who subject the Court's actions to intense scrutiny and sophisticated assessment, in light of the general requirement of continuity with the written Constitution and the history of its interpretation. And there is ultimately the need for the acquiescence of the government officials who must enforce the Court's decisions and of the general public who must generally support that enforcement. When I said earlier that the Supreme Court engaging in noninterpretive review is *part* of an institutional mechanism for monitoring and correcting the conditions of legitimacy, it is this larger interacting complex of institutions and practices that I had in mind as the *whole* of which the Court is part.

It is comparatively easy to look down from the heights of theory and sketch out one's pet theory for how a government should be organized. It is quite a bit harder to design an actual institutional complex that—subject to human frailty and unanticipated circumstances—is actually likely to realize any given set of moral ideals over time. This was the goal of the framers of our Constitution They were practical political philosophers concerned not with drawing beautiful Platonic republics in the air, but with designing a real republic that—given people's actual capabilities and foibles—would not be likely to decay into tryanny for ages to come.

None of this guarantees that our or any other set of institutions will always come up with the right answers, that they will always identify and protect our real basic rights. But that is an impossible requirement. It would be like insisting that the criminal trial system be designed so that no innocent person would ever be found guilty and no guilty person ever be acquitted. What we can do is design institutions that actually keep alive a wide-ranging public and professional moral conversation about the nature of our basic rights, and that effectively translates the conclusions of that conversation into legal reality. If it be granted that a legitimate state is one that includes an institutional mechanism for effectively monitoring and where necessary correcting the conditions of its legitimacy, then a mechanism must be designed such that it is actually likely to keep alive and effective the ongoing moral conversation, though it be operated by mere mortals and though it reflect the conflicts in that conversation that have not yet been resolved. If, even now, one were to sit down and try to come up with such a design for real people, I find it hard to imagine that he or she will come up with anything appreciably better than a politically insulated Supreme Court wedged between an elected government and a free and fractious populace.

Notes

1. Michael J. Perry, *The Constitution, the Courts, and Human Rights* (New Haven: Yale University Press, 1982), 2.

2. Ibid., 2–3.

3. Cf., Ibid., 15–16, 172n21.

4. Ibid., 61–65, 194n26.

5. Forrest Macdonald, *Novus Ordo Seclorum: The Intellectual Origins of the Constitution* (Lawrence: University Press of Kansas, 1985), 15–16, 17n.

6. Perry, *The Constitution, the Courts, and Human Rights*, 10.

7. For a sampling of authorities who have argued to this effect, see Ibid., 28–29, and accompanying notes.

8. Ibid., 92.

9. One author who maintains that the putative obligation in the concept of legitimacy is absolute is Robert Paul Wolff, in *In Defense of Anarchism* (New York: Harper & Row, 1970). I have argued against this extreme claim (and the anarchism to which Wolff contends it leads for those who accept their responsibility to make their own moral choices) in Jeffrey Reiman, *In Defense of Political Philosophy* (New York: Harper & Row, 1972).

10. Zechariah Chafee, Jr., *How Human Rights Got Into the Constitution* (Boston: Boston University Press, 1952), 4.

11. Thus I disagree with the Court's ruling in the recent case of *Bowers v. Hardwick* (92 L. Ed. 2d 140 (1986)), decided on June 30, 1986; and I agree broadly with the conclusions of David A.J. Richards, concerning the appropriateness of reading the Constitution as implicitly containing some version of John Stuart Mill's principle that the state only has the right to limit the freedom of sane adults to prevent harm to others. David A.J. Richards, *Sex, Drugs, Death, and the Law* (Totowa, NJ: Rowman and Littlefield, 1982), 1–83. While my conclusions converge generally with Richards', note that he reaches them by a different route than I do. He starts by arguing that the Constitution implicitly embodies a commitment to the notion of individual rights against government. My argument starts from the claim that the Constitution (as moral promise) embodies an implicit commitment to establish the conditions of legitimate, nonsubjugating governance, and moves from there to the notion of rights against government. One consequence of this difference is that while Richards is willing to appeal to a variety of foundations for a rights-based moral theory of the Constitution, of which contractarianism is one such foundation, my emphasis on the centrality of the question of legitimacy leads me—for reasons soon to be presented—to emphasize the unique appropriateness of contractarian theory for constitutional interpretation.

12. Alexander Hamilton, James Madison and John Jay, *The Federalist Papers* (New York: New American Library, 1961), 465.

13. Perry, *The Constitution, the Courts, and Human Rights*, 101.

14. Ibid., 123.

15. I refer here generally to Paul Brest, "The Fundamental Rights Controversy: The Essential Contradictions of Normative Constitutional Scholarship," *Yale Law Journal* 90 (1981): 1063–1109; Duncan Kennedy, "The Structure of Blackstone's Commentaries," *Buffalo Law Review* 28 (1979): 205–382; Robert Unger, *The Critical Legal Studies Movement* (Cambridge: Harvard University Press, 1986); and the essays in David Kairys, ed., *The Politics of Law* (New York: Pantheon, 1982).

16. I have developed this argument in a different context in, Jeffrey Reiman, "Law Rights, Community, and the Structure of Liberal Legal Justification," in J.R. Pennock and J.W. Chapman, eds., *Justification: Nomos XXVIII* (New York: New York University Press, 1986) 178–203.

8

Constitutionalism and Critical Legal Studies

Mark Tushnet

Tushnet proposes the following thesis: constitutionalism is impossible, despite its being indispensable in preventing oppressive government. He explains that the social stability a legal institution is presumed to provide is ultimately undermined by the inevitable lack of controls on its power to interpret and specify what protected rights and liberties citizens possess. The interesting result for Tushnet, as for some other luminaries of the Critical Legal Studies Movement, is "a government of men not law." In disclosing the basis for his claim, Tushnet examines three leading theories of how the courts are supposed to be sufficiently constrained to fulfill their social purpose.

Critical legal studies has emerged in recent years as an important and somewhat novel perspective on the law. Proponents and critics of that perspective offer varying defintions of critical legal studies. For purposes of this essay I take critical legal studies as having two elements. First, it is an effort to identify fundamental or central difficulties in the intellectual project of liberal legal thought, with the latter defined as the main tradition of Western social and political thought about law. Second, after identifying those difficulties, critical legal studies attempts to provide a socioeconomic explanation for the centrality of those difficulties and for the inability of liberal legal thought to resolve them.

This essay applies the critical legal studies approach to the concept of constitutionalism, defined here as the ideal of "a government of laws and not men." Judges and judicial review play crucial roles in the implementation of that ideal, which is itself one of the fundamental concepts of liberal thought. I will argue that, because of some fundamental assumptions we make about people and government, constitutionalism is necessary to avoid kinds of oppression that we fear, and that the same fundamental assumptions make constitutionalism impossible. First I explain the *necessity* for judicial review, and then I turn to a somewhat more detailed discussion of its *impossibility*.[1]

Constitutionalism, which I will generally reduce to the special judicial role in enforcing legal limitations on the activities of private and public actors, is necessary because of the nature of social life. We all need each other, but we also pose threats to each other. This combination of need and threat can be described in *psychological* and *game-theoretic* terms. We exist in a social world that creates the conditions under which we come to understand ourselves. Our self-understanding—the meaning that we give our lives— therefore necessarily depends on others, that is, on those who constitute our social world. That in turn means that we are always at risk: the others may, entirely without our consent or participation, redefine the social world in which we are located, and thereby destroy our self-understandings.[2] Constitutionalism is an effort to create social institutions that stabilize the social world by placing the definition of the social order beyond willful transformation.

The game-theoretic version of the need-threat combination helps elaborate the structure of institutions that express the constitutional ideal.[3] We need each other to enable us to carry on joint projects that will improve our position in ways that we could not do, acting alone. By cooperating with each other, we can produce more than we can produce independently. We can agree on a joint project because, at its outset, we see the prospect of ending up better off. And we can also agree, at the outset, on what the proper division of the net benefit is.[4] Consider what happens, however, when the project is over. With the need to cooperate at an end, there is no need to comply with our prior agreement. The strongest member can simply walk away with all of the net benefit.

Often, however, the need to cooperate on additional projects will continue. Then the strongest has to figure out a way to keep us cooperating. The solution is for the strongest party to walk away with all but a little bit of the net benefit. That way, the weaker are indeed better off than they would have been if they had not cooperated, because they, each one, get a share—small though it be—of the net benefit. Yet, because the weaker will get only a small share of the benefit they produce, they need not produce as much as they could. That is not to the advantage of the stronger party, because there will not be as much net benefit to walk away with. This gives the stronger party an incentive to keep the prior agreement: he or she can walk away with as much as possible, because everyone has the maximum incentive to cooperate.[5]

This picture of cooperation and self-regulation is coherent only if people are going to cooperate with each other over a relatively extended period. Because as a practical matter extended cooperation is unlikely,[6] we must devise some other way to make sure that the stronger parties comply with the agreements they have made. That way is a system of enforceable law. Such a system says to people, "If you don't want to comply with your agreements, we're going to force you to anyway."

Now notice the new problem we have. The system of enforceable law has to have enough power to force stronger parties to do what they do not want to do. Unfortunately, "systems" do not have power; people do. So what we have to do is give *more* power to those people who we are going to use to make sure that agreements are honored. The problem is that those people—the government—might decide to seize the net benefits for themselves.

Once again, we can reduce the problem by counting on the need for repeated cooperation. If the government gets greedy, people will stop making agreements and producing net benefits for the government to seize.[7] In general, that is probably enough to keep the government in line most of the time. Occasionally, however, the people in the government will see really attractive opportunities—a really large net benefit produced by a despised minority, and the like. The government can then seize that, and say to the rest of us, "Look, don't worry. You can keep cooperating; we won't do this sort of thing very often, so you'll be better off running the risk that, sometime in the future, you'll have the bad luck to have your stuff grabbed from you." By introducing some uncertainty into the production system, this reduces somewhat the incentive to produce. There might be a better way to guarantee that everyone has the incentive to produce as much as possible.

To recapitulate the game-theoretic argument: people make agreements, and they create governments to provide the framework within which they can be sure that those agreements will be honored. Governments have the power to force people to act appropriately. At this point, the problem is to figure out how we can control the government. The solution is obvious: we create a government strong enough to do what we want, but then we specify limits on what it can do. This is the Constitution.

There are two kinds of limits. There are elements of the structural design—federalism and the separation of powers[8]—and there is the specification of protected rights and liberties. The structural elements make it hard for the government to misbehave. The rights and liberties say, "Even if you overcome those hurdles, there are some things you can't do." Once again that creates a problem as we have to figure out what those things are. Not, I should stress, that we cannot devise some general form of words to cover or define these rights but rather that we must figure out what exactly those rights are in particular contexts. We can agree that it is a bad thing for government to infringe the right of free speech, but does that right cover obscenity, or libel, or language critical of the government?

We need a way to answer that kind of question. Once again, we have an institution that we use for this. We count on the courts to specify what these rights are. Thus, judicial review is necessary, because it is what we use to make sure that the government, which is itself necessary, doesn't get out of hand.

I can now state the reason why judicial review is, though necessary, also impossible. It is impossible because we do not have any way to control the courts when they go about specifying what those protected rights are. What that means is either that judges will become powerful—able to keep the rest of the government from acting—and uncontrolled, or that judges will be impotent—unable to keep the government from seizing our goods and violating our rights.

The most important methods of controlling the courts are theories about the proper methods of constitutional interpretation.[9] Therefore, I consider next three of the major theories of interpretation:[10] (1) *Originalism*—the theory that the Constitution should be interpreted according to the intent of its drafters; (2) *Representation-Reinforcing Review*—the theory that it should be interpreted to remove obstacles to the expression of the democratic will; and (3) *Moral Philosophy*—the theory that it should be interpreted to guarantee that we live in a just, or at least a not seriously unjust, society.[11]

ORIGINALISM

Originalism claims that the courts should invalidate legislation only if it is inconsistent with the text of the Constitution as understood by those who wrote and adopted it. What are the problems with originalism?

Historical Investigation

There are some straightforward problems of historical investigation. We know something about what some people said about some provisions of the Constitution,[12] but how do we put together all the various views to come up with a single original understanding? For example, when the Fourteenth Amendment was adopted in 1868, everyone knew that it had something to do with promoting racial equality. But at that time people distinguished among equality of civil rights, political equality, and social equality. They had not sorted out which exactly the Fourteenth Amendment promoted. Indeed, they probably could not have sorted that out, because concepts of equality were quite fluid at the time. Second, consider the establishment clause of the First Amendment. James Madison did not believe that it was necessary to include a bill of rights in the Constitution, because the enumeration of a limited list of powers Congress had would be sufficient. But, to make adoption of the Constitution easier, he and others promised that a bill of rights would be added after the Constitution went into effect. And, as a member of the House of Representatives, Madison did introduce a bill of rights—but, remember, because he did not think it was necessary, he did not care much about many of its details. The debate in the House on the establishment clause is quite brief. It can be described with only slight distortions like this: Representative A says, "I'll vote for the clause because it means X." Madison says, "Fine." Representative B says, "No, no, it doesn't mean X at all. It means Y, and because it means Y, I'll vote for it." And Madison, who does not care about what it means but just wants to get it adopted, says, "Fine."[13] Under these circumstances, it is difficult to know what the House of Representatives as a whole understood the clause to mean.

Technological and Social Change

A second problem arises from what we might call technological and social change. In today's world, there are things that the framers could not have imagined. The usual example is wiretapping, a technological change. Social change can make a difference too. For example, the framers thought about problems of religious liberty in a country characterized by an almost entirely Protestant population divided into different denominations. Today, religious diversity covers a broader spectrum, and the breadth is not something that the framers had in mind. How does an originalist handle these problems of technological and social change?

One course, which no one has defended because it is normatively unattractive, is to say, "Too bad." The courts, on this view, would be authorized to invalidate statutes only if such statutes were precisely what the framers had in mind when they wrote the Constitution: because they did not have wiretapping in mind, it cannot be invalidated.

A second course is to say that the courts *can* invalidate things that are just like—are functionally equivalent to—what the framers had in mind. Wiretapping is just like a search, in terms of the reasons it is done and the values it threatens; problems of religious liberty in today's society of broad religious diversity are functionally equivalent to problems of religious liberty in a society of multidenominational Protestant diversity. But then the theoretical difficulty arises: as far as I know, no one has been able to come up with a decent way to keep these "functional equivalents" under control.[14]

The functional equivalents approach is a way to handle another vexing problem for originalists. Although we may be unable to tell what the framers thought was *un*constitutional, we often can find out what they thought would remain permissible. Unfortunately, on a normative level, what we find out is often quite troubling. For example, it seems reasonably clear that in 1789, when the First Amendment was sent to the states for ratification, people did not think that it violated fundamental principles of free speech to send people to jail for criticizing the government.[15] And it seems equally clear—that is, not absolutely certain but reasonably clear— that people in 1868 did not think that principles of racial equality were violated by segregation in public schools.[16]

Again, there are several ways to handle this. One is to swallow hard and say, "So be it—*Brown v. Board of Education* was wrong." And again, I know of no one who is willing to do that, because it is so normatively unattractive. A second way is to distinguish, as Ronald Dworkin has, between conceptions of free speech *or* equality, and the concepts of free speech and equality.[17] The conceptions are the particular examples the framers had in mind—"Racial equality means that blacks can testify in court, but it doesn't mean that they can go to integrated schools"—while the concepts are the philosophically defensible generalizations of those examples. The concepts are embodied in the Constitution. The difficulty is that there is no stopping point that keeps the courts from moving up from the mundane examples into the grandest stratosphere of abstract concepts that will let them find anything unconstitutional that they disapprove of—or from moving up to exactly that level of abstraction that lets them do what they want.

Functional Equivalents

A third course is a version of the functional equivalents argument again. This is, I believe, what Chief Justice Warren used in *Brown v. Board of Education,* when he said that in deciding on the constitutionality of school segregation in the 1950s we cannot turn the clock back to 1868 when the Fourteenth Amendment was adopted; we have to consider the issue in light of what public schools are today.[18] His claim, as I interpret it, is that in 1868 the framers thought about buildings with children in them that performed certain social functions. Today, however, the buildings with children in them perform a different, greatly expanded set of functions. And, to put it back in originalist terms, if we could ask the framers what they thought about segregation with respect to that expanded set of functions, they would have said, it is *not* permissible to segregate.

Here again the uncontrollability of the method makes it unsuitable as a method that will keep courts from getting out of hand. Nothing constrains the judges' definition of the functions served by X in the past, which the framers thought was permissible *or* unconstitutional, to be the functions served by Y today, thereby making Y permissible or not to depend entirely on the functional linkage today's judge decides to create. Consider for example the implications of involving the functional equivalent idea in connection with newspapers in 1789 and the mass media today.

All of these difficulties lead to the identification of the most fundamental problem with originalism as a theory of constitutional interpretation. There are two ways to do originalist analysis. The more common is to identify a clause, such as the establishment clause, and then to look for what the framers had to say about that clause. The fundamental problem is that what they thought about *that* clause was set in a much larger matrix of political theory that made sense to them overall and therefore made sense of the particular clause at issue. One cannot rip what they thought about the establishment clause out of the matrix, apply it to today's problems, and think that one is actually being faithful to the framers' intent. One must instead reconstruct and apply that entire overall structure.

At that point the difficulty becomes the one that I have labelled the problem of conceptual change. Intellectual historians do this sort of overall reconstruction. They have found out enough to make overall originalism impossible. The matrix of political theory of the 1780s and 1790s is almost incomprehensible in its assumptions about how people are and how governments behave, and in its assumptions about the distribution of wealth that, while perhaps realistic then, are entirely unrealistic now.[19] Thus, every plausible solution to these problems of originalism opens the way to letting judges do what they want—which is what we were trying to avoid.

REPRESENTATION-REINFORCING REVIEW

The idea behind *representation-reinforcing review* is this: We have a democratic system, and when it works well, the courts should not overturn whatever it produces. Here, though, working well does not mean "producing good laws." It means functioning as a democratic system, in terms of process.[20] In such a system, all views are heard and considered and then we decide what we want to do.

A democratic system can work badly in several ways. If people are not allowed to try to get support for their political programs, not all views will be taken into account; similarly if some people are not allowed to vote, or when they vote, what they want is not taken seriously. The present theory says that the courts can reinforce or strengthen the operation of the democratic system by guaranteeing that these sorts of impediments to proper functioning are removed.[21]

What might be unconstitutional under this approach? It can be shown that this approach allows the courts to invalidate only national sedition laws and exclusions from the national franchise.[22] The reason for stressing "national" here is that if something goes wrong on the state or local level, Congress can rectify it. If it goes wrong on the national level, however, there is no higher legislature to go to. If this conclusion is right, the approach has a troublingly narrow range of application, for there are no controversial exclusions from the national franchise, and whatever problems of restrictions of free speech there are, they do not involve national sedition laws.

Many proponents of this theory believe that it invalidates discrimination, against blacks or women or whoever, in substantive laws; however, because we have a pluralist political system, they are wrong. In a pluralist system, every group that has the vote, no matter how small the group, has a chance to have its policies adopted. It does so by finding another group, or coalition, that is just short of a majority to enact that group or coalition's policy. The tiny group then offers a deal, "We'll put you over the top for *your* policy, if you'll back us on ours." Particularly because policy coalitions in our society are fluid, combining and recombining different groups on different issues, the opportunity for this sort of horse-trading arises all the time. So, as long as a minority group has the vote, the pluralist political system guarantees that its interests will be taken into account through these deals.

Much in this picture rings true. If we consider the classic example of a discriminated-against group, we might observe that the worst excessess occurred precisely when blacks were effectively disfranchised in the South, and that as effective black enfranchisement took place, blacks became an important element in the Democratic Party coalition, which then began to support programs favored by the black community. Nor is it sufficient to undermine this account to note that minority groups do not always get what they want. Of course they do not; in a democratic society no one wins all the time. Defeats on particular issues may mean only that the minority group did not care as much about those issues as it did about other issues on which it won because of deals to win the latter and failure to make deals to win the former.

Still, virtually everyone who has worked with this theory of judicial review thinks that sometimes things do not work so well. They think that sometimes the pluralist democratic process does not work as it should. although it is difficult to work out why the process fails, the leading idea is that discrimination occurs when certain voters somehow do not count as much as they should. It is as if they have to care twice as much about an issue as anyone else before they can make the pluralist deal.

Why might that happen? The best explanation comes from the area of economic regulation, where the Supreme Court has said in effect that anything goes. Much economic regulation is producer-protective. That is, producers—optometrists or insurance agents—get together and decide that it would be a good idea to limit the competition they face. So they pool their political resources, become a single-interest pressure group, and persuade the legislature to prevent opticians, in one case, or funeral directors, in the other, from entering certain aspects of their business.[23] Who suffers from this? The opticians and funeral directors, of course, but they can raise their rates for the services they continue to perform. The true victims are the consumers, who have to pay higher prices when competition is reduced. The problem for democratic politics here is that consumers have less incentive to organize to oppose the single-interest producer-protective lobbyists. Each consumer pays only a little more for glasses or insurance and it is not worth it to invest effort in counter-lobbying. That is, the cost to each individual consumer of lobbying is greater than the extra cost of glasses, even though the increased costs to consumers as a whole are substantial.[24]

This provides a representation-reinforcing justification for aggressive judicial review of much economic regulation: the democratic process does not work to represent consumer interests adequately. This justification relies on a description of how politics actually works, rather than the formal model of pluralist politics. The problem now can be stated. Once judges can overturn statutes because of their understanding of how politics actually works—an understanding in which they can find that some groups are not represented fully—they are unconstrained. It is relatively easy to develop the "actual politics" argument to show why the poor are systematically underrepresented vis-à-vis the rich, or workers as against employers.[25] Thus, once judges can take informal obstacles to representation into account, the theory can no longer satisfy the requirement that we have an approach to constitutional interpretation that lets courts invalidate some statutes but keeps them from doing whatever they want.

MORAL PHILOSOPHY

My analysis of *moral philosophy* as a method of constitutional interpretation begins by identifying two of several different ways that we could use moral theory to guide constitutional decisions.

Conventional Moral Philosophy

The first involves conventional moral philosophy. Under this approach, the courts would invalidate statutes that are seriously out of line with what the large majority of the American people believe is morally permissible. The best example of this is *Moore v. City of East Cleveland.*[26] There the city had a zoning ordinance that was interpreted in a way that prohibited a grandmother from living with two of her grandchildren who were first cousins. This case is particularly interesting because virtually everyone believes that the Court was right to hold the ordinance unconstitutional under these circumstances, and because it is difficult to explain why such an ordinance would be unconstitutional under an originalist or a representation-reinforcing theory. Thus, people have come to agree that *Moore v. City of East Cleveland* must be defended, if at all, along the lines of moral philosophy.

The defense, in terms of conventional moral philosophy, is straightforward. Simply put, the ordinance is an outrage to the sensibilities of the vast majority of the American people. But we have gone too fast. First, there are going to be rather few issues on which there is that sort of general agreement. In addition, how are the courts supposed to know what the American people think? The courts, which cannot take polls that address the precise issues before them, can only rely on their sense of what the American people think and they might not be very good at doing that. For example, one justification of the Court's original set of death penalty decisions was that the people of the United States no longer believed in the death penalty. Polls and the increasing reluctance, at that time, to impose the death penalty demonstrated the people's misgivings about its morality.[27] It turned out that the Court was wrong. After the first set of death penalty decisions, state legislatures reenacted capital punishment statutes. When those statutes came before the Court again, the Court said that they were constitutionally acceptable—in part at least because the reenactments showed that the Court's initial judgment had been wrong.[28]

There is a more serious and more general problem, which applies even to *Moore v. City of East Cleveland.* That case implicated more values than the integrity of families. It also involved the value of federalism. A federal system allows different communities to choose different policies. If people do not like the policy in one community, they can move to another that is more congenial. No one has ever been able to explain, for example, what is so troubling about telling Mrs. Moore that if she wants to live with her grandchildren she merely must move across the city line to Cleveland.

We can generalize this point. Every state statute or local ordinance advances a complex set of values, the substantive purposes of the statute plus the value of federalism. I doubt that we would be able to find *any* statute that was inconsistent with the conventional morality of the American people once we made it clear that part of that conventional morality with respect to any particular statute would be respect for the value of federalism.

That leaves us with a theory that would allow the Court to invalidate only national statutes. But when would a national statute be inconsistent with the conventional morality of the American people? Surely no recently enacted statute could meet that standard. Perhaps some old ones could, and indeed it does seem to be the case that a disproportionate number of invalidations of national statutes come in cases involving old statutes.[29] That is not a very robust theory of judicial review.

Systematic Moral Philosophy

The version of moral philosophy as a theory of judicial review that people find more attractive, because it seems to handle more of the kinds of problems that they find troubling, is systematic moral philosophy. The idea here is that courts should find out what the best moral philosophers have to say about the permissibility of such laws as those restricting the availability of abortion or penalizing homosexual sodomy. If the moral philosophers say that restricting the availability of abortion violates women's rights to control their bodies, even if that infringes on some interests of fetuses—which seems to be the prevailing position among contemporary philosophers—then statutes restricting the availability of abortions are unconstitutional. In contrast, if the philosophers conclude that the problem involves competing interests of women and fetuses, as some have, then restrictive abortion laws are constitutional. Indeed, it could be the case that philosophers concluded that abortion violated rights of the fetus without advancing equally strong rights or interests of women (I take this to be Catholic doctrine) in which case it might violate the Constitution for a state *not* to have a restrictive abortion law.

There are a number of difficulties with this version of moral philosophy as a theory of constitutional interpretation. What are the implications, for example, of lack of agreement among philosophers? Are the courts to count heads? If not, are they supposed to determine for themselves which of the philosophers is right? We can identify three relatively narrow difficulties— narrow in the sense that they do not go to the heart of the theory, but raise important questions about whether we really want to accept it.

The first of these narrow difficulties is one that has been identified by a number of writers, including Judge Learned Hand. Assume that there really are moral truths and that judges can determine what they are, by reasoning for themselves or by relying on philosophers for guidance. And assume that a legislature enacts an immoral statute, in the appropriate sense. We could correct that enactment in two ways. We could rely on the courts to invalidate the statute. Alternatively, we could hope that the legislature would see the error of its ways. Of course that is not going to happen immediately, because the legislature enacted the statute. But perhaps it would be better in the long run if people knew that no one was going to bail them out if they acted immorally. That is, it might promote greater democratic responsibility, producing better statutes in the long run, if the courts said, "Look, you're on your own. If you make mistakes, you're going to be stuck with them, so you should be pretty careful about what you enact." Judicial review, this criticism goes, may make the people less responsible, which is not a good thing. Indeed, it may be so bad a thing as to outweigh the harm that occurs during the time between the enactment of an immoral statute and its repeal by a more enlightened legislature.

A second difficulty with this theory is that it depends on the proposition that there are morally correct answers to questions like those involved in the abortion or sodomy issues. Metaethical skepticism denies that there are such answers. Many philosophers today think that metaethical skepticism is a bad theory about the nature of moral inquiry. They think, that is, that there *are* answers to moral questions. Some moral philosophers have recently tried to defend versions of metaethical skepticism, and, if they are right, this approach cannot get off the ground.

Even if the philosophers who criticize skepticism are correct, still there is a strong strain of ethical skepticism in American culture. Many people do not think that there really are answers to ethical questions. They think that all there is, is the play of political power. Given the presence of so many people holding these views in the American public, a court will be hard-pressed to defend its reliance on moral philosophy as a theory of constitutional interpretation. It might be correct in the abstract, but its political position will be a difficult one. The people who disagree with the Court's disposition of the moral question will join the ethical skeptics, who think the whole enterprise is silly and undermines the Court's authority.

A third difficulty arises even if there are right answers to moral questions. When a court is presented with a constitutional issue, there are two candidates for the governmental body authorized to decide what the right answer is. The statute at issue can be taken to represent the legislature's judgment about the morally correct result. Thus, when the court invalidates a statute using this theory, it is necessarily claiming that *it* is better at moral philosophy than the legislature is. Typically this claim has been defended by saying that judges, who are removed from the hurly-burly of daily political life, are able to examine the moral issues in greater detail and are able to see them in a purer light, undistorted by the political pressures on legislators. We could wonder, however, whether those circumstances are actually likely to lead judges to make better moral decisions than legislators do. What this defense characterizes as undesirable political pressure might alternatively be characterized as information relevant to an accurate moral assessment of what is at stake. Consider, for example, the possibility that pressure on legislators from victims of crime, pressure that courts indeed feel much less substantially, actually makes legislators better at understanding the moral dimensions of problems of criminal procedure.

More generally, perhaps better moral answers are given by people who are very close to the messy details of life than are given by those who think about them in the abstract. Here one might consider controversies over whether criminal sentences should be set by the legislature or should be more individualized. The defense of individualized sentencing is precisely that circumstances vary so widely that we want someone who knows all the details to make the relevant decision.[30]

I have called the preceding difficulties narrow ones. They are serious, and raise questions about the theory of relying on systematic moral philosophy. But they only raise questions, and are not dispositive. There might be answers to all these questions: the cost of waiting for legislatures to correct immoral statutes might outweigh the cost to democratic responsibility occasioned by judicial review; there might be right answers to moral questions; and the detachment of judges might make them better moral reasoners than the legislators.

However, there is a general problem with this theory. Moral philosophers' works have two parts, the general philosophy and the applications to real problems. The general philosophy produces some general statements about what political morality requires. For example, the current favorite is the proposition that government must act with equal respect and concern for all people it affects (or sometimes, more narrowly, for all citizens).[31] Judges, who are asked to resolve concrete real-world problems presented to them by allegedly unconstitutional statutes, must connect the general propositions of political morality to those real-world problems. That has not yet been done in a credible way. The second half of the philosophers' works, the particular applications, consists of a series of obviously ad hoc judgments. Some will say that equal concern and respect implies that certain statutes are morally unacceptable. When translated into this theory, it means that such statutes are unconstitutional. But in the argument connecting equal concern and respect to the outcome, there are obvious points at which one could rather readily depart from the authors' line of argument.

One way to sketch this difficulty is to refer to a different sort of controversy among the philosophers. Often philosophers who agree on the fundamentals disagree on the deductions. For example, that appears to describe most of the philosophers' writings about the abortion issue. They all agree that the fundamental principle is equal concern and respect. The problem is that they cannot figure out what equal concern and respect implies for the resolution of the abortion controversy. Similarly in connection with the problem of affirmative action: everyone agrees that discrimination is a bad thing, but disagreement rages over what constitutes discrimination. Again, a principle like equal concern and respect can tell us that we should not discriminate but, at least as I read the philosophers, it does not tell them—and therefore it cannot tell the judges—whether affirmative action violates the principle of equal concern and respect.

Asking the judges to rely on moral philosophy as the basis of constitutional interpretation, then, will not work. It cannot be done in a way that will keep judges from doing whatever they want, under the guise of enforcing the conventional morality of the American people or, more likely, under the guise of making sure that legislatures do not enact immoral statutes—which, it turns out, might well simply be statutes that the judges do not like.

Let me try to summarize the argument about impossibility in this way.

Our premises about government require us to conclude that politics will not work perfectly and that at least occasionally the courts will have to invalidate a statute. Once we identify a statute and explain why it should be invalidated, our explanation will give us a theory of constitutional interpretation. And once we have that theory, whatever it is, judges will be able to use it to invalidate any statutes they do not like. The Archimedean principle of constitutional law is, "Give a judge an example of a justified invalidation of a statute, and an explanation of why it is justified, and he or she will be able to do anything he or she wants."

The preceding arguments deal with the *logical* impossibility of judicial review. We should be skeptical about that type of argument, however, because we all know that judicial review is certainly *not* impossible. The courts exercise that power all the time, and it does not seem as if the judges are doing *whatever* they want; there do seem to be some limits to what they do. If the logical arguments are right, this cannot be the result of the fact that one side or interpretation of the Constitution is correct.

Rather, it happens because of what I will call *sociological* reasons. That is, judges are able to settle on outcomes and interpretations and do not do *whatever* they want, because they are all persons unwilling to pursue the implications of their theories too far. They do not want to do everything they could do. One dimension of this is purely demographic. Judges are mostly well-to-do white men and they are all lawyers. These demographic characteristics mean that judges share a certain ethos or outlook on the world, which reduces the likelihood that deep disagreements will arise, particularly with respect to issues touching the vital interests of people who have *different* demographic characteristics—the poor, minorities, the relatively less well-to-do. Another dimension might be called *political*—the process by which people become judges screens out potential judges whose approaches to judicial review are, so to speak, too eccentric.

These sociological—demographic and political—points are, in themselves, quite accurate. They serve to stabilize the constitutional system. But notice the difficulties that occur when the constitutional system is stabilized by these sociological factors. One difficulty can be captured in a phrase. It becomes a government of men, not a government of laws. And that was precisely what we created a Constitution to avoid. True, the *range* of men is somewhat broader than might otherwise be the case. Complete arbitrariness by a single person or a small group is pretty much avoided.

But that helps to identify another difficulty with the sociological justification for judicial review. To be satisfied with it, we would have to agree that the range of people who become judges is broad enough to cover all the values that we think are important. Obviously people will disagree in making that judgment. Nonetheless, the demographic point deprives the sociological argument of almost all of its normative force. The fact that people like *that* happen to agree on what they think are important values—such as, unsurprisingly for them *and* me—the preservation of the existing distribution of wealth, has rather little moral force.

The problem for a theory of constitutionalism is deeper than mere disagreement about the moral implications of the narrow range of characteristics shared by contemporary judges, however. I began my argument with the stipulation that, for present purposes, constitutionalism meant "the rule of law and not of men." I have argued that ideal cannot be achieved because rules of law constrain only when, and to the extent that, they are implemented by a group of people who share certain values—that is, the rule of law *must be* the rule of men. And that opens up all the problems of oppression by the people who rule—whether called Leviathan, legislators, or judges— that constitutionalism was designed to avoid. Thus, I have argued, constitutionalism, though necessary, is impossible.

Notes

1. The arguments in this chapter are developed in more detail in my forthcoming book, Mark Tushnet, *Red, White, and Blue: A Critical Analysis of Constitutional Law* (Harvard University Press, 1988).

2. *See* Duncan Kennedy, "The Structure of Blackstone's Commentaries," 28 *Buffalo Law Review* 205 (1979): 211–14.

3. *See* Gregory Kavka, "Hobbes's War of All Against All," *Ethics* 93 (1983): 291.

4. By net benefit, I mean the amount made available by our joint production in excess of the total that each of us could produce on his own.

5. Note that, under this scenario, the stronger party gains nothing from his or her strength per se.

6. A technical reason for the unlikelihood of extended cooperation is the end period problem: no one has an incentive to comply with the last of a series of agreements, and no one can know whether or not the present agreement will be the last one.

7. In this context, the net benefits are seized in the form of taxes on production.

8. Although these limits are not discussed in this chapter, the analysis developed here is applicable to them as well, because we need some institution to tell us what constitutes a violation of the principles of federalism and the separation of powers. For illustrations of the general theoretical problems with respect to these limits, see *Garcia v. San Antonio Metropolitan Transit Authority*, 469 U.S. 528 (1985); *Immigration and Naturalization Service v. Chadha*, 462 U.S. 919 (1983).

9. Other methods of controlling the judges include the formal mechanisms of impeachment and restriction of the jurisdiction of the courts. These have proven to be completely ineffective. For a more extended discussion, see Tushnet *Red, White, and Blue*, chap. 6.

10. Other theories, and more nuanced versions of these theories, are also discussed in more detail in Tushnet *Red, White, and Blue*.

11. In this chapter, I do not consider whether any of these theories is affirmatively attractive. Instead, I assume that each has some merit in itself and examine whether

the theories can be implemented so as to achieve the desired goal of constraining legislative choice without licensing judicial willfulness.

12. James Hutson, "The Creation of the Constitution: The Integrity of the Documentary Record," *Texas Law Review* 65 (1986): 1, has recently shown that the documentary record of the Constitutional Convention of 1787 is distorted in ways that caution against relying on it for evidence about questions of constitutional interpretation focused on quite specific points.

13. *See* Thomas Curry, *The First Freedoms: Church and State in America to the Passage of the First Amendment,* (New York: Oxford University Press 1986) 200–02.

14. That is, a decent way within the confines of an originalist theory. Ronald Dworkin's work, which is a form of the theory of moral philosophy, does offer a method—identifying the best moral philosophy consistent with the decided cases—for constraining the choice of functional equivalents. This succeeds, however, only if Dworkin's theory as a whole succeeds, and in any event is plainly a nonoriginalist approach.

15. *See* Leonard Levy, *Emergence of a Free Press* (New York: Oxford University Press, 1986).

16. *See* Michael Perry,"Interpretivism, Freedom of Expression, and Equal Protection," *Ohio State Law Journal* 42 (1981): 261.

17. Ronald Dworkin, *Taking Rights Seriously* (Cambridge: Harvard University Press, 1977) 134–36.

18. *Brown v. Board of Education,* 347 U.S. 483, 492–93 (1954).

19. *See,* for example, Robert Shalhope, "Toward a Republican Synthesis: The Emergence of an Understanding of Republicanism in American Historiography," *William & Mary Quarterly* 29 (3d ser. 1972): 49; Robert Shalhope, "Republicanism and Early American Historiography," *William & Mary Quarterly* 39 (1982): 334; Similar, though somewhat less acute, problems attend the effort to retrieve the overall political theory of the Reconstruction era.

20. The now classic presentation is John Hart Ely, *Democracy and Distrust* (Cambridge: Harvard University Press, 1980).

21. One minor objection to this approach should be noted. Although most theories of democracy say that it consists of representation plus some substantive guarantees (such as some forms of personal privacy), the present theory says that courts can only remedy problems of representation and should not concern themselves with those substantive dimensions of democracy. Thus, it is not a theory that relates judicial review to democracy in the whole; some parts of what political theorists say is essential to democracy fall outside the scope of permissible judicial review. The theory's proponents claim that the courts can handle the representation part of democracy pretty well but cannot handle the substantive part. The latter claim is discussed in the next section of this chapter in connection with moral philosophy as a theory of constitutional interpretation. The present discussion considers the former claim.

22. For a more complete discussion and a defense of this assertion, see Tushnet, *Red, White, and Blue,* chap. 2.

23. The cases alluded to are *Williamson v. Lee Optical Co.,* 348 U.S. 483 (1955); and *Daniel v. Family Security Life Insurance Co.,* 336 U.S. 220 (1949).

24. *See* Mancur Olson, *The Logic of Collective Action* (Cambridge: Harvard University Press, 1965).

25. *See,* for example, Charles Lindblom, *Politics and Markets* (New York: Basic Books, 1977).

26. *Moore v. City of East Cleveland,* 431 U.S. 494 (1977).

27. *Furman v. Georgia,* 408 U.S. 238, 360–69 (1972) (Marshall, J., concurring).

28. *Gregg v. Georgia,* 428 U.S. 153, 179–80 (1976).

29. *See,* for example, *Bolger v. Youngs Drug Products Co.,* 463 U.S. 60 (1983), invalidating a statute adopted in the 1870s that restricted the distribution of information relating to contraceptives.

30. The example is not precise, because sentencing involves a situation in which judges are closer to the details of the problem with which they must deal, while in the most interesting cases, such as *Moore v. City of East Cleveland,* legislators are likely to be closer to the morally relevant details.

31. For present purposes I put aside the problem raised by the fact that philosophers disagree about what even the most general formulation of this principle might mean and assume that judges can somehow adjudicate the controversies among the philosophers.

9

Property, Economy, and the State

Milton Fisk

Fisk analyzes the idea of constitutionalism from the perspective of its function as a form of government that mediates the inevitable social conflicts in a private property economy. He argues that, as circumstances change, certain modifications in property are required if constitutionalism is to be preserved against tendencies towards authoritarian rule. His analysis highlights two leading defenses of private property rights and concludes with a unique claim that a genuine justification of property rights lies in a blending of these defenses.

THE DEFENSE OF PROPERTY RIGHTS

Property plays an important role in many societies. It is a mistake to think that in the United States today property has lost the importance it had a century ago. Property, in the general sense dealt with here, exists whenever support is given to claims by people in certain circumstances to control processes, people or things. A pattern of support for these claims to control is normally taken to indicate that those who make the claims have property rights. On an overly narrow view of what property is, it might be correct to say that it has been displaced from the preeminent position it once had. But this narrow view ignores the changes that property has undergone. Older property rights (which determined what property was) may well have been displaced by newer ones (which determined what it became) but both are property rights.

There are two sources for such changes. Changes in the circumstances surrounding the underlying economic system have made changes in property necessary. But property, however changed, has retained its importance as vital to the flourishing of the underlying economic system. An underlying economic system will be taken to involve both a division of roles in regard to the broadest aspects of production and a division of the product in a way related to those roles.

Also, property has changed in order to preserve the rule of law. For, when people are ready to rebel against a system of property, two avenues are open to a government. It can modify a burdensome system of property or it can try to preserve it unchanged by authoritarian measures. To preserve the rule of law established on the basis of some system of representation, and to curb state authoritarianism, may make a modification of property necessary. In short, to preserve constitutionalism may make a modification of property necessary. The upshot of the argument that follows will be that changes in property are closely linked not just to the vitality of the economy but also to preserving constitutionalism.

The topic here is not property in general but property restricted in two significant ways. First, it is property associated with the various types of production characteristic of a given economy. This *productive property* involves control for the sake of such production, and is then to be distinguished from *user property,* which does not involve control over things, processes,and people for production of the kind characteristic of the economy. This distinction rests on an appeal to the idea of an underlying economic system, that will be discussed further on. (Starting with it here might help exposition but would not be satisfactory theorectically.)

There are several ways that private productive property rights have been defended. (A defense or justification of property rights is given when reasons are advanced that show support is warranted for the corresponding claims to control processes, people, or things.) It will be well to begin by reviewing several of these ways. The purpose of this paper is to show that a satisfactory justification of property rights must blend together two of these avenues of defense.[1]

An Economist Justification

One of these avenues leads to an *economist justification* of property. It treats property rights as justified on the grounds that they facilitate the continuation of the underlying economy. This avenue leads to the implication that property rights are changeable in response to the obstacles that in different periods are placed before the underlying economy.

A Statist Justification

The other avenue of defense leads to a *statist justification* of property that treats property rights as justified on the grounds that they facilitate the legitimation of the state in the eyes of the diverse groups over which it rules. If a major group, advantaged or not, sees the state as supporting a system of property that is in conflict with its interests, then that group could withold its acceptance of the state unless the state moves to modify that system of property. The property rights justified on the basis of state legitimacy are in potential conflict with the property rights justified on economist grounds. In practice, the two justifications are blended together serially with the requirements of legitimation modifying what promotes the economy. However, the results of this blending may be property rights that actually endanger the underlying economy.

The Human-Nature Justification

These two are of course not the only ways property rights have been justified. One familiar theory is that something important about human nature would have to be sacrificed if private productive property rights were forfeited. We have then the *human-nature justification.* One version of this theory of justification is the libertarian view that human liberty would be forfeited unless there were a defense of property rights. Another version of this theory of justification is the self-realizationist view that without property rights humans would be frustrated in their effort to realize that part of their essence which leads them to take entrepreneurial initiative.[2]

Justifications based on human nature are notoriously tricky, for it is difficult to be sure that such justifications have avoided the fallacy of circularity. Is the conception of human nature appealed to a reflection of what humans are only in a society of the sort that this conception of human nature is intended to justify? What is needed is a proof that the aspect of human nature on which the justification turns is more than a socially relative aspect of what humans are. Yet any such proof runs the risk of assuming that the relevant social institutions are valid for all time, and hence of assuming the justification of these institutions that was to be based on human nature. Fortunately, however, the human-nature justification of property rights is not necessary since, as sketched above, we can anticipate another successful justification.

The Contribution Justification

But prior to getting back to the economist and the statist justifications, there is another familiar form of justification, the *contribution justification.* It is designed to justify both property and property inequality in one stroke. According to it, people have property according to their contribution to things produced or to their benefiting from transfers of property made to them by others. Hard work, initiative, greater skill, and commercial shrewdness become the basis for having more property. Both the contribution and the transfer parts of this justification have been sources of difficulty.

On the one hand, suppose the division of the product is to be made according to some criterion of contribution. But which criterion shall be used? How much of the product is to be distributed to each of the various agents in production? How much is the contribution of entrepreneurship, of technical skill, of so-called unskilled labor? It would appear that the basis for choosing one criterion over another is that it does a better job of rationalizing what the various agents in production actually get.

This leads one to consider, on the other hand, the possibility that the distribution of property after production depends on the transfers made by those who contribute to the product. In this case, the transfers are made for a consideration, thereby not unduly depriving those who make them. Those who bring investment funds to production receive interest as part of a contractual arrangement by which the contribution their funds make to the product is transferred to the entrepreneur. Similarly, the worker contracts for a wage in return for transferring his or her contribution to production to the entrepreneur. The problem of justifying property is then displaced to the problem of justifying the contractual arrangements through which transfers of the contributions of various agents are made. These contracts are not incidental arrangements since they are the ones that determine the very nature of the underlying economy. Thus, instead of having the problem of justifying property rights, we now have the problem of justifying the whole economic system.[3] In sum, the contribution justification of property leads to a dead end whether it emphasizes contribution or transfer.

The Utility Justification

There is then some reason to look more closely at the economist and the statist justifications of property. The former is in fact one division within a broader category of justifications which shall be called the *utility justification* since, it appeals to considerations of utility. Property would have a utility justification if, once the institution of property were widespread, there was a higher level of well-being, higher productivity, or a maximizing of the advantages of the least-well-off. In addition to these social goods, there is also the social good of continuing the underlying economic system. This social good is the one appealed to by the economist justification of property. Property has no independent sanctity under the utility justification. There may be periods during which private productive property does not help to realize any prominent social good, and in such a period there would be no private productive property rights. In particular, there might be economic systems for which the institution of property would be dysfunctional; for in such systems there would be no economist justification of property rights. To escape the relativity implicit in such a justification it is tempting to hark back to the human-nature or the contribution justification, but we have already seen the pitfalls threatening them.

The statist justification is designed to answer an objection to the economist justification of property. The continuation of the underlying economy may be a social good, but that is no guarantee it is a good for all the individuals of the society. A conception of property that places no limits on the losses of those with little or no property, or on the losses of those whose property is no longer of the dominant form, will not be a good for those individuals. Such a conception of property is not then adequately justified until it has been modified. The state has been the vehicle through which such modifications take place. It makes these modifications not out of a dedication to ideals but out of the practical necessity to rule over all its subjects. Those who suffer from the implementation of a conception of property that makes no concessions to them will be reluctant to give their allegiance to a state that mobilizes its might to protect such a conception of property. The need of the state for legitimacy leads it to modify property rights justified along economist lines in ways that make concessions to the property-less and to those whose property is no longer of the dominant form. It is in the intersection of economist and statist justifications that we must look for a genuine justification of property rights. We are thus separating ourselves from those who say that property is a pure creation of the state.[4] Rather, the state must limit itself to developing a conception of property in terms of features of the economy that can be abstracted from the state.

A GENERAL CONCEPTION OF PROPERTY RIGHTS

Before going more fully into the issue of justification, it is necessary to say what it is that property rights enable people to do. Property rights give people with property some level of control over something. There is no basis for saying that the control is total. In the property holder's vision of an ideal world, his level of control is greater than it is in the actual world. But it is not obvious that such an idea of total control is even coherent, since total control by one property holder might well imply the possibility of taking actions that impinge upon another property holder in such a way as to undermine total control for the second property holder. The right of a downstream landowner to control the water in a stream adjoining his or her property by building a dam for powering a mill might limit the control of the stream's water by an upstream land owner who has already built a dam, by reducing the height of the waterfall at the upstream dam and hence reducing the power generated at the upstream dam.

Total control might be rescued however, by changing the focus away from other property holders toward the property-less. The control of property holders would then be total in the sense that property holders decide what they are going to do with their property, and in the process make no concessions to the property-less. However, there is always some level of workers' control on the shop floor of an enterprise. This varies depending on the political and the economic nature of the period, without ever disappearing. The fact that there is such workers' control is testimony to the partial character of the control that property holders actually exercise in the production process. For all these reasons, then, it is best to say that property rights imply some level of control rather than total control over the relevant factors of production.

What, precisely, is it that property holders control? The answer to this question has traditionally been much too narrow. It is an answer that derives from an attempt to treat productive property like user property. The traditional answer is that the property holder has control over the use of things he or she owns. If we stay with this response, we face insuperable problems immediately. Although the key thing about productive property is the product itself, yet control over the use of productive property implies nothing about control over the product. In principle, control over the use of productive property gives a property holder the option of closing down his or her establishment, of moving it from one area to another, and of allowing it to harm the community with pollution. Considerations about the product remain outside this concern with use. For productive property in our economy, the scope of control must be extended to include control over the product. Otherwise, there would be no basis for distinguishing productive property from user property. It is *control over the product* that determines the direction of an enterprise. If the product is sold in order to invest in a new way, the nature of the enterprise changes.

If we consider only user property, we will miss sight of another distinction. Control over the use of productive property is a complex matter. First, there is control of the use of productive resources—plant, equipment, and materials—through controlling their status. Locking the factory gate, moving the equipment to a new plant, speeding up the machinery, or making the process less polluting, changes the status of the productive resources. So we shall speak of *control of the status of productive resources* to refer to this aspect of property.

Second, there is control of the use of productive resources through controlling the way labor is applied to them. *Control of the application of labor* falls under the broad heading of control of the use of plant, equipment and materials, since to use these resources to realize a certain goal will require that labor be applied in an appropriate fashion. For example, to use the productive resources in the most profitable way might require that there be no restrictions on layoffs and this in turn might require that owners be allowed to prohibit the organization of unions. When, in the first quarter of the 20th century, the U.S. Supreme Court upheld the yellow-dog contract, it did so on the grounds that state legislation prohibiting the yellow-dog contract was an unconstitutional restraint on personal liberty and private property.[5] Thus we have, under the heading of control of the use of productive resources, both control of their use through controlling their status and control of their use through controlling the application of labor to them.

The control of labor is understandable as a feature of productive property since, without it, there is no guarantee that the property holder will make a profit. Minimal control of labor might result in loitering, featherbedding, absenteeism, working to rule, and exclusion of management from the shop floor. Owners can employ a number of devices by which their agents—from general managers to shop floor supervisors—can control labor. They will typically control the application of labor to productive resources through hiring, firing, work schedules, and work pace. As emphasized above, such controls are never total and the kinds of control will vary with the circumstances.

In sum, property holders will have some level of control over a variety of factors of the production process. Each of these factors of control will correspond to a property right. There will be a property right that insures a certain level of control over the product, one that insures a certain level of control over the status of productive resources, and one that insures a certain level of control over labor. What determines the level of control insured by a property right? What aspects of labor activity are controlled and, if they are controlled, how tightly are they controlled? At any given time there is a basis for giving reasonably good answers to such questions. It takes us beyond a general conception of property rights to ask what is the control insured by such rights in the first place? Since control never exists for its own sake, where should we look for its purpose?

THE ECONOMIST JUSTIFICATION OF PROPERTY RIGHTS

In order to explain fully the economist justification, a distinction must be drawn between the underlying economy and the control mechanisms that promote it. This is not a distinction that is often made but the result of not making it has been considerable confusion about the role of property in the economy. Whether we think of a slave economy, a serf economy, or a wage-labor economy, the distinctive transactions within the economy can be described without entering into questions of control. In short, we can treat the agents entering into those distinctive transactions as automata programmed to carry out the main roles within the economy. The serf would deliver the product of a share of his efforts to the lord without our having to go into the question of the relationship between the serf and the lord that provides a motive for such action. Admittedly, such a view of things is not a realistic one, since people are not automata who enter into the transactions characteristic of a given economy either because of a pattern of expected benefits or, where the benefits are minimal, because of a pattern of discipline that puts some people in control of others. The very fact that such a view is not realistic tells us something important; it tells us that control relations are needed to insure that the transactions characteristic of an economy will go on.

In the last section we characterized property in terms of control over certain aspects of the productive process. It follows from this that property does not in any way enter into an economy understood simply as a set of tendencies for certain kinds of transactions. Instead, institutions of property develop a response to challenges to a given underlying economy. When habitual human behavior or older property institutions are no longer able to protect the economy, an adjustment can be expected in the form of new property institutions.

In the first half of the 19th century in the United States the economy was promoted by a transformation of the conception of property that had been current in the 18th century. In a situation of emerging capitalism characterized by capital scarcity, investors had to be encouraged. They were encouraged by reducing the number of damage judgments against them. The damage their investments did to holders of land or of technically less-developed enterprises had to be absorbed by the victims. In other words, by having the right to invest regardless of injury, investors could force those whose holdings were damaged to invest simply by leaving their damages uncompensated. The property concept appropriate to the 18th century agrarian economy, which insured the quiet enjoyment of one's property, was transformed into the aggressive property concept appropriate to the industrial growth of the early 19th century, which insured the owner against ruinous settlements for damages. This shift marked a change in the control of the status of productive resources. Whereas previously an owner's control of resources was bolstered by another's liability for damages if they were harmed, the new property concept allowed an owner to control resources in a way that put another at risk with impunity. It was thought by the courts that this shift of control promoted social utility. In the mind of the courts, the continuation of the economy was the social utility that was to be promoted by the new concept of property.[6]

Different theorists will have different views on how an underlying economy is to be described. It would be pointless here to enter into the disputes between theorists on the nature of capitalism or the nature of feudalism. Still, it is worth mentioning what might enter into such a description in order to resolve doubts whether control must enter into such a description. In a capitalist economy, there are some who work directly in production and there are some who direct the application of labor to the productive resources or choose what products are to be made. The costs of production should amount to less than the total costs of the product, so that there will be a surplus that can be made part of an expanded base of productive resources. There are then roles for different agents to play, but unless much more is read into this description than is actually there, we cannot say that some of these agents must be challenging others in a way that calls for institutions of control or domination. There is, to be sure, a fuller description in which those who put labor to work on productive resources will indeed control those resources as property holders. Yet, within our partial and abstract description consisting only of the underlying economic system, those who put labor to work on productive resources are simply playing a role in respect to those productive resources. Of course the surplus is, in a fuller account, privately appropriated, though in this partial account it is allocated by those whose unchallenged role it is to allocate a surplus. In the world of environmentalist protests, escalating welfare demands, and anticapitalist revolutions, those who play the role of allocating the surplus do not go unchallenged, and to meet these challenges a variety of institutions of control are created. That is, however, not the world of the underlying economy.

With all this by way of clarification, we are prepared to give the economist justification of property rights. This justification starts from the assumption of the utility justification, that controls over factors of the productive process are warranted when they contribute to a significant social goal. The controls are not warranted in their own right but only if they help advance some goal. What the economist justification does is to make a specific proposal as to what that goal is. For it, the social goal is the continuation of the underlying economy, understood in the abstract sense sketched above. *Thus, there is a property right when there is a right to control an aspect of the productive process, and that right is justified by the fact that such a control contributes to the continuation of the given underlying economy.* There is no presumption that a property right be associated with a form of control that is *necessary* for the economy, for otherwise there could be no reform of existing property without overturning the existing economic system. All we require is that the form of control associated with a property right generally promote the continuation of the underlying economy rather than put an obstacle in its way. Moreover, there is no presumption that forms of control that at an earlier time were associated with property rights will continue to be associated with property rights. For, it might be the case that with changing circumstances the same forms of control that once had promoted the continuation of the underlying economy no longer do so. The right of an employer *not* to have to make provision for his or her workers in a possible period of unemployment through contributing to unemployment insurance may have been justified by its potential for promoting the economy in a period when industrialization demanded the greatest flexibility in control over the investment of available resources. But during a time of development industrialization it would seem to be impossible to argue that unemployment insurance is an attack upon property.

To get a perspective on the economist justification, consider some of the difficulties of looking at property as though it were a primary feature of, rather than a derivative one from, the economy. Such was the approach of Max Weber and of the current group calling themselves "analytical Marxists," who follow Weber in this regard.[7] On this alternative approach, it is assumed in defining an economy that the population is divided into groups with differing amounts of property. The behavior of the members of one of these groups is then determined by their possessions; this behavior becomes the behavior of a class. It is the interaction of these classes that then provides us with an economic system. There is no question on this view of an economist justification of property rights, since various property distributions give rise to different and indeed incompatible economies.

This alternative is unworkable for the following reason. Differential possession of property determines on this approach different kinds of behavior, and among these kinds of behavior is control behavior. The problem with this approach emerges when we ask why different behaviors get forced on those with different property. The modern wage laborer has only his or her labor power and is thus unlike the serf who has at least partial ownership of some land and implements. Does this mean that the person who has only labor power must in general sell that labor power in order to gain a living? Not at all; he or she might get the owner of plant and equipment to decide to let those resources be run under workers' control. It might be objected that this is inconsistent with the expected capitalist behavior of the owner of these resources. True enough; but recall that we are only assuming unequally distributed property and are not assuming an underlying economic system that would determine how it is to be used. So, letting the plant and equipment be run under workers' control cannot be inconsistent with the mere assumption that the worker has only labor power and someone else has, in addition, plant and equipment. The conclusion to this thought experiment is that the assumption of unequal property does not force on its possessors the behaviors typified by particular classes, and hence does not give rise to any particular form of economic system. Conversely, if the assumption of unequal property does force on its possessors the behaviors typified by particular classes and gives rise to a particular form of economic system, this will be because it is assumed to be unequal property of a specific economic type. That is, the property will be constituted by controls that protect a specific form of underlying economy. Then, far from being able to get a class system and an economy out of property, property remains nothing more than a vague notion of possession until it is relativized to a specific form of economy.[8]

The animus of the analytical Marxists against the use of the notions of control and domination is misplaced. They limit control to control by supervisory personnel over labor in the workplace, and they then argue, correctly, that such control by itself is inadequate to account for property. But control should be allowed a broader scope such as we have given it here, where it includes not only control over labor but also control over the status of productive resources and control over the product. With this broader scope, control can then account for property in the way indicated above. Even control is not enough, however, if we fail to insist that property is control for the continuation of the underlying economy. A property concept detached from this purpose becomes, like that of the analytical Marxists, too general to be useful in determining behavior.

THE STATIST MODIFICATION OF PROPERTY RIGHTS

There are several ways the state affects property. The state here is taken to be a complex institution with forms of representation, of internal organization, and of social intervention. In the case of most modern states, laws— including constitutional, statutory, and court-made laws—specify these three forms. It is through forms of social intervention in particular that the state affects property. First, the courts, the legislature, and the regulatory agencies need not wait until new forms of control, making up a new aspect of property, have been established in the society in order to give them official recognition. If they had to wait, then there would be a bifurcation between "real" property as exemplified in economic behavior and an "official" property that is its juridical reflection. Empirically, such a distinction is not warranted since it turns out that the so-called juridical reflection regularly antedates the economic behavior. The economist justification enables us to make this intelligible. When the state, through the legislature, the courts, or the regulatory agencies, takes away certain controls from property holders, or provides them with new controls, its basis for doing this may well be that it sees such controls as obstructing (or promoting) the underlying economic system. The underlying economy's health was seen by us in the previous section to be the basis for the shift by the courts in the first half of the 19th century from an agrarian to an aggressive property system. This is related to the widely recognized fact that one of the roles a modern state plays is to facilitate the continuation of the existing economy. When it takes away controls or adds new ones, thereby changing property, it may well be acting in this role of promoter of the economy. Controls of the sort needed at a given time to promote the economy may face the determined opposition of the property-less or of holders of property in a form that is no longer dominant.

The state provides a powerful means for cutting through this opposition before the underlying economy is weakened.

Second, the state need not act in its role of promoter of the economy when it initiates changes in controls making up property. It has another role that may be the basis of its actions in changing property. The state must be able to rule if it is to play the role of promoter of the economy, and in order to rule it must, if it is to have stability, be widely accepted. However, the requirements of gaining the sort of acceptance needed and the demands of a healthy economy are two quite different things. An economic system may be such that it cannot be promoted by a state without the state undermining its legitimacy; conversely, to legitimate itself the state may have to take measures that undermine the economy.[9] So we are dealing here with two quite different roles and with demands that, although they may overlap, are in principle quite different.

In its role of assuring its own ability to rule, the state has often modified property rights that might otherwise seem nicely designed to continue the underlying economy. The courts have in the recent past shown a willingness to hold manufacturers and suppliers of defective products strictly liable to consumers and users for injuries caused by the defects. They have not required negligence or an explicit warranty in order to hold manufacturers and suppliers liable.[10] The heightened awareness of consumers and their activism in lobbying and boycotting has offset considerations of the sort that, when laissez-faire still dominated, limited liability. Making the corporations and the economy more vulnerable can be interpreted here as a response to the need for governability.

The response to this may be that it is a dodge to suggest that the legitimacy of the state can justify new property rights or the denial of old ones. Is it not justice that provides the justification of property rights here? Well, if justice means the limits imposed by the state on the benefits of some and the losses of others for the sake of its being able to rule, then certainly justice is the basis for at least part of property. Clearly, this is not what the response intended. The root of the response is an appeal to an ideal of justice distinguished from the mere official justice of the state.

The problem of finding such an ideal of justice is analogous to the problem we faced earlier of finding a conception of human nature on which to base property that did not assume the system of property it was to justify. In the case of justice, the problem takes the form of asking whether ideal justice amounts to more than a pattern of benefits and losses that permits orderly rule. Since orderly rule will call for different patterns of benefits and losses in different circumstances, ideal justice then turns out to be the form of justice that permits legitimacy either for a given state, or possibly for an alternative to it, being promoted by an internal opposition. Circularity stalks us again. Once it is clear how difficult it is to avoid circularity in appealing to ideal justice, we should be content to recognize that it is adequate justification of the state's modifications of property that they promote the state's legitimacy.

These modifications will fail to satisfy everyone, although they will certainly satisfy or at least immobilize enough to allow the state to rule. Those who remain actively dissatisfied will project a new conception of property that would change controls in their favor.[11] This will be a conception that they are sure more and more of those currently acquiescing in the current conception of property as a result of state modifications will come to accept and struggle for because it favors their interests as well. Nothing about such an alternative conception of property calls for ideal justice; it originates in the quite real interests of those who do not acquiesce in the state's modifications of a property concept that promoted the underlying economy. These interests may also have to be curtailed should those with them become a ruling group within a new state, for such a state, like the one it replaced, will have to rule through general acceptance and will be able to do this only by modifications of the new conception of property. And so, both official and radical conceptions of property can be justified without getting entangled in the circular appeal to ideal justice.

It needs emphasizing that the welfare state has involved the most systematic modification of property the state has undertaken. Those who resist modifying property for legitimacy and defend a solidly economist basis for property charge that the welfare state has been an attack upon property that has done the economic system serious harm. They are both right and wrong. Yes, it has been an attack upon economist-based property. That is, it has removed some controls that could be said to have a positive effect on continuing the economy. Yet it is the argument of this section that an economist-based conception of property is too narrow since it ignores the need of the very state that protects property to be legitimate. It cannot provide stable protection for property if it fails for lack of legitimacy. To gain legitimacy, however, the state makes adjustments in the economist-based conception of property that become the basis for justifiable conception of property. So, the welfare state, as such, is not an attack on property but only on a narrow version of it. (It is assumed here that the welfare measures taken are limited to those defended as needed for legitimacy.)

What about the rest of the objection, that the welfare state has done the underlying economy serious harm? Employer contributions to various social security programs for workers reduce the owner's control over the product and would appear to make less capital available for investment. It is far from clear, however, that aggregate investment capital is reduced. Economies within states that have pushed welfare measures have performed as well as, or better than, those within states where welfare programs amount to a smaller share of the national product. Moreover, the money that goes into welfare programs does not simply dissappear; it contributes to demand for products on the market or goes into funds that provide a basis for investment capital. So, from the perspective of its effect on aggregate investment capital, the case has not been made that the welfare state is undermining capitalism.

But is control over the product reduced? In the welfare state part of the product is dedicated to benefit programs, part is dedicated to the construction of social infrastructure—schools, transportation, water—and part is dedicated to meeting minimum-wage standards and contractual wage agreements the state will back up. The owner has suffered a drastic loss of control in these regards through modifications of property by the state in the interest of its own legitimacy. This loss of control reduces the flexibility of the owner in a period of recession; he or she cannot unilaterally stop the drain to welfare benefits and social infrastructure programs and begin to lower wages protected by statute or contract. In addition to this threat to the system, as a greater share of the product is dedicated in advance of private investment decisions, the state, rather than private entrepreneurs, begins to make a greater share of investment decisions, either directly or indirectly. This undermines the ability of the private owner to cut costs in times of exigency and to set the direction of the economy through investment decisions. Carried to an extreme, this loss of controls could coincide with the passing of capitalism.

It has, of course, been true that during the slowdown of the American economy in the 1970s and 1980s strenuous efforts have been made to curb the American welfare state. During such a slowdown, the effect of these controls becomes much more obvious to the owner, and his or her will to fight against them becomes stronger. In fact, during such a period, it is likely that there could be a reversion to an earlier property concept. This is because two new conditions have been met that affect the justification of property. First, the justification of property on economist grounds calls for tighter controls due to the difficulty of carrying on business in a climate of stagnation. Second, the justification of property on statist ground calls for fewer modifications for the sake of legitimacy. This is because of chronically high unemployment and a new resolve on the part of the employing class to win concessions and break unions. Those who at another time would not give their allegiance to a state that overtly supports the economist property concept of the employing class will have become so demoralized by their own personal defeat and the defeat of their leaders that they acquiesce in the rule of this state. These new conditions call for reversion to a traditional conception of property. It is these conditions, not tradition itself, that might justify this reversion.

THE CONSISTENCY OF THE PROPOSED JUSTIFICATION

Putting together the views of the last two sections yields what we have set out to get—a serial view of property in two steps: the economist part and the statist part.

The first step consists in showing that a certain set of controls plays a role in continuing the underlying economy. They are controls over factors of production, such as labor, productive resources, and the product. The second step consists in showing that the property rights to be justified are modifications of the initial set of controls that make them compatible with the state's ability to rule.

It is assumed that the state does function to promote the underlying economy and hence to protect the controls that promote it. So the second step in the serial account serves to indicate how far the state can go in performing this function while retaining legitimacy. Only those controls that pass through both steps can be called genuine property rights, but for convenience we can call the controls that pass through the first step "initial" property rights. Normally, then initial property rights are modified to yield property rights.

The second step in the serial view of property rights would cause no problems if there were some guarantee inherent in the notion of state legitimacy against steps undermining the economy. But state legitimacy, like state security, is an open-ended aspect of the state as far as the preservation of the economy is concerned. In securing itself against possible enemies the state may take measures that threaten its form of economy. The imperatives of security are based on the goal of saving the state even though the means may turn out to be incompatible with a feature of the society, such as the economy, that it is the state's role to promote. In the same way, the imperatives of gaining legitimacy are based on the goal of enabling the state to rule events though the means may undermine some aspect of society that it is the state's role to promote. So there is no way to guarantee that the property rights justified by the two-step procedure must end up consistent with the underlying economy. These rights may not allow controls sufficiently strong to continue the economy, or they may introduce controls that are not compatible with those needed to continue the economy.

This creates a practical problem of consistency. The two-step procedure is not itself internally inconsistent; the initial rights that may be incompatible with the ultimate property rights are, as we saw, simply not real property rights. The inconsistency arises, rather, from the double role of the state. The state must see to it that it can rule, yet it is the guardian of the existing social order, including the underlying economy. In its role of seeing to its own legitimation it helps devise—through legislation and through its various agencies—property rights that limit the benefits of some while limiting the losses of others. In the interest of its own ability to rule, it must stand by such property rights against efforts to violate them. Yet, in its role as guardian of the current social order, the state will find itself protecting those controls over factors of production that enable the economy to be continued. If there are to be modifications in these controls, consistency requires that they be minimal modifications, allowing the controls to remain strong enough to help promote the economy.[12] Still, there remains the possibility that the state will have to stand by the property it calls for in order to rule even when this undermines the control necessary for continuing the economy for which it is the guardian.

This inconsistency should not be treated as merely a logical possibility. It has its basis in concrete social tensions, a crucial element of which is the control that is part of the general concept of property. Some have more control than others over both things and people, and this disparity is the essence of property in societies of the industrial period. Those who lack control and are in fact controlled will regularly challenge this arrangement and either attempt to eliminate or at least to reduce the burden of their position. But it is through controls like these that it is possible to continue the underlying economy. So pressure against them is, at least indirectly, pressure against the underlying economy. In short, there is no magic correspondence between those levels of control that are found onerous enough to agitate against and those that are unnecessary for continuing the underlying economy. The controls implicit in private productive property create a widespread pressure which becomes more and more difficult for the state to eliminate through minor modifications. The extent of the modifications introduced by the welfare state attests to this difficulty. These modifications are now criticized as being the result of capitulation to pressures from the majority, an indication that property may have been weakened enough for the economic system to have been challenged. Whether the challenge is as yet real or not, the system of controls is such that restlessness under it will soon reemerge to exact new inroads into property that might weaken the economic system. The response might be to curb these mass pressures by a retreat from constitutionalism to authoritarianism. This would be a retreat from a form of government that is limited by laws established on some basis of representation to a form of government that puts state power above such laws. To preserve the tradition of constitutionalism against such a threat of authoritarianism, it would be necessary to consider whether the pressure against the controls needed for the underlying economy could or should be reduced by further modifying or restructuring the underlying economy.

Notes

1. The traditions behind the statist and the economist justifications of property go back, respectively, to Thomas Hobbes *Leviathan*, Part II (Indianapolis: Bobbs-Merrill Co., 1958) chap. 24; and John Locke (*The Second Treatise of Government* chap. 5, sections 35–37).

2. For this type of self-realization justification of property, see Ernest Barker, *Principles of Social and Political Theory*, (London: Oxford University Press, 1951), 158, 249.

3. Robert Nozick's entitlement theory has a structure similar to contribution

theory and is thus subject to this difficulty. See R. Nozick, *Anarchy, State, and Utopia,* (New York: Basic Books, 1974), 155–180.

4. For the pure state view of property, see C.B. Macpherson, "The Meaning of Property," in *Property: Mainstream and Critical Positions,* ed. C.B. Macpherson (Toronto: University of Toronto Press, 1983), 1–13.

5. *Adair v. United States,* 208 U.S. 161 (1908), 4, 209; and *Coppage v. Kansas,* 236 U.S. 1 (1915), 209.

6. Morton J. Horwitz, *The Transformation of American Law, 1780–1860* (Cambridge, MA: Harvard University Press, 1977), chap. 3.

7. Jon Elster, *Making Sense of Marx* (Cambridge: Cambridge University Press, 1985), 105, 169, 199, 254, and 331. Also John Roemer, "New Directions in Marxian Theory of Exploitation and Class," in *Analytical Marxism,* ed. J. Roemer (Cambridge: Cambridge University Press, 1986), 84–86 and 106–108.

8. For a full-blown version of an argument like this that can be directed at the analytical Marxists, see Robert Brenner, "The Social Basis of Economic Development," in *Analytical Marxism,* ed. J. Roemer, 36–40.

9. Claus Offe, "'Ungovernability': The Renaissance of Conservative Theories of Crisis," in his *Contradictions of the Welfare State,* ed. J. Keane (Cambridge, MA: MIT Press, 1984), chap. 2.

10. *Greenman v. Yuba Power Products,* 59 Cal. 2d 57 (1962); and *Phipps v. General Motors Corp.,* 278 Md. 337, 363, A. 2d 955 (1976).

11. Charles A. Reich, for example, would like to see state benefits to individuals vested in them so that they have the stability of property. See C.A. Reich, "The New Property," *Yale Law Journal, 73* (1964): 733–787.

12. The Christian Democratic critique of "absolute," "rigid," or "exclusive" private property promotes reforms in property for the common good that by some unexplained harmony never undermine the capitalist economy (for example, John Paul II, *Laborem Exercens,* Part III, Sections 13–15, in *National Catholic Reporter, 25* September 1981).

10

Constitutionalism and Military Justice: Making Justice from Military Justice

Peter A. French

American constitutionalism is premised on the belief that its fundamental principles should extend to all citizens. The independence of the military legal system, however, under conditions of both war and peace, typically places military personnel beyond the reach of the most important constitutional provisions, to their detriment. In his essay, French offers a brief history of the two separate systems of law, and he assesses some of the leading arguments for and against the continued maintenance of this difference. A highlight of French's essay is the justification of his proposal for increasingly "constitutionalizing" the military justice system, despite recent Supreme Court decisions to the contrary.

In Title 1 of Book II of the *Theodosian Code*, the issue of jurisdiction is tackled. The second edict under that title, attributed to Emperor Constantius Augustus on July 25, 355, contains the following:

> In criminal cases, if any person in the imperial service should prosecute an accused person, the governor of the province shall try the case. If it should be affirmed that any military man has committed *any crime* [italics mine], it shall be tried by the person to whom the direction of military affairs has been entrusted.[1]

The accompanying interpretation of Constantius Augustus' edict, supplied by the Theodosian scholars, made crystal clear the intent and force of the edict. It was that civil cases and military cases were to be treated as falling under separate jurisdictions. If a private citizen were to bring criminal charges against a military person, the case was heard before military superiors. Only if the military person were to initiate an action against a private citizen was the case removed to the civilian courts. Furthermore, the only two kinds of cases in which the military person was assured of the same outcome as the civilian were established in the next entry in the *Code:* forceful violation of the chastity of anyone (rape) and robbery. All other cases were, apparently, left to the wisdom of the courts-martial.

It is not difficult to conjure up reasons why the Romans and most other succeeding societies have maintained a distinction between civilian and military justice. Discipline, which usually translates to "obedience to superiors," surely is essential to successful military operations. It is believed that direct access to nonmilitary courts and civilian rights protections could lead to difficult command situations. The military has been traditionally viewed as a body of persons apart from the ordinary members of society. Maintaining a self-contained judicial control, since the earliest times, has been seen by the military hierarchy as crucial, if not essential, to good order, high morale, and the self-discipline of the service person. In other words, it is believed (and stated in the Naval Institute's comprehensive work on *Military Law*[2]) that military justice is intended to promote the state of mind in the individual service person "so that he (or she) will instantly obey a lawful order, no matter how unpleasant or dangerous the task may be . . . In this way, law supports the military mission, which it must do if the nation's freedom is to be protected and preserved."[3]

SOURCES

Congressional enactments are almost the exclusive source of American military law. Congressional authority is derived from the Constitution (Section 8 of Article I) in which the Congress is empowered to raise, support, and maintain army and naval forces and to govern those employed in service by making all laws "necessary and proper."

From 1789 to 1862, Congress enacted a number of pieces of legislation in the area of naval law. The common characteristic of these statutes was that each aimed at decreasing navy law's dependence on British maritime customs and the common law. In 1862, Congress passed the "Articles for the Government of the Navy" ("Rocks and Shoals"). These were superseded in 1951 by the "Uniform Code of Military Justice" (hereafter UCMJ).

The history of American army law is comparable to, if rather more active than, its naval counterpart. The British "Articles of War" (1765), which contained a section on military justice, were the model for the first American military code, adopted by the Continental Congress in 1775. That code was revised in 1776 into the American "Articles of War," which remained in force until 1806, when a new code was adopted. That code was superseded by the "Articles of War" of 1874. They were in turn replaced by new articles in 1917, then again in 1921 and 1948. The "Uniform Code" superseded the 1948 articles and was made applicable to all branches of the armed services. In 1962, the "Uniform Code" was amended, and in 1968 it was significantly altered by the Military Justice Act. In 1969, the executive branch, in the name of the President, drafted the *Manual for Courts-Martial,* directives that implement the UCMJ.

The Constitution is the authoritative source of American military law, just as it is the source of the authority of the President, Congress, and the Supreme Court. It is of interest that, in the UCMJ, Congress delegates its constitutional authority in substantial areas of military justice to the President. Article 36 of the UCMJ is of particular import. It reads:

> Pre-trial, trial, and post-trial procedures, including modes of proof for cases arising under this chapter triable in courts-martial, military commissions, and other military tribunals and procedures for courts of inquiry, may be prescribed by the President by regulations which shall, so far as he considers practicable, apply the principles of law and the rules of evidence generally recognized in the trial of criminal cases in the United States district courts, but which may not be contrary to or inconsistent with this chapter.

Article 36 of the UCMJ thereby empowers the President to create the *Manual.* Article 56 further delegates to the President the authority to set the maximum punishments for violations of the Code. It has been argued, though without vigor, that Congress cannot constitutionally transfer its powers in this area to the executive branch, and so both the UCMJ and the *Manual for Courts-Martial* should be declared unconstitutional. There is little reason here, however, to pursue this argument, for it is most unlikely that the titanic military justice system will founder on such an ice cube. Our more practical focus should be on the difficulties that have been associated with the attempt to reconcile military justice with the provisions of the Constitution.

JURISDICTION AND RIGHTS OF THE ACCUSED

Two problems seem prominent, even dominant, for the constitutionalist confronting military law. One is jurisdictional, and the other concerns the extent to which constitutional rights and protections can and ought to be available under the UCMJ to those accused and standing trial in the military justice system. As is well known, many, if not most of those rights are not encoded in military law. Interestingly, the jurisdictional and rights issues are entangled in a number of landmark military law cases of both the Supreme Court and the Court of Military Appeals (CoMA). I hope to tell a story that interrelates a few of those cases and highlights the constitutional development.

Before doing so, it is important to remember that in the struggle to "constitutionalize" military law there are (and certainly have been) two main combatants. I refrain from identifying them with political positions because, where the military is concerned, matters of constitutionality are political footballs. Conservatives might be expected to support only that level of constitutional protection that is consistent with full-fledged support of the defense establishment. On the other hand, however, support of personal constitutional rights frequently has been a conservative rallying cry. In any event, I am uncomfortable with trying to pin political labels on the polar positions.

Suffice it to say that, on the one side, a military law in which constitutional protections are not provided is defended (perhaps on utilitarian grounds) as essential to the constitutional purpose of the military. This argument typically contains the claim that armed service personnel must forego the constitutional protections of civilians in order that those protections can be preserved for civilians. The constitutionalist's position, on the other hand, argues that military law not only ought to incorporate the rights and protections of the Constitution, except perhaps in time of war, but that military law must be absorbed into the federal court system where constitutional remedies will be available to military personnel as a part of our fundamental law. Francis X. Gindhart, Clerk of the Court of Military Appeals (CoMA) has written:

> How ironic it is that the dedicated and valiant members of the armed forces, on whom we all ultimately depend to preserve and defend our constitutional government and way of life, must spend their own personal and professional lives in constitutional alienage.[4]

The constitutionalist's argument is that just entering military service ought not constitute renouncing one's rights as an American.

As in most debates of this type, the middle ground, though severely trampled and shellshocked, is regarded an uninhabitable without much investigation by the polar combatants. I think a story can be told in terms of CoMA cases that shows our military justice system actually has been rather consistently moving to occupy the middle ground and, with one major adjustment, that ground should be viewed as the appropriate location with respect to justice, equity, and fairness.

CONSTITUTIONAL PROTECTIONS

It should be remembered that because CoMA is a product of the UCMJ, it exists solely at the will of the Congress. (It is an Article I court.) The UCMJ states that CoMA decisions are final, and the Supreme Court has made only a few attempts since the early 50s to intercede or supervise CoMA's administration of justice. Jurisdictional issues, however, have prompted the most significant constitutional attention. It is on such cases that I shall focus.

The 1955 case of *Toth v. Quarles*[5] is the earliest major decision after the UCMJ was enacted in which the Supreme Court intervened in a CoMA case. The confrontation was over Article 3(a) of the UCMJ. Robert Toth and a fellow airman, while serving as security guards on a post in Korea, murdered a Korean. By the time the crime was discovered, Toth had been honorably discharged and returned to civilian life in Pittsburgh. Article 3(a) states that a person charged with committing an offense against the code while in military service can be tried by court-martial, even though that person has left the services. The Air Police were sent to apprehend Toth and bring him back to Korea to stand trial. Toth's sister filed for a writ of habeas corpus in federal district court in Washington, D.C., claiming Article 3(a) is unconstitutional.

The District Court issued the writ on the grounds that the arresting officers had not followed the Federal Rules for Criminal Procedure because Toth had not been brought before a federal commissioner. The Air Force appealed. The Court of Appeals reversed the lower court decision and remanded Toth to Air Force custody. The appeals court's primary reason was that an accused is customarily subject to stand trial in the jurisdiction in which the offense was committed. (That, by the way, is a principle also to be found spelled out in the *Codex Theodosianus*[6]) Toth's sister was not deterred. She appealed to the Supreme Court, which ruled Article 3(a) unconstitutional.

The Supreme Court applied a jurisdictional test to Toth, but not the Theodosian test of location of the crime. Instead of the facts of the offense being the determining factor, the status of the accused was made the central test for jurisdiction. The Supreme Court (by a 6 to 3 margin) found that Toth was lacking in the requisite status because he had been honorably discharged, so he "could not constitutionally be subjected to trial by court-martial." He was set free.

Associate Justice Hugo Black's opinion for the majority contained a number of points relative to our concerns. He maintained that the assertion of military authority over civilians cannot rest on the President's powers nor on any theory of martial law. The Fifth Amendment, he argued, does not grant to Congress court-martial power with respect to the Due Process Clause. Furthermore, Black stated that considerations of military discipline cannot warrant the expansion of military legal jurisdiction at the expense of the constitutionally preferable system of trial by jury. All civilians, including exservice personnel, must have all benefits afforded by the constitutional courts (Article III).[7]

In effect, Black was voicing (for the majority of the Court) the view that military law was not good enough for civilians, even if it suffices for those in the armed services, given the need to maintain discipline, and so forth. Associate Justices Reed and Minton wrote dissenting views. Reed's opinion ostensibly focused on the heinous character of the crime and on the fact it would now go unpunished, but beneath the surface was the jurisdictional issue:

> If Congress enacts the substitute law as the Court suggests (i.e., trial by federal district court) . . . the accused must face a jury far removed from the scene of the alleged crime and before jurors without the understanding of the quality and character of a military crime . . . Or perhaps those accused will be extradited and tried by foreign law.[8]

The elements that fueled Reed's opinion are obvious. He defined jurisdiction not primarily in terms of status but, traditionally, in terms of the location of the crime. Secondly, he opted for a United States military court rather than trial under a foreign legal code. We may assume that Reed believed that military law is more likely to protect a U.S. citizen's rights than is any foreign legal system. He was probably right, at least with respect to many countries in which the military has a presence. Although there are, as mentioned above, no constitutional protections in military justice, many of the rights associated with the Constitution are available to armed service personnel, and some of the provisions for the accused in the civilian courts, that is, being represented by counsel, are arguably better supplied in the military courts.

Toth was used by the attorney for Dorothy Krueger Smith to gain a Supreme Court reversal of a court-martial sentence against her. Dorothy Smith, a civilian, murdered her husband, a colonel, while they were stationed in Japan. She was tried by court-martial under Article 2 (11) of the UCMJ and convicted. Her attorney filed for a writ of habeas corpus. The Supreme Court consolidated the case with a similar one from Europe (*Reid v. Covert*) and on June 11, 1956, decided (5 to 4) not to intervene. Justice Clark, writing for the majority, maintained that Americans accompanying our troops overseas "would enjoy greater protections under the UCMJ than in foreign courts."[9]

Mrs. Smith's attorney petitioned for a rehearing, which was granted. After the new hearing on June 10, 1957, the Court reversed its earlier decision. Justice Black wrote the principal opinion, arguing that the Constitution permits only Congress to regulate land and naval forces, not those who might have some relationship with them. No statute, Black maintained, can be framed to force a civilian to submit to a court-martial. He continued by noting the constitutional inadequacies of military law: no trial by jury, no indictment by grand jury, no Bill of Rights protections.

There can be little doubt that in 1957 the Supreme Court had every good reason to denigrate military justice. But the military law did not remain intransigent in the face of constitutional criticism. The CoMA case of *Jacoby* in 1960 marks a significant move towards the Constitution.

Loretta Jacoby was an Airman Third Class. In a special, not a general, court-martial,[10] she was convicted on charges of violating Article 134 of the UCMJ by bouncing checks. She received a bad-conduct discharge, forfeiture of $70 per month for four months, confinement at hard labor for four months, and reduction to the grade of basic airman. The issue on which the CoMA decision on her appeal turned was whether "it was proper to receive in evidence certain dispositions taken upon written interrogatories over the accused's objection that she was thereby denied her constitutional right to be confronted by the witnesses against her."[11]

Over the objections of Jacoby's attorney, three bank officials testified against Jacoby by written deposition. The trial counsel cited two CoMA decisions (*Sutton*, 1953, and *Parrish*, 1956) as *stare decisis* for permitting the admission of written depositions even though the accused and her counsel were not present at the time the depositions were taken. CoMA Judge Ferguson noted that Jacoby's position had merit and that "in the light of the Constitution," he was convinced that CoMA had "erred in so giving effect to the doctrine of *stare decisis*"[12] (with respect to *Sutton* and *Parrish*). He went on to argue that though *stare decisis* generally ought to apply, that it should not in military law "perpetrate a mistaken view," especially when it stands in direct opposition to both the letter and the spirit of the Constitution. In *Jacoby* (as well as *Sutton* and *Parrish*), the Sixth Amendment right that guarantees the accused confrontation with the witnesses was clearly abridged.

Ferguson wrote, quoting from the Supreme Court decision in the *Mattox* case (1895):

> The substance of [The Sixth Amendment's] ... protection is preserved to the prisoner in the advantage he had once had of seeing the witness face to face, and of subjecting him to the ordeal of cross-examination. This, the law says, he shall under no circumstances be deprived of, and many of the very cases which hold testimony such as this to be admissible also hold that not the substance of his testimony only, but the very words of the witness, shall be proven.[13]

The majority in *Jacoby* ruled that the UCMJ with respect to Article 49 conflicted with the Sixth Amendment and reversed the finding of the review board on Jacoby's court-martial and ordered that the case be returned to the

Judge Advocate General of the Air Force to determine whether a new court-martial proceeding against the accused would be initiated.

CoMA did a number of significant things with *Jacoby*, but perhaps the most important was to identify the Constitution as overriding expediency and the UCMJ with respect to rights. In effect, CoMA ruled that the UCMJ has to pass constitutional muster and, as in Article 49, it frequently cannot do so.

The *Jacoby* decision, however, was not a unanimous one. Judge George Latimer wrote the dissenting opinion. He strongly objected to what he called the "civilianizing" of the interpretation of military justice, to warping "the Code to make military law on all fours with civilian law."[14] The military, Latimer argued, cannot be removed from military law; hence there must be a "fundamental distinction between the two." The Constitution, he maintained, "entrusted to Congress the task of striking a precise balance between the rights of men in service and the overriding demands of discipline and duty."[15] It is of some note that, though Latimer expressed such a sweeping defense of the separation of the courts doctrine, he actually justified his dissent in *Jacoby* on the narrow point that the evidence gathered in the interrogatories was redundant because the accused had herself testified to its truth during the trial. Latimer, nonetheless, endorsed the traditionalist's view that Article 49 properly relieves the military of the onerous burden of transporting an accused under guard in the company of attorneys to take depositions at locations remote from the base at which the court-martial is to occur. Given the frequency of military personnel relocations, the costs of transporting and prosecuting these offenses could become excessive. Hence, many crimes might go unpunished and the disciplinary structure of the military, consequently, could be severely weakened. Even Latimer allowed, however, that if the accused could demonstrate before the convening authority that "the taking of depositions might make it impossible for him to defend (himself) properly,"[16] relief from Article 49 could be granted. That had not been the case in *Jacoby*; hence, Latimer argued, the lower court decision should have been affirmed.

Jacoby's major effect was the further extension of the Constitution over the UCMJ. Nufer writes:

> The Opinion of the Court declared that Article 49 of the UCMJ *infringed* on a service member's *inherent* rights under the Sixth Amendment: that anyone, whether civilian or military, should be able to "confront witnesses against him . . ."[17]

Simply, *Jacoby* establishes that constitutional relief is always available to the accused service person who feels his or her basic liberties and rights have been unduly restricted or abridged by military law. It is especially noteworthy that it was the highest military court, and not a civilian court, that put forth this doctrine. The military courts were moving military law into the middle ground.

The story continues into the midseventies with the "watershed" case of *McCarthy* (1976), in which CoMA had to deal with the extent to which military justice extends into the civilian community when the accused is a soldier and the offense occurs off-post. Again, the issue was jurisdictional.

McCarthy was convicted by a general court-martial at Fort Campbell, Kentucky, of selling marijuana to a fellow soldier outside the gate of the fort. McCarthy contended that the offense was not service-connected and so not properly heard in a military court. He cited the Supreme Court's 5 to 3 decision in *O'Callahan v. Parker*[18] in which the court held that a service member is entitled to a civilian court for nonservice connected crimes. In the civilian system, the Supreme Court stressed, the service member's constitutional rights to a grand jury indictment and trial by jury are protected. In fact, the court maintained, "the expansion of military discipline beyond its proper domain is a threat to liberty,"[19] and "courts-martial are singularly inept in dealing with the nice subtleties of constitutional law."[20] The *O'Callahan* decision produced a series of criteria for determining whether an offense was nonservice connected: the service member had to be properly absent from the base, the crime had to be committed off-base in an area not under military control, and in the United States in peacetime. There must be no connection between the accused's military duties and the crime. There must be an available civilian court in which the case can be prosecuted, and the alleged crime must not involve a threat to the military post or military property.

CoMA had to admit that the fact that McCarthy was a soldier was not sufficient to establish the service connection, but it added a new factor to the "*O'Callahan* criteria": "whether the military interest in deterring the offense is distinct from and greater than that of civilian society and whether the military interest can be vindicated adequately in civilian courts."[21] This turned out to be a reformulation of the old argument against assuring that constitutional protections are provided to the military because authority and discipline could be severely disrupted.

CoMA ruled in *McCarthy* that, despite an apparent passing of the *O'Callahan* tests, McCarthy was properly tried in a court-martial. They set forth two rather different sets of reasons (actually two different opinions, one by Chief Judge Albert Fletcher and one from Judge William Cook) in support of the same result. Fletcher accepted the Supreme Court's "*O'Callahan* criteria" as governing jurisdiction, but went on to argue that *McCarthy* did not meet the criteria in crucial ways. According to Fletcher, the formation of the criminal intent must have occurred on the base and there was a distinct threat to the military personnel by the introduction of marijuana to the base.

Judge Cook first attacked the earlier Supreme Court's denegation of the military courts. He argued that courts-martial members are "the functional equivalents of the jurors in a civilian criminal trial."[22] Hence, trial by jury was provided in the military courts. Judge Fletcher himself had decried such a preposterous claim, but Cook was undeterred. He sallied on with the contention that the civilian courts are too lenient with respect to punishing marijuana trafficking (as is evident at rock concerts); so, to let such courts prosecute military personnel would "foster disregard of and even contempt for the military prohibitions."[23] Retreat to the necessity of maintaining discipline! But surely not an unreasonable way of showing that the military interest in the case was distinct from the civilian.

Cook's opinion aside, the important step taken in *McCarthy* was that the highest military court acknowledged the superseding authority of the Supreme Court in jurisdictional matters and the relevance of the "*O'Callahan* criteria." In so doing, it again limited the exercise of its own authority over those in uniform, edging further into the middle ground.

SOME DIFFERENCES BETWEEN CONSTITUTIONAL AND MILITARY LAW

These cases cannot adequately represent nearly four decades of military law decisions, but they do tell a coherent story of a movement down a certain track that was not derailed by other decisions of either CoMA or the Supreme Court. The story is one of the "civilianization" (using Latimer's term) of military justice, or rather, it is the story of the rapid movement since the UCMJ toward constitutional protection during military prosecution. It is of note that these decisions do not call for recasting of the military law to include a military version of the constitutional rights. They, instead, attest to the authority of the Constitution over the military justice system. In simple terms, they reject the notion that military law must be distinct from civilian law, regardless of what the old soldiers claim about discipline and morale.

But elements of these cases, and especially the "*O'Callahan* criteria," suggest that there should be some significant differences between military law and constitutional law. The military discipline argument has never been totally discredited, and it is not likely to be. Who could doubt that the military must have far more control over the prerogatives of soldiers, sailors, and aviators than a wide open extension of constitutional rights would permit? Clearly, I should think, no one would disagree that, in wartime, fine points of constitutionalism cannot be allowed to deter, or interfere with, military action.

There is, however, a major difficulty with the wartime necessity defense of the suspension of constitutional rights in military law. When is the military in a state of war? As is well known, the power to declare a state of war constitutionally resides with the Congress. Since the Second World

War, however, there have been precious few days in which the American military has not been in combat or stationed under arms in volatile regions in which hostilities against them can and do erupt at any moment. An argument might be mounted to the effect that if there is no official state of war, then there is not sufficient legal reason to enforce substitution of military regulations for constitutional protections. The war-peace distinction that is crucial to such an argument is, however, for all practical purposes a distinction without a difference. The age of executive-ordered engagements, missions, and alerts has been upon us for nearly four decades. Hence, if the military law defender (hereafter militarist) is right that war-time conditions require strict adherence to the Code, no room would seem open for the constitutionalist. Still, we must not forget that the conditions of undeclared warfare which prompt support for the militarist's views are created by actions of dubious constitutional status by the executive. One of the effects of the militarist's position, then, might be the destruction of the authority of the fundamental law of the land, the very law the military is maintained to protect.

The framers of the Constitution could not have imagined that the country would have a large standing armed force in a time when no war has been declared. This could also explain why the framers say so little about military law and justice. The world they knew was one in which the military was to be active only in declared wars, during which it would handle offenses within its ranks as expeditiously as possible and with little concern for the niceties of judicial review. Standing armed forces, and a world spasmodically erupting in the kind of hostilities to which executive order is the only effective response, are so alien to the underlying conceptions of the Constitution that hope of salvaging constitutionality in military law may be a pipe dream.

THE MILITARY JUSTICE ACT OF 1968

The military justice system (since 1951) has shown remarkable flexibility and little resistance to being molded by Supreme Court interventions on behalf of personal rights. But how far has military law really come? The case of Lieutenant William Calley (USCMA 534, 48 CMR (1973)) provided an excellent test. In 1971, Calley was found guilty by a general court-martial held at Fort Benning, Georgia, of the murder of 22 Vietnamese civilians in the village of My Lai. Calley's attorney went collateral by seeking a writ of habeas corpus from the U.S. District Court at Columbus, Georgia. The writ was obtained and a federal judge ordered Calley released. The Army refused to honor the order and appealed to the Circuit Court of Appeals in New Orleans, which sustained the court-martial verdict. The Army's primary reason for appealing the District Court order was to derail a precedent that would have occurred—that a civilian court other than the Supreme Court could overrule a military court's decision. The Supreme Court refused to review the Calley conviction, thereby sustaining the Circuit Court and the general court-martial.

The Calley case is important for reasons beyond the high court's sustaining of the court-martial verdict, in other words, that civilian inferior court collateral interference in the case was disallowed. Of particular note is that *Calley* was one of the first cases to come to trial after the enactment of the Military Justice Act of 1968 in which independent single-officer courts and trained counsel for defendants were provided. Calley's defense rested on the claim that he was following superior orders and that the massacre at My Lai was nothing more than an instance of ordinary Army operations in Vietnam. A defense of this type would not likely have been used in a court-martial before 1968. The reason is, as noted by Generous, that until that time the law officer in a court-martial was appointed from the local staff judge advocate's office. "He was normally subject to the convening authority, [and] would risk his career if he permitted a defense such as the one Calley used."[24] Because the Act of 1968 made the military judge independent of command pressure, the door was opened for most any defense, even one intended to draw the military itself into the dock with the accused.

This freedom granted, the military judge responded to Supreme Court complaints in *O'Callahan* about tribunals appointed by the very commander who had preferred the charges. Independent judges are not exactly jury trials, but they are laudable improvements on the past.

Much more important than the independence of the judges to the reform of military law would be getting all offenses in the armed services within the jurisdiction of the reformed UCMJ. Even critics agree that "once a GI's case reaches a point where the Uniform Code takes over, he will be treated about as fairly as he might be on any other jurisdiction."[25] Requiring that all cases, whether of senior officers or buck privates, be brought before a court-martial would work wonders with respect to fairness. As it stands, senior officers often void court-martial for offenses for which lower ranking service members stand trial.

ASSUMPTION OF RISK

Suggestions of the previous sort, though practical, do not go to the heart of the real issue. They do only a little interior decorating within the military justice system, rather than confront the major constitutional inadequacies cited by the Supreme Court. The hard fact is that, at least intuitively, it seems unfair to subject those in the armed service of their country to a legal code that is basically alien to all of their previous legal experiences. A simple distinction is sometimes drawn to defeat this objection. The armed forces usually are composed of two different types of service persons—those who entered the military by free enlistment and those conscripted. The draft now is inactive, but registration is still required and the draft may be revived if conditions are perceived to warrant it, so the distinction does not seem to be an artificial one. It can be persuasively argued, those who volunteered for military service of their own free will expressly agreed to abide by all of the rules and regulations of the armed forces, including especially the UCMJ. That commitment should stand, this argument continues, despite the fact that it means losing some, even all, constitutional protections of ordinary citizens. Enlistees should be viewed as responsible adults contracting, in part, to be bound to the decisions of an alternative way of resolving disputes, the UCMJ. The model here might be a private arbitration court to which parties to a conflict submit their cases and agree to be bound by the arbitrator's judgment without recourse to the federal system and its rights. The idea is that of justice between consenting adults based on contract. The only segment of the military for whom the constitutional inadequacies of the UCMJ might then need to be remedied are those who did not freely accept the authority of the code—those conscripted.

But this bounds too fast and too far. We may imagine two sorts of arguments put forth to buttress the significance of the enlistment or conscription distinction. The first, suggested above—that a contractual relationship exists for the enlistee that has the effect of superseding the constitutional protections—looks specious. Admittedly, there are superficial similarities between ordinary contractual relationships and enlistments. Crucial conditions are missing, however, to support the conclusion that the enlistee, in the UCMJ, gets what he or she contracted for. It is a cornerstone of the theory of contract, for example, that contracts without consideration are legally unenforceable. Consideration in contract is typically taken to involve a benefit conferred by the promisee on the promisor or a detriment incurred by the promisee. In fact, as Holmes noted, "It is ... thought that every consideration may be reduced to a case of the latter sort, using the word "detriment" in a somewhat broad sense."[26] In enlistment, who is the promisor? Who the promisee? It seems reasonable to say that the enlistee promises to serve the military and abide by the UCMJ. That would make the enlistee the promisor conferring a benefit upon the military. After all, the enlistee usually initiates the relationship. The TV recruitment spots would constitute binding offers to the general public only if they are "clear, definite, and explicit and leave nothing open for negotiation," and "show that some performance was promised in positive terms in return for something requested." Could a Navy enlistee sue for breach of contract if he joined because, after seeing the TV ad, he decided he wanted to see the world and yet he was never stationed outside of Norfork, Virginia (which happened to be his hometown)? In enlistment, which is the detriment incurred by the military? This business begins to stretch the normal notions well out of fit. Still, Holmes, it may be remembered, rejected the account of consideration in terms of benefits and detriments. In its place he offered the "bargain theory," the view that "the root of the whole matter [of consideration] is the relation of reciprocal conventional inducement, each for the other, between consideration and promise."[27] Here again, however, the enlistment situation satisfies the criteria only if we perform semantic gymnastics. An enlistment may surely have elements of reciprocal inducement (especially in times of peace and an all-volunteer force) but these are far from essential to the enlistment. A private citizen motivated by patriotism, or just down on his luck, wanders into a recruitment center and signs up for three years in the Army. Maybe the Army has induced him by posters and slick TV advertisements, but how has he induced the Army? By being able-bodied? The more one tries to fit the situation into contract, the further from "conventional" it moves; and that is not to ignore the fact that the Army provides food, shelter, training, and pay in return for services.

I am not, of course, arguing that enlistment does not create a very binding commitment. It surely does. But it seems to do so outside of contract law. When the Army prosecutes an AWOL soldier, it does not plead breach of contract. That is one of the reasons why military law was created.

It might further be argued (though I think the point of doing so is not lost) that even if enlistment creates, or is, a contract, it cannot be one that places one of the parties, the enlistee, even if voluntarily, outside the realm of basic constitutional rights. It cannot alienate that party from the fundamental protections of the basic law of the society. Contract law is neither as powerful as that, nor should it be.

The second sort of argument that might be set forth to buttress the enlistment or conscription distinction under military law associates military service with ordinary employment. In fact, there seems to me to be a good deal of virtue in thinking in such terms about the military. The soldier does have something like an employment relationship to the Army. But we should not press this too far, or we will be in danger of losing the distinction between soldiers and mercenaries where the contractual description is most clearly appropriate. Still, if we say that enlistees are, in important ways, seeking employment in the military, we might go so far as to invoke an assumption of risk doctrine to cover their dealings with the Code.

Enlistees should know, it might be argued, that while in service they will be governed by the UCMJ. They assume the risk that is coincident with the loss of constitutional protections. Drafted soldiers do not assume such a risk, as they did not seek association with the military.

The old doctrine of assumption of risk was captured in *Farwell v. The Boston and Worcester Rail Road Corp.* by Chief Justice Shaw of the Supreme Judicial Court of Massachusetts, (1842).

> The general rule, resulting from considerations as well of justice as of policy, is, that he who engages in the employment of another for the performance of specified duties and services . . . takes upon himself the natural and ordinary risks and perils incident to the performance of such services.[28]

The test is whether the employment was voluntary and whether the perils were likely to be known to the employee. In 1960, in *Pouliot v. Black*, the Massachusetts court affirmed the doctrine.

> As a matter of law, by his voluntary conduct in exposing himself to a known and appreciated risk, plaintiff assumed the risk . . .[29]

One might, of course, wonder if the risks the enlistee assumes when entering the military should include those of its judicial system. The enlistee, we may suppose, is well aware of the dangers of combat and accepts those, but should the doctrine be extended to the administration of the UCMJ's brand of justice? Actually, something very strange would occur were we to apply the assumption of risk doctrine to the enlistee. Consider what we then must do with the conscripted soldier. The draftee certainly did not voluntarily assume any risks, yet in combat and during other military duties, there is practically no way to distinguish the risk assumers from those who did not assume the risk. Should draftees have the right to remedies that enlistees do not when work conditions produce injuries?

The assumption of risk doctrine, however, has been significantly reformulated since *Siragusa* (1962). Workmen's compensation legislation, the doctrine that "an employer has a duty to his employees to exercise reasonable care to furnish them with a reasonably safe place to work,"[30] and contributory negligence have rendered assumption of risk a bit of a relic in the work place. Of course, one could claim that because such doctrines are hardly at home in the military, assumption of risk should still govern there. The retention of the doctrine to preserve an impractical distinction intended to overcome an unfairness has little to recommend it. We cannot escape the fact that both enlisted and conscripted service members stand in the same position vis-à-vis military law's lack of constitutional protections. If it is unfair to impose such a legal system on a draftee, it is equally unfair to impose it on an enlistee.

It would not be unfair to deprive service members of constitutional rights, I assume, on at least two counts. One would be if the rights themselves were trivial, meaningless, vacuous, or inherently distributable only in such a way as to foster untoward or inequitable conditions between the members of the society. Surely the basic constitutional rights cannot be described in any such fashion. A second case in which deprivation might not be unfair would be if rights were substituted that were as good or better in promoting fairness, justice, equity, and so on, as those in the Constitution. That, as noted in a number of Supreme Court decisions, does not come close to being the case. Yet there remains the persuasive consequentialistic argument of the militarist: there are important and undeniable military reasons for military law. The continuing advance of military court decisions towards the standard of the federal courts seems destined to be repelled when it finally reaches the lines of military necessity. But a compromise might still be reached. I shall conclude by sketching what it might look like.

SKETCH OF A COMPROMISE

Let us grant that the military legal system must be, to some extent, independent of the civilian courts for legitimate command and discipline reasons. To achieve that end, appeals of courts-martial decisions should run only through the superior military courts, and only CoMA decisions should be appealable into the federal system, and then directly to the Supreme Court. This would disallow collateral attacks on military court decisions in the federal district courts. "Going collateral, however, will not be a viable option if the offenses tried by courts-martial are restricted to genuine military crimes, that is, crimes peculiar to military service. In that category there will be two types of offenses—those that do and those that do not place the lives of other military personnel in jeopardy. In the former type will be such offenses as failure to show appropriate respect for a superior officer; failing to obey certain kinds of orders in noncombat situations (for example, not swabbing a deck when ordered); and wearing an improper uniform (for example, wearing a yarmulke[31]). In the latter type will be such offenses as failure to obey a direct order in combat; willfully disobeying such an order; and being AWOL or sleeping on watch in a war zone. More specifically with reference to the UCMJ, the first category would consist of crimes set forth in Articles 88, contempt toward officers; 89, disrespect toward superior commissioned officers; 90, willfully disobeying a superior commissioned officer; 91, insubordinate conduct toward a warrant officer, noncommissioned officer, or petty officer; 112, drunk on duty; and 115, malingering. The second group would contain UCMJ crimes set forth in Articles 85, desertion; 86, absence without leave; 87, missing movement; 94, mutiny or sedition; 99, misbehavior before the enemy; 100, subordinate compelling surrender; 101, improper use of a countersign; 102, forcing a safeguard; and 104, aiding the enemy.[32]

If military courts were to deal exclusively with military crimes, then all other criminal cases that involve military personnel would be tried in the federal district courts or other civilian courts, regardless of whether the crime were committed on a military post. Found under the Punitive Articles of the UCMJ[33] are murder, manslaughter, rape, larceny, robbery, forgery, maiming, sodomy, arson, extortion, assault, burglary, housebreaking and the like. These would fall to the jurisdiction of civilian courts, in effect, removing the status of the accused test for jurisdiction and excluding military property as a relevant factor in the location test for jurisdiction. Service members would have full constitutional rights for all standard civilian crimes. Furthermore, because the usual penalties for the more heinous civilian crimes far exceed the normal time of enlistment or the length of conscripted service, military law would no longer be in the position of depriving a person of his or her liberty (in some cases for 25 years at hard labor) without constitutional protections or remedies.

Strict militarists will, no doubt, raise any number of objections to this attempt to carve out a middle position that responds to the constitutional "crisis" of military law. Assuredly, they will worry that bringing civilian law onto the base will undercut command discipline and prerogatives. That may indeed occur, but the undercutting of such prerogatives also has been a product of the UCMJ and the Military Justice Act of 1968. We may well imagine that hardline militarists would prefer the older approach of leaving *all* matters of prosecution in the hands of commanding officers. In wartime combat, the old approach may be necessary for discipline, but the peacetime standing army creates quite a different world, one that the framers of the Constitution seemed to fear.

Although the Constitution does not expressly forbid a standing army, it tries to exert legislative control by requiring that military appropriations never be for a period in excess of two years. Presumably, at that time the need to maintain a large standing force would be evaluated. Hamilton, in *Federalist* Number 8, goes much further. He writes:

> Standing armies, it is said, are not provided against in the new Constitution; and it is therefore inferred that they may exist under it. Their existence, however, from the very terms of the proposition, is, at most, problematical and uncertain.[34]

Hamilton warns that standing armies necessarily strengthen the executive arm of government at the expense of the legislature, and so the state will "acquire a progressive direction toward monarchy." In straightforward terms, Hamilton regards a standing army as the "engine of despotism". At the very least, the world the framers did not want to be actualized is the world of a bifurcated society under parallel legal codes. In wartime, the civilian and military populations can be efficiently disjoined, but in peacetime mischief spills over the borderline.

It should be noted that the civilian criminal codes are not now, and should not become, very interested in the purely military crimes mentioned above. While it is the treatment of just those sorts of crime that provides the militarist with his strongest case, the ways they are handled would seem likely to affect the maintenance of discipline and morale. Hence, military law ought to focus in that direction, but its administration of justice should be as much a mirror of fundamental fairness and due process as circumstances will allow. Enormous discretionary latitude must be extended to commanding officers in combat, but for the sake of the constitutional aim of a unified society under law, the movement in military law to incorporate its own versions of the constitutional protections afforded the accused must be continually encouraged.

REMARKS ON THE CONSTITUTIONS OF CLARENDON (HENRY II)

There is a striking similarity between the military-civilian legal bifurcation in our society and the dual and separate jurisdictional issue that confronted early Plantagenet Britain. Henry II "came face to face with the fact that a large and important part of the people were beyond the control of the state courts."[35] Those in religious orders who committed crimes were tried only in the ecclesiastical courts. Henry decided to act because, as William of Newburgh notes, "criminous clerks" had committed hundreds of murders and were receiving nothing greater than prison sentences on reduced diets.[36] Henry's response to this situation was the monumental Constitutions of Clarendon (1164).

The first Article of the Constitutions established that the right of advowson[37] belonged not to the church, but to the landowner. Disputes over the right (even if both parties were members of the clergy) had to be heard in the King's Court, not in the ecclesiastical courts. Article 3 became the most famous part of the Constitutions. It required that when a cleric was suspected of a crime he was accused in a lay court where he entered his plea. If he pleaded innocence, he was taken to an ecclesiastical court for trial. If found guilty there, he was defrocked, but then returned to the King's court where either the results of the church court were accepted or a further trial was conducted, and if the accused were found guilty, he would receive the same kind of sentence an ordinary layperson would receive for the crime. As is well known, the Archbishop of Canterbury, Thomas à Becket, refused to assent to the Constitutions, defending to the death the separation of the Church Courts from the King's Court. The murder of Becket tempered the King's attempt to unify the jurisdiction of criminal law under his own court, for it gave birth to the infamous doctrine of "benefit of clergy" which allowed a cleric to be tried for any felony less than treason in the ecclesiastical courts. Treason and all misdemeanor charges against those in holy orders were, however, heard in the lay courts. The church courts were left to deal with purely ecclesiastical matters in whatever ways they felt to be consistent with their institutional purposes. (It was not until 1826, when the "benefit" was abolished by statute, that Henry's goal of joining the two major segments of his society under a common legal system was finally accomplished.)

My proposal for reforming military law with respect to the Constitution is very much within the general framework of Henry's conception of how a second legal system ought to function. A version of the defrocking exercise for the guilty in the Constitutions of Clarendon should also be adopted. If a service member is convicted in the civilian court of a crime that warrants long term incarceration or supervised probation, then a discharge from the service should be forthcoming. (I agree with Generous that distinctions among types of discharges should be eliminated.[38]) Minor offenses such as disturbing the peace and public drunkenness, if they were prosecuted at all, would occasion little interruption in service duties, though the conviction would be a matter of public record and may be noted with interest by the offender's superiors.

What Henry II saw as definite injustice—a virtual guarantee of unequal treatment in parallel courts for the same offense—we can explicate in more extensive legal terms. Not only are dual legal systems liable to deal differently with similar offenses, they are likely to have incompatible rules of evidence, different notions of due process, dissimilar senses of fairness and equity, and different conceptions of fundamental rights. In a society that believes that its law ought to deliver the basic principles of the Constitution to all of its citizens, such rifts between legal systems must be minimized. As I have tried to highlight, the military courts themselves have been steadily moving in that direction, but they are confined to act upon the UCMJ, which is distinctly socially disjunctive. The proposal I have outlined recognizes the fact that military law's only constitutional raison d'être is to promote the efficient operation of the land and naval forces analogous to the ecclesiastical law's legitimate purpose (in Henry's eyes) of regulating the religious lives of those in holy orders. But my proposal also affords military personnel with the fullest extent of the rights guaranteed by the Constitution that are consistent with their service duties. To do less is to relegate those in the armed forces to second class citizenship, and that is most definitely unconstitutional.

AMERICAN MILITARY PERSONNEL ABROAD

In closing, another issue should be confronted; it is, in fact, one raised by Associate Justice Stanley Reed in the *Toth* case. My proposal focuses only on peacetime applications of military law within the territory of the United States. It should be remembered that one of Reed's concerns with the majority opinion in *Toth* was that if the military were not granted jurisdiction over nonmilitary crimes committed by those in service while stationed in a foreign country, the accused's fate would rest with a foreign legal system in which our constitutional guarantees may be totally absent. Would it be fair to place an American service person, even one accused of a heinous crime, under the jurisdiction of foreign law? I see no reason why this is a problem. The American in the armed forces in this regard is no worse off than a private American citizen who, while living or traveling in a foreign country, violates its criminal code. The Constitution does not protect Americans everywhere on earth. Why should American military law do so? Military personnel should be subject to the criminal code of whatever jurisdiction they are based in, whether at home or abroad. At home, like all other American citizens, however, they should, in as full a measure as possible, enjoy the rights, privileges, and protections of the Constitution.

Notes

1. *The Theodosian Code*, translated by Clyde Pharr (New Jersey: Princeton University Press, 1952) Book II, Title 1.

2. Edward M. Byrne, *Military Law* (Annapolis: The Moral Institute Press, 1981), chap. I.

3. Ibid., 1.

4. Francis X. Gindhart, "Foreword" to Harlod F. Nufer, *American Servicemember's Supreme Court* (Washington, D.C: University Press of America, 1981), vii.

5. *Toth v. Quarles*, 350 US 11 (1955).

6. *The Theodosian Code*, Book IX, Title 1, Edict 10.

7. *Toth v. Quarles*.

8. Ibid., 24.

9. See William T. Generous, Jr., *Swords and Scales* (Port Washington, NY: 1973), 178.

10. There are three types of courts-martial: summary, special, and general. Officers are not subject to summary courts. Special courts-martial may award up to six month's confinement at hard labor, while the general courts-martial are the highest trial courts of the military system and they can award any sentence permitted in military law. Another difference is that the trial and defense counsel and the judge at a general court-martial are always certified military lawyers.

11. *United States v. Jacoby*, 11 U.S.C.M.A. 428, 29 C.M.R. 244 (1960), 429.

12. Ibid., 429-30.

13. *Mattox v. United States*, 156 U.S. 237, 15 S. Ct. 337, 39 L. ed. 409 (1895), 242-244.

14. *United States v. Jacoby*, 441.

15. Ibid.

16. Ibid., 442.

17. Nufer, *American Servicemember's Supreme Court*, 87-88.

18. *O'Callahan v. Parker*, 395 U.S. 258 (1969).

19. See John T. Willis, "The United States Court of Military Appeals: 'Born Again,'" *Indiana Law Journal*, LII, 1 (Fall, 1976): 168.

20. Ibid.

21. *United States v. McCarthy*, 2 M.J. 26 (U.S.C.M.A. 1976) 28.

22. Ibid., 30.

23. Ibid., 31.

24. Generous, *Swords and Scales*, 199.

25. Ibid., 201.

26. Oliver Wendall Holmes, Jr., "The Elements of Contract," *The Common Law* (Boston: Little, Brown & Co., 1881), 227.

27. Ibid., 230.

28. *Farwell v. The Boston and Worcester Rail Road Corp.* (Supreme Judicial Court of Massachusetts, 1842) 45 Mass. 4 (Metc.) 49.

29. *Pouliot v. Black*, 341 Mass. 531, 170 N.E. 2d 709 (1960).

30. *Siragusa v. Swedish Hospital*, (Supreme Court of Washington, 1962) 60 Wash. 2d 310, 373 P. 2d 767.

31. Note *S. Simcha Goldman v. Caspar W. Weinberger, Secretary of Defense, et al.* (1986) in which the Supreme Court held that the First Amendment did not prohibit application of the Air Force regulation to prevent the wearing of a yarmulke by the plaintiff while on duty and in uniform.

32. I do not mean these to be exclusive lists, but they are representative.

33. *The Uniform Code of Military Justice*, (1950) Subchapter X, Articles 77-134.

34. Alexander Hamilton, *The Federalist*, Number 8, (New York, 1788) (New American Library, 1961).

35. Geroge Burton Adams, *Constitutional History of England* (New York: H. Holt, 1921), 95.

36. William of Newburgh, *Historia rerum anglicorum* (1016-1198) in *Chronicles of the Reigns of Stephen, Henry II, and Richard I*, ed. Richard Howlett (London: 1884-85) vol. I, 140.

37. The right to name the candidate for a vacancy in a parish church.

38. Generous, *Swords and Scales*, 206.

11

The Extension of Law to Foreign Policy: The Next Constitutional Challenge

Richard A. Falk

The central focus of Falk's essay is the issue of whether there are sufficient constitutional grounds for democratically controlling the increasingly dangerous and widening discretionary power of the American Presidency in the deployment of the armed forces in foreign affairs. Falk traces the recent political and legal developments which he believes render ineffective the envisioned role of Congress as the primary constitutional guardian of presidential accountability. In keeping with the values of democracy, he offers some challenging arguments regarding how the proper respect for international law, coupled with a reconsideration of citizen participation and of judicial review, may reinvigorate a more effective legal response to unchecked presidential power.

In Federalist #1, Alexander Hamilton raises the foundational question as to "whether societies of men [sic] are really capable or not, of establishing good government from reflection and choice, or whether they are forever destined to depend, for their political constitutions, on accident and force." The adoption of the Constitution, and the generally favorable experience over the course of two subsequent centuries, have created an overall conviction that the framework adopted for the governance of the country has worked remarkably well. The Constitution has served as an inspiration to numerous other peoples who have more recently achieved independence, and this, despite the otherwise controversial status of the United States as a political actor.

Granting this unprecedented success in state-building, the viewpoint of Federalist #1 needs to be tested these days in a context of calls for reassessment and renewal. A group of individuals no matter how prophetic, or how careful to preserve room for maneuver on the part of succeeding generations, cannot do away with the challenge of a fundamental shift in circumstance. In the face of such a challenge, the question posited is whether the society of men and women that constitutes America is capable of renewing their social contract on behalf of the safety, well-being, and public good of the citizenry conceived of both as a whole and individually.

The thesis of this chapter is that the constitutional treatment of foreign policy, its execution and restraint, was contoured around a specific set of eighteenth-century concerns of the postrevolutionary colonists—mainly, how to achieve republican control over war making without losing entirely the efficiency associated with royalist or monarchical concentrations of authority in the crown. Ever since the earliest days of the republic, it has been commonly supposed that a weakness of the constitutional arrangement has been this commitment to decenter war making, and foreign policy more generally, that is, to apply the principle of separation of powers (and the complementary friction of checks and balances) to the external conduct of public affairs.

The main positive and practical rationale for the Constitutional arrangement is that it was desirable to make recourse to war as deliberative as possible, even semipopulist, relying heavily on the legislative branch acting in its representational role, to restrain an impulsive presidency. At the same time, the conduct of war, once properly declared, should be primarily entrusted to the unified control of the President in his (her) role as Commander-in-Chief, with even here a serious legislative check existing in the form of a continuing Congressional control over the appropriations power.

THE "IMPERIAL PRESIDENCY," INTERNATIONAL LAW, AND THE LIMITED ROLE OF AMERICAN COURTS

In this century, such a solution for issues of war and peace seems increasingly unworkable given changes in the world, in the character of war, in the role of the United States as a global superpower, and in the resultant formation of a powerful segment of government that has a definite vocational and ideological stake in a hostile world and in a permanent military buildup based on continuing international tensions. The problem of "the imperial presidency" is one dimension of what has emerged to unbalance the original constitutional arrangement, but this might be rectified by pursuing the largely unexplored option of reinterpretation, leading to an expanded role for courts *within* the four corners of the space of the Constitution as enacted. Such an option suggests that the existing style of judicial deference on foreign policy issues was never unconditionally mandated by either authoritative text or unambiguous intentions of the founders, and that there exists interpretative space to reassess the appropriate judicial role in light of the policy imperatives of today and the long-term well-being of the citizenry, conceived as "the public good."

But beyond this effort to provide through reinterpretation a new constitutional equilibrium in the form of counterweights to the growth of the executive branch, there lies a more fundamental, largely substantive problem. The basic assumption embodied in the Constitution is that the government as a sovereign entity has discretion to use force when the appropriate institutional mechanisms so decree as serving the national interests. True, American presidents, even Ronald Reagan, claim to possess a foundation in international law for their most controversial uses of force. Reagan alleged that inter-American collective security arrangements authorized the invasion of Grenada in 1983, and that the self-defense provisions of the United Nations Charter were an adequate legal basis for the air attack on Libya in April 1986.

But to provide legal cover is not to acknowledge a constraining framework of international law as applicable to foreign policy. Such a framework would involve some type of review process to enable challenged policies to be assessed impartially. At minimum, an international law framework would mean the possibility of judicial review of executive policy decision in domestic courts and, as well, a show of respect for adverse rulings of competent international bodies, especially the International Court of Justice (ICJ).

The guiding assumption of this essay is that such a failure to abide by disinterested interpretations of international law increasingly badly serves the national interest and the well-being of the citizenry.[1] This legalist critique of constitutionalism in foreign policy can be regarded as seeking two types of reform: reinterpretation of the separation of powers in the setting of foreign policy to upgrade the role of courts, and a possible structural reform, but not necessarily by formal amendment, that would assure disinterested judicial review of contested foreign policy decision under international law. The goal here is part of a larger plan for greater responsiveness by governments to disinterested assessments of international law, acknowledging an interest by citizens in establishing a framework in which one's own government is constrained by international law.

The constitutional process has, of course, exhibited remarkable flexibility in accommodating normative sea-changes during the life of the republic. Assuring individual liberties, extending the franchise to women, offering protection of law to racial minorities, and providing welfare benefits to the poor have all been achieved in accordance with changing mores, popular pressures, militant social movements, and shifting images of the appropriate role of government. True, the emancipation of blacks has depended mainly upon the successful recourse to extraordinary means outside the constitutional process—a long, bloody civil war. And in one crucial instance—the oppression of native American peoples—the Constitution has never offered protection for basic rights.

The subject matter of foreign affairs has not been generally perceived as presenting a structural challenge of accommodation, so much as presenting recurrent crises of mediation, in the relations between the Presidency and the Congress as to the proper distribution of function. Most debate continues to concentrate upon the appropriate contours of respective roles for the distinct branches of government, a shifting set of boundaries reflecting changes in public mood, the impact of particular leaders, the success or failure of a given initiative especially in the area of war and peace, the ebb and flow of power between coordinate branches of government, and the degree of activism of the United States in controversial matters beyond its borders. During these two centuries of practice, there has also been a spiral, cumulative trend toward the concentration of power in the executive branch, creating a growing sense that Congress is grasping awkwardly after power, but without the will or capacity to perform successfully if it extends its prerogative in foreign policy matters beyond a distinctly subordinate and essentially passive role. On the one side, the executive claims virtual supremecy over the execution of foreign policy initiatives, even if at variance with congressional will and public preferences, and on the other, Congress is continuously criticized for trying to micromanage foreign policy. Congress, itself, is ambivalent, not wanting the responsibility associated with questioning fundamental premises of foreign policy in the national security area (should the United States engage in covert operations? rely on nuclear weapons? intervene on behalf of democracy?) and yet seeking the prominence arising from meaningful participation. Generally, then, the tug-of-war has been over the quality of participation—in the procedural realm of policymaking—rather than being resolved by reference to matters of substance.

True, if a presidential policy backfires or breaks down, Congress can, especially through its hearing process in an age of television, briefly occupy center stage. In this way, Congress can expose, challenge, discredit those who carry out foreign policy, including even the President. Both the long ordeal of the Vietnam War and the extraordinary departures from normalcy disclosed by the Iran-Contra hearings are suggestive of this potential congressional role. But note that this role is also consumed by considerations of domestic process, and only tangentially touches on matters of substance or on the excesses of foreign policy per se. To build an impeachment consensus against Nixon in the aftermath of Watergate, it was necessary at the last instance to drop the count pertaining to combat operations in Cambodia, despite clear evidence of presidential deceit in the execution of a policy that cost many lives, American and Cambodian.

The main effort of Congress during the last twenty years has been to resist erosion of its constitutional role in an era of expanding executive claims to act in foreign affairs. Congress wants to be in on the action, to participate, to know state secrets, and to share the war making prerogatives with the Executive. By and large, Congress remains content to be subordinate on substance so long as it is consulted and its dignity respected. The Iran-Contra disclosures suggest a special instance of aggravated assault on constitutional expectations because even responsible cabinet ministers in Departments of State and Defense were shut out by the White House acting through particular individuals on the National Security Council who, in turn, relied upon a private network of shadowy operatives to carry out foreign policy initiatives that enjoyed neither public backing nor congressional approval, although they did seem to reflect the overall preferences of the President.[2]

My focus here is upon the underlying structural problems that have emerged over the course of decades both from the limitations in the constitutional arrangement itself and from a pattern of understandable, yet arbitrarily narrow, lines of interpretative practice in the courts. These interpretations are arbitrary in the sense that a far more expansive view of judicial function could have evolved quite legitimately. As matters now stand, a serious constitutional inadequacy that involves a great risk to public safety and to the well-being of the national political community has resulted from the self-denying definition of function that has been generally offered by the courts.

TWENTIETH CENTURY CHANGES OF SITUATION

Here, then is the crux of the problem. The Constitution was drafted at a time when recourse to war and force as an instrument was a matter of national discretion *under international law* and when the role of the United States was largely hemispheric, deliberately opting (via Washington's Farewell Address and subsequent policy) to avoid the maelstrom of geopolitics, historically associated with Eurocentric conflict. As a result, the prospects of war were closely connected with the territorial defense of the country and its citizens, with brief assertions of military power to uphold hemispheric interests against European encroachment and, as time went by, with an expanding Pacific naval presence.

The change of circumstance came in this century, especially with the two world wars, and with an expanding U.S. involvement with geopolitics since 1945. In each of the world wars, the United States was drawn out of its isolationist stance to intervene, as it turned out decisively, to alter the course of conflict in Europe and to take part in the shaping of peace. After World

War II, the United States emerged as the dominant world power, not only militarily but economically and diplomatically as well. It also emerged with a national leadership convinced that interwar isolationism was no longer viable, and that the United States needed to remain a presence in Europe during peacetime to avoid yet another breakdown of international order at its center. Such an outlook coincided with the view of the Soviet Union and the ideology of Communism as expansive and hostile, with the collapse of the colonial hold over the Third World, and with the availability of weaponry of mass destruction on a scale that made warfare between strategic rivals a manifestly self-destructive, if not a suicidal, venture.

Without entering into detail, the post-1945 role of the United States in the world has underscored the inadequacy of the constitutional framework that has evolved, either to secure the national interest or to enable the kind of mediation between the coordinate branches of government that was originally envisioned. Indeed, the original preoccupation of the Constitution-makers was tilted toward checks upon executive prerogative. The American Revolution brought to power and influence a group of citizens who risked their lives to detach the United States from a royalist system in which the citizenry had no effective check over the ruler. One thing the framers were agreed upon was that they didn't want a king when it came to initiating war, although arguably, the Hamiltonian wing wanted something that was functionally equivalent to kingship. But the basic consensus at Philadelphia was determined to vest the power to declare war in the Congress, and to limit the President in foreign affairs to designated roles as Commander-in-Chief and principal negotiator.

Yet, there was a degree of incoherence, perhaps inevitably so, from the outset of the republic. The Hamiltonian perspective was powerfully asserted in early patterns of state practice, and quickly became ascendent: the country, to be successful, needed a unified foreign policy that could provide the stability required for the growth of commerce and trade, the key to influence and prosperity for a republic. Even Jefferson, the arch foe of Hamilton, largely capitulated to this view during his presidency, expressed in foreign affairs by sending American naval units far off to engage the Barbary pirates off the shores of North Africa. In the 19th century, congress collaborated with the executive in a course of foreign policy that was rarely controversial and involved no sustained foreign wars.

What was more important for our purposes, there were no legal criteria that could have provided limits on the extension of presidential power or, more generally, on governmental power. International law did not purport to regulate recourse to force beyond the vague directives of the just war doctrine directed at the heads of sovereign states, and relying upon an appeal to a Christian conscience supposedly held in common. Out of such a context, courts naturally were led to perceive and treat foreign policy controversies as matters of judgment within the domain of leadership and as "political questions" not susceptible to judicial assessment. Individual citizens were to be protected by representative institutions and were generally denied standing to challenge foreign policy, lacking a legally defined right. The perverse result was that only in the property area did individual citizens discover some basis in international law to challenge foreign policy initiatives.

In the famous *Steel Seizure* case, a majority in the U.S. Supreme Court held that President Truman could not send federal troops into the steel mills so as to assure the flow of war equipment needed by soldiers fighting in Korea.[3] Another case (*Flast v. Cohen*) held that a taxpayer with a general grievance could make a claim, even if lacking a specific interest arising from some severe loss.[4] On the other side, especially in a series of cases involving citizens objecting to a call to serve in Vietnam, courts found that the objections were "political" or that the litigants lacked "standing." Similarly, in more recent years, a series of antinuclear cases have generally, but not invariably, denied citizens any opportunity to present their legal grievances to a court, and have imposed prison sentences on individuals who, on the basis of their conscience and their understanding of international law, have believed it was their duty to obstruct the deployment or operation of weapons systems.[5]

In the background is the development of international law and its reinforcement within the political culture, especially by religious organizations. Beginning with the Hague Conventions of 1899 and 1907 there were agreed a series of limits on the *conduct* of warfare, especially a variety of rules designed to prohibit tactics that didn't distinguish military from civilian targets. Later came the Pact of Paris or Kellogg-Briand Pact of 1928 that limited *recourse* to force as an instrument of foreign policy to situations of self-defense. This conception became the cornerstone of modern international law governing the use of force, and is embodied in Articles 2(4) and 51 of the United Nations Charter.

A further twentieth-century development has been the creation of international political and judicial institutions with the competence to pass on contested claims to use force in international relations. This development enables, but does not prescribe, an escape from the subjectivity associated with each government deciding for itself that *its* uses of force were *defensive* and those of its opponent were *aggressive*.

On another front, the governments of the world, and especially the United States, agreed in the wake of World War II that policymakers, including the heads of state, were individually liable for crimes of state committed in relation to war. The Nuremberg (and Tokyo) experiences were landmark developments that planted seeds of a new understanding on the part of citizens as to their political obligations. The Nuremberg concept was extended down the ladder of responsibility from the level of primary leaders, and applied to doctors, judges, and business executives who were associated with implementing one or another facet of officially sanctioned

Nazi (and Japanese imperial) policies.[6] The logic of Nuremberg is even wider, suggesting that anyone with knowledge of crimes of state has a responsibility to act to prevent their continuation, and that no superior order or sense of nationalistic identity should inhibit this primary duty.[7]

BUREAUCRATIC AND TECHNOLOGICAL CHANGES IN THE CHARACTER OF STATE POWER

These broad legal developments have been reinforced by some crucial bureaucratic and technological changes in the character of state power. Since 1945, the United States has assumed a peacetime role as guardian of the status quo in large portions of the non-Communist world. This has produced the need for a permanently rising military budget and capability, as well as for a major intelligence network to provide information about developments everywhere. Framed by notions of territorial sovereignty, rights of self-determination, and the renunciation of force, the world political system is contrary to the drift of an interventionary diplomacy, no matter what the character of the moral and strategic claims of the intervening side. There is no persuasive way to reconcile respect for international law with a foreign policy role that includes the mission to resist political movements in foreign countries whose program and outlook are deemed hostile to U.S. national interests.

Two effects ensue. The first is pressure to keep the interventionary policies as secret as possible. The United States government attempted, by way of "covert operations," to uphold its geopolitical role without acting in a manner that directly flouted the UN Charter. The interventions in Iran (1953) to restore the Shah, and in Guatemala (1954) to overthrow a leftist government, were typical of this new approach to foreign policy. Secrecy was not needed to the extent that containment was challenged directly in Korea (1950-53), when the North attacked the South; the U.S. response was generally deemed appropriate and "legal," being a response to a prior military initiative across an internationally recognized boundary, making the response an instance of collective self-defense, an interpretation upheld by the United Nations and a consensus of governments.

The second effect of the pressure to intervene is to regress in relation to the Rule of Law, especially when international institutions do not give their blessings to a more controversial undertaking of American foreign policy. This loss of diplomatic leverage by the United States correlated especially with the decolonization process, the postwar recovery of Europe and Japan, and the persisting rivalry with the Soviet Union and with left-oriented politics. From the mid-1960s onward, the United Nations could no longer be counted on to rubber-stamp United States foreign policy and indeed began to be an arena that gave voice to harsh criticism. The Vietnam War was a watershed in this process of legalist disenchantment by the U.S. government. The attempts by government lawyers and civilian apologists to reconcile U.S. war policies in Indochina with international law seemed empty rationalizations outside the United States, and have been virtually disregarded in non-Anglo-American scholarship. In the Reagan years, the process of disenchantment has become explicit, even shrill—the invasion of Grenada (1983), the air attack on Libya (1986), and the interventionary policy of support for anti-Sandinista forces have only the slenderest basis in international law. What is more clear, the World Court decision, in a carefully reasoned judgment supported by 12 of the 15 participating judges, has found the U.S. intervention in Central America to be a serious and multiple violation of international law. Even more significantly, the adverse judgment has been repudiated by the United States government without any serious backlash even among the mainstream opponents of the Reagan policies, political forces critical of support for the *contras* with the aim of overthrowing the Sandinista government in Nicaragua. It is almost as if there exists a national consensus that the policy should be debated "on its merits," without considering the merits as including matters of the legal status of the policy itself.[8]

The evolving technology of war, especially its nuclear dimension, has undermined the constitutional idea of war making in fundamental, yet largely unacknowledged, respects. Even without nuclear weaponry, missiles and rockets, when used in conjunction with modern guidance and delivery systems, produce a situation in which neither time nor space could give the United States any secure period between "peace" and "war." These developments were underscored by the lesson of Pearl Harbor, which suggested to the postwar generation that vulnerability to surprise attack existed, despite the oceanic buffers, if the country did not maintain a posture of military readiness.

Nuclear weapons in a bipolar world emphasized this new reality. Wartime, or at least the prewar posture of an imaginary war constantly being rehearsed, became the norm.[9] Such a new reality meant a large, enduring, and unavoidable influence for the military, a recurrent argument about the extent to which the government should be able to take special action beneath the banner of "national security," as well as an unbalancing of the governmental arrangement of checks and balances envisaged at the outset of the republic.

Arising out of this situation have been associated developments pertaining to nuclear weapons. Because these weapons are so gruesomely destructive, there has been a special inhibition on discussing their strategic role in foreign policy, including occasions of threat and possible use. Given the nature of modern conflict, there would likely be no opportunity for wider consultation and participation during an international crisis, and certainly not once such weapons are used. The secret, decisive character of this prerogative to shape nuclear weapons policy lodged in the presidency without prior discussion, without guidelines for use, and without notions of accountability, is an unprecedented erosion of both popular sovereignty and separation of powers.

In sum, the Constitution arose at a time when the country was weak and modest in capacity, when it was insulated from war by oceans, and when the status of war could be sharply differentiated from a normally prevailing condition of peace, enabling a clear possibility under most circumstances of making a reflective decision to have recourse to war. In the nuclear age and in the setting of the United States as a global power with an ambitious overt and covert interventionary agenda (recently reaffirmed and extended in the form of the Reagan Doctrine), the loose structure of the Constitution no longer serves our citizenry well. This assessment is confirmed by the growth and development of legal rules and international institutions that withdraw discretion from governments, but also provides national policymakers and judges with legal criteria and procedures by which to assess objectively the propriety of foreign policy. In light of all this, it is time that courts reinterpret the judicial function in relation to foreign policy. A strong argument now supports advocates of a creative judicial role, for an approach, in this setting, that rejects Alexander Bickel's affirmation of the call in Federalist #79 to develop "the passive virtues." The time is now ripe for judicial expansion, for a dramatic acquisition of the active virtues.

RATIONALIZATION FOR PRESIDENTIAL CONTROL OF FOREIGN POLICY: LOUIS HENKIN'S POSITION

Louis Henkin's influential writing on the Constitution and foreign policy rests on an essential confirmation of the viability of existing arrangements and the absence of either political will or normative necessity to make major changes.[10] Henkin discounts the view that the Vietnam War provoked "a constitutional crisis," arguing instead that the Constitution envisaged the push-and-pull of congressional-executive relations, weighted in favor of the presidency, in the event that a foreign policy initiative came under heavy fire. He also is scornful of judicial efforts to resolve such tensions by passing judgment on the relative merits of contested institutional positions.[11] In effect, this general assessment allows the play of governmental forces to shape the direction of United States foreign policy which, effectively, leaves the locus of authority to initiate and sustain war making in the executive bureaucracy.

This conclusion is bolstered by Henkin's view that the overall system "cannot be effectively improved by constitutional amendment," an attitude that expresses both a confidence in muddling through and "a perhaps tired conclusion that that is the best one can hope for in human government."[12]

Such a deposition leaves a governmental control of foreign policy about where Justice Sutherland left it in his famous majority opinion in *U.S. v. Curtiss-Wright*, a rationalization of presidential hegemony that has been extended far beyond the holding of the case. An oft-quoted dictum captures the spirit of Sutherland's attitude:

> Not only, as we have shown, is the federal power over external affairs in origin and essential character different from that over internal affairs, but participation in the exercise of the power is significantly different. In this vast external realm, with its important, complicated, delicate and manifold problems, the President alone has the power to speak or listen as a representative of the nation.[13]

The reach of *Curtiss-Wright* was exhibited by Lt. Col. Oliver North's reliance on its authority to justify his various undertakings disclosed in the course of the Iran-Contra hearings.[14] The scholarly views of *Curtiss-Wright* are more critical and circumscribed, giving the basis for either narrowing its influence to its holding (bearing on the constitutionality of a delegation of authority that allowed the President to use discretion to restrict export licenses for arms sales to a war zone in South America) or disregarding its dicta on the broad theory of external relations.[15]

It seems correct to conclude that it is not currently feasible to contemplate a formal revision of the Constitution by resort to the amendment process, nor even to suppose that congress is likely to do more than assert its prerogatives vis-à-vis the executive. Such assertions, although likely to be resisted at every stage, are nevertheless essentially defensive in character. The cumulative tendency is assuredly to reinforce ever more the actuality of presidential hegemony—by way of secrecy, the national security doctrine, the manipulation of information and the media, the projection of bureaucratic influence, and the undermining of congressional independence by special interest to lobbies and through new patterns of political financing. After policy failures and revelations of presidential excess, brief periods of reaction occur, as has happened in the aftermaths of Vietnam, Watergate, and Iran-Contra, enabling Congress to extend its role concerning executive action—but the main effect is to alter the *form* of interaction without touching on its substance. The War Powers Act of 1975 and the legislative effort to constrain covert action by the CIA are illustrative settings. The Executive objects to congressional interference, but, in fact, is not challenged at all and, at most, alters patterns of consultation and reporting. That is, the political consensus within government and among contending political parties is content with existing arrangements applicable to foreign affairs, including the ebb and flow of congressional-executive assertiveness and the overall drift toward structural control of foreign policy in the presidency.

For reasons suggested earlier, this prospect seems unsatisfactory: there is a growing gap between functional and normative imperatives that call for constitutional reforms of a fundamental character and the political stasis that precludes reform. The statist-realist response is to accept the political constraints evident in Washington and confine attention to small adjustments at the margin.

CONCLUSION

My argument here is that the energy for constitutional reform is being assembled at the grassroots level of citizen action. Whether this assembly process will culminate in a political climate that would make projects of constitutional reform practical is impossible to assess at present. At the same time, it is misleading to discount altogether such grassroots ferment, or to assume that only what seems realistic at the governmental center of state power establishes political limits. Especially in a democratic society, it is the exercise of popular sovereignty that ultimately provides the basis for both governmental legitimacy and social change. Such a perspective seems appropriate here, where the old framework is rigidly confined to the old patterns despite the pressures mounted by a more interdependent and fragile world.

Without entering into detailed argument here, the reshaping of our world view has to do with both the *globalization of the common good* and, consequently, *the necessity for placing limits on governmental discretion* in the area of war and peace. In such a process of reshaping, the political culture of modernism that continues to dominate bureaucratic and institutional politics is challenged as well as its notions of unconditional statism and its confidence that reason, science, technology can preserve the common good even though political leaders act out of circumscribed laissez-faire assessments of national interest.[16]

To prepare the political ground for a Magna Carta of the nuclear age requires a continuous process of reflection on activity at the grassroots as well as analysis of the formal outcomes by the constitutional structure. The resistance of institutions to these new claims by the citizenry is not the last word. The process of political renewal at every crucial stage of the normative development of democratic practice has depended on a push-and-pull interplay between state and civil society carried on beyond the limits of routine electoral politics. The Civil Rights Movement is a recent instance of such a process on the setting of race relations. The quest by women and gay people for an economic and political order that is more receptive to their needs is being partly played out in the streets as an aspect of the quest for formal legislative acknowledgment and reform. Such a dynamic is also visible in the area of war and peace—societal pressures for normative constraint (both legal and moral) are being mounted on a largely extralegal basis with a declining show of concern about the workings of the apparatus of government, including party rivalry for control of elective office.

Here is the point. The national security consensus flowing from Washington—especially from its bureaucratic recesses of power—has successfully disciplined the formal political process, including elections and representative institutions. As a result, shifts in the degree of discretion to use force in foreign policy are not even on the agenda of mainstream politics. Two illustrations might help clarify this assertion. Despite the recurrent discrediting of covert action, its unconditional repudiation by government is never seriously discussed even by those most critical of a particular instance of excess. In the Iran-Contra hearings, for instance, the sole focus was on the degrees of presidential knowledge and on the consequence of circumventing CIA management of covert action. At no time was the issue raised as to the long-term damage done to the United States reputation as a result of covert action or even to assess particular instances as contributing, or not, to the realization of U.S. foreign policy goals. And never was the substantial question raised as to whether covert action could be reconciled with law, morality, and United States expectations about appropriate behavior of foreign governments.

A second illustration relates to the use of nuclear weapons. Apparently most Americans think that the policy of the United States is to use nuclear weapons only in retaliation against a nuclear attack, but never first. In actuality, the official doctrine in Europe and elsewhere is to retain a first-use option, and to convey such a threat. Such a crucial matter, as to whether nuclear weapons are legitimate instruments of foreign policy, has never been challenged in the course of presidential debate or even concerted congressional discussion. Again, this absence of challenge flies in the face of prudential as well as normative considerations—to reduce the risk of nuclear war.

Yet, there are citizens raising these and related questions, acting out of moral conviction and increasingly from a sense of legal right and duty. These actions are fairly widespread, but they are reported only locally, or in poorly distributed shoestring operations in the form of newsletters.[17]

The reason that these barely visible developments at the edges of the political process deserve attention is two-fold: the moral-legal coherence of their claims and the practical implications of redefining security in a more normative, less militaristic fashion. Expressing the position differently, current boundaries on political discourse as a result of the national security consensus require us to examine these claims for reform being mounted at the margin.

It is not feasible to examine here the numerous legal cases that have been decided over the past decade or so, or even to assess whether there is a gradual trend toward endowing these claims with an increased legitimacy. Suffice it to say that these cases cluster into several categories of resistance to official policy: first, resistance to various dimensions of nuclear weapons policy, especially the development and deployment of allegedly first-strike weapon systems;[18] second, resistance to covert action and forcible intervention in Third World countries; and third, resistance to policies associated with severe abuse of human rights, especially those connected with "constructive engagement" in South Africa or the return of "illegals" to Central America where they face a prospect of destitution, even persecution. What is relevant to this argument for constitutional reform is the underlying rationale which bears upon the nature of citizenship, patriotism, and the rule of law as expressed in the legal defenses mounted by defendants and their counsel.

There are two closely interconnected lines of argument in these cases that bear fundamentally on the central theme of bringing law to bear on foreign policy. The first argument empowers any citizen with the authority to oppose *on constitutional grounds* a policy that is *reasonably believed* to violate applicable treaty and customary rules of international law. In effect, each citizen has an enforceable claim to a lawful foreign policy to be processed through the courts. This claim is not a *substantive* innovation, as treaty rules of international law are already "the supreme law of the land" by virtue of Article VI, clause 2, of the Constitution, and customary rules are binding as a result of consistent Supreme Court practice. It is a procedural innovation, however, to the extent that it depends on reversing a line of judicial decisions that affirms presidential supremacy in the area of foreign affairs. Either by denying the citizen as possessed of standing, or by accepting the view that the policy in question is a "political question," the governmental obligation to uphold international law is relegated to the status of nonjusticiable issue. In effect, the presidency is given discretion to interpret the implications of applicable international law, including an option of flagrant violation. This treatment is reinforced by an implicit taboo across the whole political spectrum upon criticism of government policy on the ground that it is in violation of international law. The strength of this taboo was manifested by the absence of any call for respect of the 1986 World Court judgment calling on the U.S. government to terminate its illegal support of Contra resistance activity.

The second strand here arises from the authority of the Nuremberg Principles applied to govern the outcome of domestic legal controversy. In essence, after 1945, by prosecuting German and Japanese leaders and policymakers for their failures to uphold international law, a strong step in the direction of individual accountability was taken. Although this step has not been reinforced by internationalization (that is, an international criminal court with independent financing and enforcement), it has been received into the body of international law in an authoritative manner.[19] The Nuremberg Principles set limits on governmental actors, but they also provide a criterion for law that is outside the state and gives citizens an objective basis on which to rest claims of disobedience.

Although this kind of refusal to respect domestic law is often considered to be "civil disobedience," it rests its claims on another logic. Ever since Thoreau, the essence of civil disobedience has been to accord moral claims priority over legal claims, assuming that the moral claims are asserted non-violently. Civil disobedience calls upon citizens to honor their conscience if it conflicts with enacted law. The Nuremberg logic goes a step further. It establishes the priority of international legal claims over internal symbolic domestic legal claims. The citizen should be able, as a matter of right, to raise the question as to whether governmental conduct is in violation of international law. Such a procedural opening would compensate to a certain extent for the absence of international mechanisms of implementation. It would also reconcile the obligations to uphold international law with the statist character of world order, allowing the application of the Nuremberg Principles to be a matter of sovereign duty. Finally, the validation of the Nuremberg Principles would be a structured way of acknowledging the long-term interest possessed by all peoples in regimes of public policy that adhere to international law on matters of war and peace, thereby neutralizing tendencies of politicians to be preoccupied by consideration of short-term expediency and to be neglectful of the public good.

Citizen initiatives by way of nonviolent and symbolic action—whether trespass against official facilities to assure termination of aid to the Contras, or against CIA headquarters, or to block a train carrying Trident submarine warheads—is intended to trigger an encounter with the state that stands behind the contested policies. It is meant to be a moral and legal challenge that provokes public discussion and legal assessment in the course of judicial proceedings. The citizen activist contends that his or her action was prompted by objection to an unlawful foreign policy and is normally accompanied by offers of proof, including expert testimony to establish the reasonable basis for the belief in illegality.

The government response is one of procedural preemption, namely, that the citizen has no standing to invoke international law in relation to foreign policy, and beyond this, that the court has neither the competence nor the constitutional mandate to pass legal judgment. The disallowance of the international law argument is often reinforced in a highly contrived way by disallowing expert testimony, especially with a jury present (most judges are quite adept at listening without hearing when the occasion warrants), and by delivering jury instructions that seek to limit the assessing role to the uncontested facts of the symbolic violation of domestic law, giving the jury no space within which to return an acquittal based on the contested facts of a violation of international law.

In actuality, there are only vague precedents to validate this complex process of judicial closure, and there have already been several breaches, that is, instances where a citizen appeal to international law has been accepted as a defense in a prosecution for alleged criminal misconduct.[20] There are also indications that prosecutors have been reluctant to prosecute, juries to convict, and judges to sentence whenever the international law perspective is allowed entry. The constitutional reform needed is a legislative mandate that courts should adjudicate *substantively* whenever a defendant invokes an international law argument as a defense. Such judicial scrutiny would serve to offset some of the effects of the national security consensus that keeps challenges based on international law out of the political process. It would as well absorb into judicial practice the developments in international law over the past several decades that clarify limits on the use of force overseas and that establish human rights standards. Finally, by allowing such challenges in courts, citizens would be reempowered in a manner that would promote the revitalization of democracy and, simultaneously, promote the notion of accountability for adherence to international law at all levels of political organization. As well, the internal dynamics of adjudication would be enlivened—the courts becoming arenas for principled controversy and public education on matters of war and peace, and juries activated to serve as the conscience of the communities in settings of severe normative tension. Giving citizens the procedural basis to assert their rights to a lawful foreign policy would deepen and strengthen popular sovereignty, redressing in part the relations between state and society.

The argument of this essay is quite simple: the consistent judicial application of international law would introduce a needed check in the overall system of separatism of powers; such a check would contribute to long-term well-being, recognizing the growing practical significance of restraining uses of force overseas.[21] This development is being pioneered by small groups of individual citizens who are accepting risks of indictment and imprisonment. Giving citizens standing to raise such claims would strengthen international law in relation to national security policy and extend notions of public accountability to the domain of foreign policy, contributing both to the public good and to a needed process of adjustment at the state level.

Resistance to these claims remains overwhelming. It rests ultimately on associating sovereignty with unrestrained presidential discretion and national advantage with an unrestricted military option. To overcome this resistance will depend mainly on social struggle and only marginally on the persuasiveness of legal argument. And yet, if we look ahead to the next century, there seems little doubt that the most important contribution to the evolution of constitutional democracy at this stage would be to endow citizens with an effective right to a lawful foreign policy by way of judicial protection.

Notes

1. See generally R. Falk, *A Global Approach to National Policy*, (Cambridge MA: Harvard University Press, 1975), 146–166.

2. For an early characterization of these elements, see Jonathan Marshall, Peter Dale Scott, and Jane Hunter, *Iran-Contra Connection: Secret Teams and Covert Operations in the Reagan Era*, (Boston, MA: South End Press, 1975).

3. *Youngstown Sheet and Tube Co.* v. *Sawyer* [*The Steel Seizure Case*], 342 U.S. 579 (1952).

4. *Flast v. Cohen*, 392 U.S. 83 (1968).

5. Many of these cases are discussed in Francis Anthony Boyle, *Defending Civil Resistance Under International Law*, (Dobbs Ferry, NY: Transnational Publishers, 1987).

6. The leading decisions are collected in Leon Friedmann, ed., *The Law of War: A Documentary History*, 2 vols., (New York: Random House, 1972), esp. vol. II.

7. Compare R. Falk, "The Spirit of Thoreau in the Age of Trident," *The Agni Review* 23, 1986, 31–48.

8. Such a view is given indirect encouragement by a new current of *political* realism that has entered international legal scholarship here in the United States in recent years. See, for example, Thomas M. Franck, *Judging the World Court*, (New York: Priority Press Publications, 1986).

9. Powerfully depicted in Mary Kaldor, "The Imaginary War," in Dan Smith and E.P. Thompson, eds., *Prospectus for a Habitable Planet*, (Middlesex, England: Penguin, 1987,) 72–99.

10. See generally Louis Henkin, *Foreign Affairs and the Constitution*, (New York: Norton, 1972).

11. "The courts, despite sometimes misguided efforts to compel them to do so (as on Vietnam), are not likely to step into intense confrontations between President and the Congress, or inhibit either when the other does not object." Ibid., 274–75.

12. Ibid., 278.

13. *United States v. Curtiss-Wright Export Corp.*, 299 U.S. 304 (1936).

14. Cf Congressional Hearings, May 5–Aug 3, 1987.

15. For example, see Thomas M. Franck and Michael J. Glennon, *Foreign Relations and National Security Law*, (St. Paul, MI: West Publishing Co., 1987), 38–39, and 39–43.

16. I have made an effort to depict this path in an unpublished paper entitled "The Postmodern Possibility."

17. For example, *Ground Zero* (Bangor, Wash.): *Year One* (Jonah House, Baltimore, Md.), *The Nuclear Resister* (Tucson, Arizona).

18. Compare Robert Aldridge, *First-Strike!*, (Boston, MA: South End Press, 1982).

19. See Falk, *A Global Approach to National Policy* 146–166.

20. Well-discussed by Boyle, *Defending Civil Resistance*.

21. Such a legal acknowledgment would reinforce the declining utility of military force as a source of political leverage. This development partly registers the impact of the nuclear stalemate on international politics and partly the rising resistance capabilities associated with the sort of mobilization generated by Third World nationalism.

12

The Taming of the Technological Imperative: Constitutionalism in the Twenty-First Century

Rosemarie Tong

Tong's main focus is on the challenges to the Constitution posed by some advanced technologies. After a pithy description of these technologies, she assesses some views which claim that as First Amendment protections are gradually diminishing, the increasing weakness of the Constitution becomes more apparent. Tong argues in a "loose constructionist" vein that the Constitution can be interpreted in a way which adapts constitutional values of individual freedom, justice, and security to a world never imagined by the framers of the Constitution.

The United States Constitution has enjoyed unprecedented longevity and has served as a model for the constitutions of many other nations for two hundred years. For some of us the Constitution is a nearly sacred text: a Bible of sorts that needs no real improvement. Recent adjustments or appendages thereto are regarded as largely decorative. For others of us the Constitution is more akin to a rough draft on how to balance the values of freedom, justice, and security,[1] an evolving document that must be continually interpreted and amended if it is to go on serving a changed and changing citizenry. And, though the reality of the Constitution is probably somewhere in between the extreme of the "sacred text" and the "rough draft" theories, those who view the Constitution as evolving apparently do have history on their side. Repeatedly, the Constitution has expanded in response to political movements, economic crisis, and especially social trends.

We have been blessed, it seems, with a set of sovereign principles from which all manner and fashion of ancillary rules can be drawn as we need them.

Although this happy thought of unending Constitutional bounty may lull the sanguine among us to contented sleep, the question arises, is it possible that at some point our nation as a whole may grow so fundamentally different from what it was in 1787, and so far in spirit from the imagination of the Founding Fathers, that we may no longer be able to derive from the Constitution the rules we need to govern ourselves? Is the Constitution elastic enough to withstand the strains exerted on it by modernity? Is modernity outstripping the Constitution, rendering it impotent? If so, is there anything we can do to prepare for the moment when the law of the land grows too old—too behind the times—to govern us?

Although there are many directions from which we could approach the ability of the Constitution to withstand the assault of modernity, my focus will be on its ability—if it is indeed an ability—to meet the specific challenges posed by technology. Admittedly, this is not an entirely new concern. Already in the midnineteeth century, constitutional questions were being raised by the advent of technology. The growth of the railroad generated a host of issues, including problems of monopolies, interstate commerce, and safety and work regulations. No sooner had the Constitution set the railroad on the right track than the telegraph and telephone, and shortly thereafter the radio and television, tested its ability to accommodate not only enormously useful but also extraordinarily unwieldly vehicles of communication.

But while the challenge of technology is not a new concern, it is a broadening and deepening concern. Technologies are increasing not only in number but in kind. Specifically, developments in the areas of electronic communications, genetic engineering, and reproductive technology have the potential to fundamentally change our lives and our society. As we shall see, these developments require us to balance our traditional values of freedom, justice, and security against one another in novel ways and to reconsider the limit of our rights and the extent of our duties as people who have private as well as public lives. My purpose, therefore, is to discern whether the Constitution, as it now exists and is interpreted, is able to help us live in a world that is changing us even as we change it. Is the Constitution a machine-aged manual for a space-aged people or is it a document that, for some blessed reason or another, still has the capacity to transcend the contingencies of space and time in ways that bind us, many and diverse individuals, into a nation that can rightly describe itself as "one"?

THE CHALLENGES POSED TO THE CONSTITUTION BY THE NEW ELECTRONIC COMMUNICATIONS TECHNOLOGIES

Ithiel de Sola Pool, in his book *Technologies of Freedom,* describes the inconsistent and ill-informed manner in which government has historically responded to new technological developments in general and to new communications technologies in particular. He begins by wondering "how the clear intent of the Constitution, so well and strictly enforced in the domain of print, has been so neglected in the electronic revolution."[2] He traces the development of a "trifurcated" communications system, each part patterned after older technologies, usually inappropriately so.[3] His first model is the print model, based on newspapers, which existed at the time of the Bill of Rights. Print communication has traditionally enjoyed the greatest protection of the First Amendment, and so have other modes of communication based on the print model. Despite the fact that recent surveys indicate that 61 percent of us believe that freedom of the press means that the public has the right to hear all points of view, while only 23 percent of us believe that freedom of the press means that the press can report what it chooses,[4] our courts continue to insist that the First Amendment's guarantee of a free press embodies *equally* the two correlative goals of freeing publishers from government censorship[5] and exposing the public to diverse and robust communication.[6]

Pool's second tier of communications model is that of the common carrier defined as an individual or organization that offers itself as available for hire to the public, that transmits whatever information a person chooses to transmit, and that bases all of its policies and practices on nondiscriminatory factors, serving all members of the public indifferently.[7] Since the telegraph and telephone are classified as common carriers, their rates, for example, are subjected to strict government regulation on the grounds that since we all need the telegraph or telephone to transact our private and public business, access to these technologies must be both universal and fair. Curiously, American telegraphy is not subject to postal law but to railroad law on the theory that "telegraph companies resemble railroad companies and other common carriers, in that they are instruments of commerce."[8] In other words, like the railroad, the telegraph is a vehicle that transmits verbal packages across the country in much the same way that the railroad transmits more tangible objects of commerce across country. Similarly, since the telephone is regarded as the telegraph's successor, it is subjected to telegraph law and, therefore indirectly to railroad law. Of course, the problem with assimilating technologies like the telegraph and telephone to railroad rather than postal law is that it obscures the fact that these technologies are *communications* technologies. To view the telegraph and telephone as common carriers no different from the railroad is, among other things, to remove them from liability for message content. Unlike the press representative or broadcaster who is expected to screen transmission content for libelous, slanderous or obscene utterances, telegraph and telephone operators and companies are not similarly responsible on the grounds that, as common carriers, they may not base decisions regarding message transmission on the identity of the customer or the content of the message.

The third model Pool considers is that of broadcasting—radio and television. Of all the communications technologies, broadcasting technologies have been the most strenuously regulated on the grounds that without such regulation, the public's right to receive published materials would be seriously jeopardized. Because of the scarcity of radio frequencies in the 1930s, and because of later court decisions that valorized the public's right to receive suitable access to social, political, aesthetic, moral, and other ideas or experiences over broadcasters' right to publish,[9] broadcasters have been subjected to regulations such as the Fairness Doctrine.[10] They have also been required to give political candidates equal access to their media,[11] to ascertain what the community needs in the way of information,[12] and to present controversial public interest programming.[13] Even though spectrum scarcity is, with the advent of cable and satellite technology, clearly a myth rather than a reality,[14] and even though broadcasters complain, for example, that "instead of encouraging enlightening discussion of matters of public interest, the Fairness Doctrine provides a crutch for the kind of journalism that can be described as, at best, terminally bland,"[15] the courts continue to draw distinctions that no longer seem to make a difference between the press and broadcasting. Specifically, newspaper publishers are allowed to editorialize to their hearts' content,[16] while broadcasters are required to be considerably more objective as they supposedly struggle to remain neutral between competing versions of the truth.[17]

This trifurcated approach to communications technology makes no sense to Pool who would have all communications technologies be treated like the press.[18] As he sees it, the current ad hoc approach to communications technology owes its irrationality to the fact that courts and legislators have repeatedly failed to understand the nature and function of these technologies. In particular, they have failed to understand that what the press, the telegraph, the telephone, radio, television, and now the cable and the computer have in common is that they are all extensions of our minds and mouths—that is, means of communication or expression. Within a relatively short period of time, however, judges and legislators will not be able to persist in this misunderstanding because we are beginning to see a convergence of all modes of communications, a coming together which thwarts any attempt to make neat distinctions among models of communication whose "samenesses" far outweigh their differences. Today, for example, a newspaper story can be sent over a telegraph wire, or sent from a faraway location over a telephone hookup to the newspaper's mainframe computer via use of a modem. Thus, the distinction between the press and common carriers breaks down. Similarly, the distinction between the press and broadcasting breaks down as the number of independent presses shrinks[19] and the number of spectrums increases.

The question, then, is to determine precisely what the First Amendment protects. Clearly, the First Amendment was written at a time when newspapers were the preeminent means of communicating news to the general populace. Thus, newspaper publishers were guaranteed freedom for their presses so that citizens could be relatively certain that the presses serving them were communicating to them not some sort of standard party line but a distinctively articulated, honest *perspective* on the truth. But when the "press" is no longer a printing press, but a microchip, a telephone cable, a satellite transmission, is there any less reason to guarantee the human beings behind these technologies the constitutional protections of free expression that safeguarded their ancestors? Pool worries that our imaginations are so limited that we may fail to recognize that the press is continually assuming new forms.[20] In other words, Pool is concerned that our understanding of the press may be too literal. We need to understand the press not as a particular machine, suggests Pool, but, more abstractly, as any instrument that communicates to the public the information they need to function as an intelligent citizenry.

It seems clear that Pool's worries about literalism are not unwarranted. Recently, a collection of ethnic, racial and other jokes offensive to specific groups, put into a computer by University of Michigan students, provoked debate over freedom of speech and computer ethics and etiquette. Under pressure from university officials who claimed that such "jokes" are inappropriate on a campus troubled by racial tensions, the computer joke file was shut down by the student who started it. The freeze generated questions about a relatively new medium that allows subscribers to communicate with one another on an electronic bulletin board available to them.[21] If electronic bulletin boards are akin to the press, then their users should be accorded the same First Amendment protections that press users are. However, if electronic bulletin boards are regarded as common carriers, or as a means of broadcasting, or simply as some sort of "game," then their users' First Amendment protections are either tenuous or nonexistent. Significantly, users of electronic bulletin boards seem to believe that their favored mode of communication ought to be better protected than even the press is. In point of fact, the creator of the University of Michigan's joke file observed that his "system was designed to be wide open and not have the technology enforce social values."[22] The implication of this statement is that "anything goes" on an electronic bulletin board—that if there is any "place" that speech should be totally free it is on an electronic bulletin board that is accessible only to those who subscribe to its services.

What we see in the case of electronic communications technology, therefore, is not a failure in the principles of the Constitution but a failure in the application of adequate First Amendment protection to communications technologies other than the printing press. William E. Lee draws a parallel between some lawmakers' inability to recognize cable and electronic publishing as the newspapers of the twenty-first century and Thomas Kuhn's "concept of scientific paradigms or shared perceptions of phenomena wherein new scientific theories are often resisted, not because of their merits, but because they conflict with the accepted paradigms."[23] As Lee sees it, those who would restrict cable are operating with a paradigm that treats cable like broadcasting. So strong is this paradigm, that it effectively prevents these people from recognizing that cable is not like broadcasting but like the press.[24]

Their desire to limit the application of First Amendment protections further limits the ability of these critics to see cable for what it is. Their fear seems to be that we have enough free speech the way it is. Lee, however, is not of the opinion that speech is one of those good things that we can get enough of. Thus, he hopes that the forces of restriction will take their blinders off long enough to see that all communications technologies—the press, telephone, telegraph, radio, television, cables, electronic bulletin boards—should be located in their proper place, that is the realm of free speech. As Lee sees it, all the distinctions that have been drawn between and among these communications technologies have given the government too much control over speech. Says Lee,

> We must think in terms of government action, impermissible with all media, rather then categories of media; our hostility toward government restrictions should not diminish because of the medium invoked.[25]

Thus, our failure to understand what essential characteristics communication technologies have in common is troublesome in at least two respects: (1) it reveals our technological illiteracy—our increasing inability to correctly classify the things we make according to their nature and function, and (2) it shows how this lack of technological knowledge leads to a lack of political power since citizens who are not able to make an intelligent case for subsuming all communications technologies into the press model are probably going to experience a contraction rather than an expansion of their speech rights.

THE CHALLENGES POSED TO THE CONSTITUTION BY GENETIC EXPERIMENTATION

Another technology that requires us to stretch the constitution beyond the limits of the space and time in which it was written is genetic engineering. In his book, *Cloning and the Constitution,* Ira H. Carmen seeks to find the "parameters" of the Constitution with regard to science. Viewing the Constitution as a "living" document, he seeks "*constitutional values,*" by which he means "not only explicit standards of right and duty enunciated in our fundamental law and in judicial opinion, but also the functional rules, actions, and expectations undergirding our body politic."[26] In the same way that

Pool and others seek to define the proper relationship between government and the communications technologies, Carmen seeks to elucidate the proper relationship between government and several new scientific technologies. Although Carmen is writing about genetic experimentation in particular—the kind of experimentation which involves the recombination of DNA molecules—much of what he says with regard to the experimenter's freedom of expression protections is clearly applicable to scientific experimentation in general.

As Carmen points out, the word "science" appears only once in the Constitution, in Article I, Section 8, in which Congress is given the authority to grant patents, and to execute legislation needed to carry out this authority.[27] Although this authority clearly gives Congress the right to exercise some influence in the sphere of scientific experimentation, it implies little about the government's role in regulating the practice of science or scientific experimentation. Nevertheless, government has traditionally played an active role in the support and perpetuation of science-related activities. For one, scientific developments were seen as a positive good in the Age of Enlightenment, a logical outgrowth of the practice of Reason. In fact, a number of the Founding Fathers themselves were practicing scientists, most notably Thomas Jefferson and Benjamin Franklin. The exercise of science for them was seen as just another form of expression in the free marketplace of ideas. And their scientific outlook contained no small element of faith in science both for its theoretical value as truth—science could increase our knowledge—and for its practical value as utility—science could bring about a better life. But, as the numbers and kinds of scientific experiments that have been undertaken in the development of electronic communications technology, could not have been anticipated by the Founding Fathers—neither could the constitutional questions they would generate.

For example, when the first United States patent law was passed in 1790 protecting the invention of "any useful art, manufacture, engine, machine or device, or any improvement thereon not before known or used,"[28] it is unlikely that the Founding Fathers had in mind anything other than the protection of inanimate items of manufacture. Nevertheless, in 1930, Congress voted to approve the patenting of new plant varieties produced by grafts, cuttings, or other asexual methods. Approximately fifty years later the Supreme Court took the next step and ruled that patent law would also apply to genetically engineered microorganisms, such as a new strain of bacteria designed to eat up oil spills.[29] Finally, and most recently, the United States Patent Office seems to have taken the biggest step of them all, announcing that it "considers non-naturally occurring nonhuman multicellular living organisms, including animals, to be patentable subject matter."[30]

Although the decision to patent animals as well as microorganisms, plants, and things was regarded by some commentators simply as an incremental move to keep abreast of advances in science, to some people it seemed more like a plunge into the dark, a Faustian trip from which humanity might never return. These critics maintained that it is not only quite one thing to patent nonsentient things like plants and quite another to patent sentient creatures like animals,[31] but it is also God's job not ours to stock Noah's ark. Other critics feared that patenting new kinds of animals was simply the prologue to patenting new kinds of genetically altered human beings, despite the fact that the Patent Office statement confined itself to *nonhuman* life. Clearly, the hullabaloo is not so much about patent law, but about the limits of scientific progress. As children of the Enlightenment, the Founding Fathers had little reason to consider limiting scientific experimentation. As children of the Apocalypse—of Chernobyl, Three Mile Island, and other technological disasters—we are ready to consider such limitations simply because we fear that some of the changes we make may turn out to be not only infelicitous but irreversible.

Upon first reflection, those who would let scientists do pretty much as they please, in the privacy of their laboratories, seem to have the better case. Stephen Carter draws attention to an argument many scientists typically use to defend the view that scientific *experimentation* deserves the same level of First Amendment protection that is accorded to scientific *speech:*

> (1) Scientific speech (as opposed to scientific experiment) is entitled to a heavy degree of First Amendment protection.
> (2) If a form of speech is protected, then that which is a necessary prerequisite to it is protected.
> (3) Scientific experiment is a necessary prerequisite to scientific speech, since without the testing of hypotheses, a scientist is engaging in no more than semi-informed speculation, which is not the same as scientific speech. In other words, without scientific experiment, scientific speech is not possible.
> (4) Therefore, scientific speech is protected.[32]

But even though this argument sounds good, in Carter's opinion it is assailable at every point. First, Carter points out that there are *no* decisions holding that scientific speech is indeed covered by the First Amendment.[33] Second, it is, says Carter, not the case that simply because a form of speech is protected, then that which is its necessary prerequisite is also protected. For example, in *Houchins v. KQED*,[34] the court ruled that news *gathering* is not protected merely because news *reporting* is. Comments Carter:

> For example, the First Amendment undoubtedly protects the right of a newspaper to publish the minutes of a secret White House meeting at which sabotage of political opponents is discussed. But would the Amendment save from prosecution a reporter who was arrested breaking into the Oval Office to look for those minutes? Quite clearly it would not.[35]

Third, Carter thinks that scientific inquiry, understood as hypothesis-experiment-observation-hypothesis, is not always a prerequisite to scientific speech.[36] There are, believes Carter, other ways to achieve scientific knowledge than through the experimental method to which most western scientists subscribe. Since "arm-chair," nonexperimental science still has some virtues, it is not certain that scientific experimentation is indeed *necessary* for scientific speech.

To be sure, not everyone shares Carter's views. Ira Carmen believes, for example, that scientific experimentation should be as well-protected as scientific speech, though he admits that our courts find it difficult to conceive of scientific experimentation as speech. As Carmen sees it, our courts have always tried to draw neat and tidy distinctions between speech and action. But, says Carmen, traditional speech-action distinctions are becoming increasingly blurred, "A Jehovah's Witness parade is action, but it is also expression; picketing is economic coercion, but it also informs the public about labor grievances."[37] More and more, courtwatchers are observing the growth of so-called "speech plus" or quasi speech.

These arguments are surfacing everywhere. For example, they surface in Catharine MacKinnon's antipornography arguments at those points when she argues that pornography is not only speech but action against women. She asks:

> which is saying "kill" to a trained guard dog, a word or an act? Which is its training? How about a sign that reads "whites only"? Is that the idea or practice of segregation? Is a woman raped by an attitude or a behavior?[38]
> ... under conditions of male dominance, pornography hides and distorts truth while at the same time enforcing itself, imprinting itself on the world, making itself real. That's another way in which pornography *is* a kind of act.[39]

Carmen believes that if freedom of expression embraces not only uttered and scribbled words but the ideas, attitudes, values and emotions behind them, then the exposition of scientific ideas embraces scientific experimentation without which scientists cannot test and substantiate their ideas.[40]

One point that Carmen does not make since it would complicate and perhaps even undermine his argument is the following. If the speech-action distinction is more arbitrary than we have been led to believe, why should we feel compelled to assimilate "action" into speech rather than "speech" into action? In the past, we may have regarded a "Whites Only" sign as speech and accorded to it all the protections we typically reserve for speech, but perhaps we should now regard such signs as action and accord to them only the protection we typically give to action. Similarly, in the past we regarded scientific treatises as speech, but if some of these treatises are more like action than speech in that the technological imperatives embedded within them are akin to performative utterances that need only to be spoken to take immediate effect, then perhaps we should burden these treatises with the same restraints that we ordinarily attach to action. Of course, when Carmen is discussing the ambiguous nature of the speech or action distinction, it is his intent to assimilate scientific action (experimentation) into scientific speech, but we should give some pause to the implications of running the causal arrow in the other direction—that is, to assimilating scientific speech to scientific action.

Even though Carmen does not choose to argue that speech can be regarded as action, in the same degree that action can be regarded as speech, he does choose to reintroduce the speech-act distinction in later chapters of his book precisely because he is aware that some experiments are much more like action than speech even if many of them are really more akin to speech than to action. Conceding that nuclear physicists do not have a constitutional right to detonate atomic weapons in search of unknown chemical elements, Carmen draws a distiction between basic research (inquiry hence speech) and applied research (technology hence action). As he sees it, it is constitutionally permissible, for example, to subject cloning to state proscriptions, when necessary and proper if it is used "essentially" as "a means for intentionally producing that . . . utility," and even if it is constitutionally impermissable to subject cloning to the same kind of state proscriptions as "essentially a 'way of knowing.'"[41]

Although Carmen does not dismiss this last question as "nitpicking," he does believe that, thanks to Thomas Emerson's "preponderance test," it is relatively easy to make inquiry–technology distinctions. Emerson's test, says Carmen, was advanced for the purpose of distinguishing betwen quasi speech falling within First Amendment coverage and quasi speech falling outside constitutional bounds. If speech is the preponderant (primary) element in a speech-action hybrid, it counts as speech. But if action in its preponderant (secondary) element is a speech-action hybrid, it counts as action. Thus, according to Emerson, draft card destruction for the purpose of conveying outrage over American military involvement in Vietnam is more like speech than action, while political assassination, despite its unambiguous message, is more like action than speech. Analogously, according to Carmen, "inversion bubble" cloning experiments—the primary purpose of which is to extend our scientific knowledge pure and simple—are more like speech than action, whereas Chakrabarty's cloning experiments—the sole purpose of which was to create a marketable bacterium capable of cleaning up the environment—are more like action than speech.[42]

Of course, we can see what the problem is with Carmen's distinction. If Carmen's approach is followed, lawmakers who, on the average, do not have the kind of scientific and technological knowledge that enables Carmen to draw his distinctions between kinds of cloning experiments, will have to rely on scientists, most of whom have a vested interest in regarding scientific experimentation as *speech* rather than as *action,* to make these distinctions for them. However, as it so happens, many lawmakers—like many citizens—do not trust scientists enough to permit them to get involved in the legislative process. This is why Stephen Carter believes that scientists are not likely to gain First Amendment protection for *any* of their experiments—even the ones that are preponderantly speech—unless they regain the public trust.[43] As a result of several scientific experiments that have decreased our ability to live safely and securely, the public has become increasingly fearful that scientists are ready, willing, and able to strike Faustian deals in the name of the pursuit of knowledge even if they send not only themselves but everyone else towards the kind of hell only humans have thought to manufacture.

What makes this state of affairs even more troublesome is that the public's fears are not always rational or informed. It is one thing to limit scientific experimentation when one's fears about its potential hazards are well-founded; but it is quite another to block scientific progress for no *good* reason. Interestingly, although Carter concedes that many of the public's fears about recombinant DNA research, for example, are indeed irrational and uninformed, he maintains that scientists have to address "the reality," not "the rationality," of these fears:

> To dismiss such politically relevant characteristic . . . To dismiss such concerns as uninformed quite misses the point: The fears may exist because an adequately informed public differs with the scientific community either in moral judgment or in predictions about the future. In either event, the policy question surely is not whether the fears are sensible or not, but what to do about them.[44]

Carter goes on to suggest that scientists can regain the public's trust through public education and self-restraint. But his bias is evident—he places the burden of proof upon the scientists themselves. This may be a wise move as far as public relations is concerned, but First Amendment rights are not supposed to be earned. They are a starting point, a given. While it certainly may be true that scientists would benefit from a more friendly public image of concern regarding safety, any suggestion that scientists are obligated to prove their value in some way smacks of prior restraint. Thus we see that when it comes to scientific experimentation, the definitional issue of whether experimentation is more like action than speech or vice versa is not likely to be decided so much in the abstract as in the concrete particularly of the community's hopes for or, more especially today, fears about science.

THE CHALLENGES POSED TO THE CONSTITUTION BY THE NEW REPRODUCTIVE TECHNOLOGIES

Like genetic experimentation, the new reproductive technologies pose complex constitutional questions. When we speak of the "new" reproductive technologies, we are speaking of some relatively old technologies like artificial insemination by donor as well as about the genuinely new techniques of *in vitro* fertilization, embryo transfer, embryo freezing, and so on. All of these technologies involve deviations from the "natural" way to reproduce and all of them raise questions not only about our relatively new right to privacy as related to procreation and, in particular, to the question whether our fundamental right to reproduce protects our freedom to reproduce not only *when* we want to and *with whom* we want to, but also *how* we want to—"naturally" or "artifically."

Although only one state, Illinois, has enacted legislation or promulgated regulations directly governing human *in vitro* fertilization (IVF) and/or embryo transfer (ET), existing laws on (1) artificial insemination and (2) research involving human fetuses suggest ways in which IVF legislation could be constructed in the future. Were laws banning IVF passed, however, they would probably be challenged on constitutional grounds. Indeed, it has been so challenged in Illinois where the new legislation sought simply to regulate rather than to ban IVF. Illinois legislators decided in 1979 to make any doctor who undertakes an IVF procedure the legal custodian of the embryo—and liable for possible prosecution under an 1877 law against child abuse. As a result, many Illinois doctors decided not to practice IVF, although the state attorney general assured them that most simple IVF procedures would not violate the statute. Concerned about the chilling effect of the statute on these doctors, one couple challenged the Illinois attempt at regulation as unconstitutional. Their class action argues that such restrictions violate their fundamental right of privacy, which includes an individual's right, without unjustified state interference, to make decisions relating to marriage, procreation, contraception, abortion, family relationships, child rearing, and "the decision whether or not to bear or beget a child."[45] On the one hand, should the couple's class action succeed, then Illinois would have to show that anti-IVF legislation is not only necessary to protect a "compelling state interest" but that it is not an excessive means to do so. On the other hand, should the couple's class action fail, then Illinois would need only to demonstrate that its anti-IVF legislation is "rationally related" to a constitutionally permissible purpose it chooses to pursue.[46]

No matter the fate of the Illinois couple's specific challenge, any general argument for a constitutional right to reproduce by means of *in vitro* fertilization does indeed rest on the right to privacy as related to the right to procreate, the right to marital privacy, and the right to bear and beget a child. In *Skinner v. Oklahoma* (1942), a case striking down Oklahoma's Habitual Criminal Sterilization Act, the Supreme Court held that individuals have the right to be free from unwarranted governmental interference with procreative capabilities. In this case the State of Oklahoma demanded that Skinner submit to a vasectomy on the grounds that he was a triple felon—once he had stolen some chickens and twice he had committed robbery with firearms. The Supreme Court reasoned that Oklahoma did not have a "compelling state interest" sufficient to forever deprive Skinner of a "basic liberty," namely, the right to procreate.[47] Just because a person stole some chickens once and because he robbed two stores for food does not entitle the state to deprive him of his capability to procreate unless to argue the ridiculous, the state can prove (1) that chicken stealing genes, for example, are passed on from generation to generation and (2) that chicken stealing is a particularly harmful kind of crime. A second constitutionally protected area is the privacy of the marital relationship. In *Griswold v. Connecticut* (1965), the Supreme Court struck down the conviction of a doctor and a Planned Parenthood director who had been convicted under a Connecticut law banning not only the use of contraceptives by married couples but also the "aiding and abetting" of their use.[48] The Court reasoned that although the Constitution does not explicitly forbid state interference in family relations, it does suggest that such implicits rights as the right to marry and raise a family are on a par with explicitly protected rights like that of free speech.[49] In other words, if we protect free speech, or expression, because without it our self-identity is in jeopardy, then surely, if our identity matters to us, our right to link one's self with the self of another person and to decide with him or her whether to perpetuate one's self through procreation is just as vital a right as the right to free speech. A third right—the right for unmarried as well as married individuals to decide whether to bear or beget a child was recognized by the Supreme Court in *Eisenstadt v. Baird* (1972) and *Carey v. Population Services International* (1977) when, as an extension of *Griswold*, it reasoned that all citizens, married or not, have a right to privacy when it comes to clearly personal matters like the decision whether to bear or beget a child.[50]

In light of these court cases, proponents of IVF, assuming the stance of broad contructionists, could argue that since *Skinner* regards the ability to procreate as a fundamental human good, then infertile individuals have a right to use whatever reproductive technologies will make them fertile; that since *Griswold* encompasses a married couple's decision to use contraceptive means not to conceive a child, it also encompasses their decision to use reproductive technologies to conceive a child; and that since *Eisenstadt* and *Carey* regard as personal and private any individual's decision to bear or not to bear, to beget or not to beget, they must also regard as personal and private any individual's decision about *how* to begin or end a pregnancy. Opponents of IVF, assuming the stance of strict constructionists, could argue that *Skinner* establishes only that the State may not make infertile a fertile person and not also that the State may not regulate an infertile person's attempt to make himself or herself fertile; that *Griswold* establishes only a married couple's right to use contraceptives to prevent conception and not also their "right" to use available reproductive technologies to cause conception; and that *Eisenstadt* and *Carey* regard as personal and private only procreative decisions that involve the act of sexual intercourse and not also procreative decisions that involve "acts" of AID, IVF, and so on.

Chances are that even a broad reading of cases like *Skinner, Griswold, Eisenstadt,* and *Carey* would find arguments for the right to IVF most cogent in situations which involve use of IVF (1) by a husband and wife when (2) the ovum and sperm are donated by the husband and wife, (3) the embryo is implanted in the wife, and (4) procreation by the couple is impossible without resorting to IVF. Where there is absence of marriage, of a genetic link, of a gestational link, or of necessity, the case may be somewhat weakened. Thus, an unmarried, fertile homosexual man, who wished to transfer an embryo fertilized *in vitro* from his sperm and a donor's egg to the womb of a surrogate mother, would have difficulty establishing that his right to privacy encompasses his decision to father a child by such means. In the case of such a man, opponents to his request would probably argue that in the same way that any purported fundamental right to life-sustaining food does not necessarily support a right to foods like caviar, morels, and truffles, the fundamental right to bear and beget probably encompasses access only to those means of procreation without which the individual would necessarily, rather than as a matter of choice, remain childless. Moreover, it is not even clear that there is such a constitutional right to procreate. The plausibility of a right to procreate may rest on the fact that having children and being parents appears as such a central part of many people's lives. However, an argument from "x is central to people's life plans" to "there is a natural right to x" cannot be based merely on the fact that most people want children. Even if most people have an interest in procreating, that interest has to be balanced against the harm that future people may pose to present people as well as the harm that may be done to these future people who, after all, will be brought into existence, like all human beings, without being consulted.

CONCLUSION

Technology is putting enormous strains on the Constitution in the sense that it is challenging courts, legislators, and ordinary citizens to rethink many of the distinctions with which constitutional law has operated for two hundred years. This is most clear in the area of communications technology where we are asked to assimilate telephones, telegraphs, radios, televisions, cables, and computers into the press paradigm, and in the area of genetic experimentation where we are asked to reconceive, among other distinctions, the speech-act distinction. Technology is also forcing us to reconsider very seriously the limits of our rights, a reconsideration that is also encourged by the sociological phenomenon that goes under names like "diversity," "variety," and "plurality," and by philosophical positions that see the private merging into the public in a manner and fashion that causes us to doubt whether our purported privacy rights are nearly as "absolute" as we once believed.

When it comes to technology, interpreters of the Constitution need to be courageous—that is, they need to avoid the defect of timidity and the excess of foolhardiness. One way to respond to the challenge of technology is to err on the side of caution, to insist on the old paradigms even if the new technologies do not fit them. Such caution results in decisions like the one to fit the telegraph into the Procrustean bed of the railroad. Another way to meet the demands of technology is to err on the side of enthusiasm, to be so hospitable to the untried and untested that one finds in the penumbra of the Constitution all manner and fashion of rights that give to scientists the "full steam ahead" signal and to ordinary citizens the sense that if something is both possible and desirable, then they have a right to it. A third and preferred way to respond to technology is for judges, legislators, and citizens to become as technologically literate as possible, so that we "discover" in the Constitution only those implicit interests and rights that are really hiding between its lines to help us not only survive but also to thrive in a world the Founding Fathers never imagined.

Technology is a mighty force but it seems to have found its match in a Constitution that is able to respond to its imperatives, at least for the time being. But even if the Constitution is *able* to achieve this feat, it is not really ready or willing to do so unless we the people carefully take its interpretation into our own hands. The Constitution is as "living" as the people it rules—and so, if we want to know whether the Constitution has technology "under control," a good place to find the beginnings of an answer is in our own homes. Technology will not outstrip the Constitution unless we let it.

Notes

1. Daniel Callahan, *Ethics and Population Limitation,* An Occasional Paper of the Population Council (Philadelphia, PA: Wm. F. Fell Company, 1971), 13–14.

2. Ithiel de Sola Pool, *Technologies of Freedom,* (Cambridge, MA: Belknap Press, 1983), 3.

3. Ibid., 2–4.

4. "Freedom and Fairness: Regulating the Mass Media," in *Report from the Center for Philosophy and Public Policy,* 6, no. 4 QQ: (Fall, 1986): 2.

5. *Young v. American Mini Theaters, Inc.,* 427 U.S. 50, 76 (1976).

6. *Virginia State Bd. of Pharmacy v. Virginia Citizens Consumer Council, Inc.* 425 U.S. 748,756 (1976).

7. *National Association of Regulatory Utility Commissioners v. FCC* (NARUC I), 525 F. 2d 630 (D.C. Cir.), *cert. denied,* 425,U.S. 992 (1976) (NARUC I).

8. Pool, *Technologies of Freedom,* 95–96.

9. *Red Lion Broadcasting Co., v. FCC,* 395 U.S. 367 (1969).

10. 47 U.S.C. 315(a) (1982).

11. 47 C.F.R. 73.1940 (1984).

12. Report and Statement of Policy Re: Commission *en banc* Programming Inquiry, 22 *Rad. Reg.* (P&F) 1901, 1912 (1960).

13. 47 C.F.R. 73.1910 (1984).

14. Lynn Becker, "Electronic Publishing: First Amendment Issues in the Twenty-First Century," 13 *Fordham Urban Law Journal* (1985): 866.

15. "Freedom and Fairness: Regulating the Mass Media," 5.

16. *Miami Herald Publishing Co. v. Tornillo,* 1974. 418 U.S. 241,94 S.CT. 2831, 41 L. Ed. 2d 730.

17. *Red Lion Broadcasting Co., v. FCC,* 395 U.S. 367 (1969).

18. Pool, *Technologies of Freedom,* 8.

19. Pool, *Technologies of Freedom,* 8.

20. "Twenty corporations control more than half the 61 million daily newspapers sold every day; twenty corporations control more than half the revenues of the country's 11,000 magazines; three corporations control most of the revenues and audience in television, ten corporations in radio, eleven corporations in all kinds of books, and four corporations in motion pictures." "Freedom and Fairness: Regulating the Mass Media," 22.

21. Isabel Wilkerson, "Ethnic Jokes in Campus Computer Prompt Debate," *New York Times* (Saturday, 18 April 1987).

22. Ibid. Quote of Dr. Robert Pasner.

23. William E. Lee, "Cable Leased Access and the Conflict Among First Amendment Rights and First Amendment Values," 35, no. 3 *Emory Law Journal* (Summer 1986): 618.

24. Ibid.

25. Ibid., 618–619.

26. Ira H. Carmen, *Cloning and the Constitution* (Madison, WI: University of Wisconsin Press, 1985), xiv.

27. Ibid., 4.

28. Claudia Wallis, "Should Animals be Patented?" *Time* (4 May 1987): 110.

29. Ibid.

30. Ibid.

31. Ibid.

32. Stephen L. Carter, "The Bellman, the Snark, and the Biohazard Debate," 3 *Yale Law and Policy Review* (Spring 1985): 368–369.

33. Ibid., 370.

34. *Houchins v. KQED,* 438 U.S. 1 (1978).

35. Carter, "The Bellman, the Snark and the Biohazard Debate," 374.

36. Ibid., 376.

37. Ira H. Carmen, *Cloning and the Constitution,* 38.

38. Catharine A. MacKinnon, *Feminism Unmodified* (Cambridge, MA: Harvard University Press, 1987), 156.

39. Ibid., 138.

40. Carmen, *Cloning and the Consitution,* 4.

41. Ibid., 46.

42. Ibid., 47.

43. Carter, "The Bellman, the Snark, and the Biohazard Debate," 386.

44. Ibid., 388–389.

45. *Carey v. Population Services International,* 431 U.S. at 687 (1977); *Eisenstadt v. Baird,* 405 U.S. at 453 (1972).

46. Dennis M. Flannery et al., "Legal Issues Concerning *In Vitro* Fertilization," in Appendix: *HEW Support of Research Involving Human In Vitro Fertilization and Embryo Transfer* (Washington D.C.: U.S. Government Printing Office, 1979), 35–36 in Section 18.

47. *Skinner v. Oklahoma,* 316 U.S. 541 (1942).

48. *Griswold v. Connecticut,* 381 U.S. 480 (1965).

49. Ibid., 495–96.

50. *Carey v. Population Services International,* 431 U.S. 453 (1977).

Afterword: Constitutionalism, Moral Skepticism, and Religious Belief

Jeffrie G. Murphy

As things now stand, everything is up for grabs.
Nevertheless:
Napalming babies is bad.
Starving the poor is wicked.
Buying and selling each other is depraved.
Those who stood up to and died resisting Hitler,
Stalin, Amin, and Pol Pot—and General Custer too—have
earned salvation.
Those who acquiesced deserve to be damned.
There is in the world such a thing as evil.
(All together now:) Sez who?
God help us.

Arthur Leff*

A theme that emerges from many current philosophical writings on constitutionalism—including several in the present collection—is a certain uneasiness with respect to the idea that the basic function of a constitution is to protect fundamental moral rights of citizens. Representatives of the

*From Paul Brest, "The Fundamental Rights Controvesy," *Yale Law Journal,* 90, 1981.

Critical Legal Studies Movement are openly contemptuous of this idea—
rejecting it as either covert subjective ideology or as outright nonsense. Even
those sympathetic to and supportive of the idea, however, do not exhibit the
kind of supreme confidence in it that was once common. Ronald Dworkin,
known as the most prominent contemporary defender of the view that the
U.S. Constitution exists to protect the inherent dignity of persons, has in his
most recent book *Law's Empire* moved toward a more relativistic account of
such matters—still confident that this document exists to protect "our"
basic conventional political morality but less confident than he used to appear that this is the same as protecting an objective set of natural or basic
human rights—moral rights that persons have regardless of the particular
cultural conventions under which they live. Even John Rawls, with each
new essay, appears more relativistic in his account of morality and of law to
the degree that law depends upon or enshrines morality.[1]

This shift toward relativism and conventionalism is not, or course, cost
free with respect to the doctrines of judicial review and judicial integrity. If
courts, in decisions about rights, really are engaged in a sincere attempt to
identify and protect rights that enshrine the inherent dignity and worth of
persons, then this is indeed a powerful argument for respecting and defer-
ring to them—for allowing them to enjoy the kind of "empire" of which
Dworkin speaks. If, however, they are simply expressing relativistic and conventional values, the argument for respect and deference is much weaker. A
person who dissents from true morality is a villain; but a person who dissents from what is merely conventional is not necessarily a villain and may
even be a hero. This is surely, for example, how those who oppose the court
on such issues as school prayer or sexual privacy view themselves—as dissenting from a certain ideology or convention ("secular humanism" perhaps) that, in their view, now improperly occupies a position of influence on
the courts. If constitutional rights really are a way of expressing respect for
the inherent dignity of persons, then it is easy to see why they should trump
majoritarian preference. If they are themselves simply institutionalized
preferences, however, then majoritarian attacks upon them do not seem to
be in principle out of place. Robert Bork's well-known defense to judicial
restraint, states's rights, and majoritarian populism, for example, seems to
depend upon his deep skepticism about moral rights and the whole natural
rights tradition.[2]

Constitutional rights might, of course, incorporate second-order preferences—preferences for a certain political process (for example, democracy, a system based on its Founders' intentions, and so on) over particular
outcomes. But why, one might ask, should such a process get absolute
deference unless *it* is required by the inherent dignity of persons or some
other objective moral value? (Is not the alternative mere fetishism about
process or history?) There is a sense in which all preferences are created
equal and thus any analysis of rights in terms merely of preferences cannot

in principle proclaim its invulnerability to arguments based on other preferences and to the political *compromises* that competing preferences demand as a condition of peace and stability.

What has produced the move toward relativism on the part of scholarly writers on constitutional morality? Ironically, it can in part be traced to the writings of John Rawls. Ironic because the high methodological standards he set for moral theory, when judged (as they have been, perhaps prematurely, by many) as incapable of satisfaction, tend to undermine confidence in the strong Kantian respect-for-persons moral theory he initially wanted to use those standards to defend. Since the publication in 1971 of Rawls' *A Theory of Justice,* ethical theory has been dominated by *foundational* questions—primarily the question of whether it is possible to demonstrate that certain moral principles are correct in the sense that all rational beings have sufficient reason to give those principles their allegiance. At first, when many people thought that Rawls' argument or some variant of that argument would work, there was great optimism about the objective status of claims about social justice and human rights; and Dworkin's early work appeared during those optimistic years. Fashions in philosophy change very rapidly, however, and we at present live in a time when it is widely believed—under the impact of work by such writers in the "analytic" tradition as Gilbert Harman and John Mackie and such writers in the "pluralist" tradition as Richard Rorty and Alasdair MacIntyre—that all such attempts rationally to demonstrate the objective correctness of certain moral claims are doomed to failure. Thus moral skepticism and moral relativism are the order of the day; and it is widely assumed that there is no reason to believe that there is a single, true morality—and thus no reason to believe in the inherent dignity or sacredness of persons and the moral respect that is objectively owed to persons simply because they are persons. Whatever rights that exist are simply grounded in conventions—conventions based on historical evolution or, where some rational basis is possible, on either general utility or enlightened self-interest.

Arguments of utility and self-interest are, of course, of value and can perhaps save morality from rampant skepticism and utter moral anarchy. John Stuart Mill, for example, argued that rights are simply those freedoms that society would guarantee to persons on the grounds that such guarantees are likely to be instrumental to the general welfare; and, agreeing no doubt with his mentor Bentham that all talk of natural rights is simply "nonsense on stilts," he explicitly said that he would "forego any advantage which could be derived to (his) argument from the idea of abstract right as a thing independent of utility" (*On Liberty,* Chapter 1). On the utilitarian view, freedom is neither good in itself nor to be guaranteed to persons as a part of respecting their inherent worth or dignity. Rather freedom is *instrumentally* valuable—valuable because most people get satisfaction from free choice, get satisfaction from having their own destinies determined by their choices, and get satisfaction from the general benefits (for example, scientific progress) that tend to emerge in societies where free choice is respected. In short—freedom is valuable because it tends to maximize a variety of human preferences. Here Mill and Bentham follow in the footsteps of Hobbes who, seeking to base morality totally on man's animal nature, had in an earlier age argued in defense of certain moral conventions on the grounds that each person's self-interest is likely to be maximized in a society having such conventions.

Considerations of utility and self-interest certainly have a role to play in establishing the basic structure of society, and I would not want to minimize their importance.[3] What they establish at their strongest, however, appears to fall far short (in moral, rhetorical, and inspirational power) of the ringing claims of the natural rights tradition. This tradition began with claims about the absolute and inalienable rights with which all persons had been endowed by God and found at least a partial secular expression in the Enlightenment in Kant's writings on the inherent dignity and worth of all human beings as rational beings—the idea that all rational beings are to be treated as "ends in themselves and never as means only." It is this tradition that such writers as Rawls and Dworkin and Robert Nozick are attempting to keep alive: and their characterization of rights is thus far richer and more ambitious than anything that is likely to grow out of merely utilitarian or self-interested foundations. They wish to defend at least some rights that depend upon such concepts as human dignity, the sacredness of persons, inherent human worth, and the fundamental respect that is owed to all persons simply because they are persons—for example, Dworkin's claim that all persons have a moral right (protected by the U.S. Constitution as a legal right) never to be disadvantaged by the state because of any contempt that other persons may have for their race. Such rights *trump* considerations of utility and self-interest (which might well weigh heavily against them) and thus it is unlikely that they can themselves be based upon such considerations; for they seem to involve a totally different vision of human beings and what makes human beings important, a vision simply not captured in the idea that human beings (like all other animals) seek to maximize individual utility.[4] This explains in part why these rights claims are *inspiring* in a way that appeals to utility and self-interest are not. Margaret Macdonald, seeking to account for the continued appeal of natural rights thinking even in the face of all the skepticism directed toward it, captured this point very nicely:

> It could, perhaps, be proved hedonistically that life for most ordinary citizens is more *comfortable* in a democratic than a totalitarian state. But would an appeal for effort, on this ground, have been sanctioned between 1939–45? However true, it would have been rejected as inefficient because *uninspired*. Who could

be moved to endure "blood and toil, tears and sweat" for the sake of a little extra comfort? (*The Proceedings of the Aristotelian Society*, 1947-48).

As demonstrated in different ways by Adolf Hitler and by Jim and Tammy Faye Bakker, inspirational power is not identical with true intellectual and moral power; and thus the attempts of Rawls and Dworkin and Nozick to keep the human dignity tradition alive are in trouble if they limit themselves to being inspiring and fail to provide that tradition with intellectual and moral foundations.[5] I have come to suspect that they have failed here—a failure perhaps shared with (and even inherited from) Kant's own attempt to base a moral theory of human dignity on purely secular considerations. I will spend the remainder of this Afterword explaining what I suspect the nature of the failure to be. My remarks will be very tentative and exploratory, more a case of my ruminating aloud to stimulate further reflection than my stating any considered views. I will begin with brief (and thus necessarily superficial) discussion of Kant.

It is often said that Kant's ethical theory is an attempt to pursue Judeo-Christian morality (perhaps even a specific form of Protestant Christianity) by secular means, and I think that there is considerable insight in this observation. A core claim of Christian ethics—a claim accepted by Kant—is that there is something uniquely precious or sacred about human beings from the moral point of view. There are, for example, certain special moral requirements (rights) that attach to human beings that do not attach to any other animal—for example, the requirement that we do not kill humans and eat them for food, or hunt them for sport, or perform medical experiments on them without their consent. They are, in short, owed a special kind of respect simply because they are persons. But what is the basis for this? Not mere species membership, surely, since that property alone could hardly be morally relevant. What is needed on this view is some obviously important characteristic or property possessed by and only by members of the human species, a property that confers moral uniqueness on human beings and thus qualifies them for the special respect that morally separates them from all other animals and grounds those special rights that protect them in a way that other animals are not protected. Could sentience or preference satisfaction, the basis of utilitarian theory, do this? It seems unlikely, since the capacity to feel pleasure and pain and the capacity to have preferences are properties we share with other animals—not something that separates us from them and makes us morally unique. Thus utilitarianism is often rejected because it seems incapable of capturing the special respect that, according to Christianity and to Kant, is owed to human beings because of their special moral status.

Though Kant agrees with the Christian tradition in claiming that human beings are morally special (precious, sacred, uniquely valuable) and merit a special kind of respect, concern, and protection because of that status, he parts company with that tradition in the answer to be given to the question of exactly what it is that does (in a way that sentience and preference satisfaction do not) constitute the essence of human uniqueness. Christianity seeks to ground the morally special status of persons of the doctrines of *creation* and *ensoulment.* Human beings are the children of God and are special because of the role they play in a divine plan. God, the creator of all, has mandated human specialness and has given each human being an immortal soul—something possessed by no other animal. We human beings are precious because we each, as it were, carry within us a precious jewel (the immortal soul) and are valuable because *it* is valuable and because *God* is valuable. Human beings are sacred because of the status they occupy in this divinely ordered world.

Given that Kant regarded the epistemological foundations for religious belief as flimsy, and given that he wanted the moral view of human dignity to rest on secure foundations, it is natural that he attempted to develop a secular foundation for the moral view to which he was committed. There is a sense, of course, in which the enterprise was doomed from the outset; for how can one expect to dump God and a religious vision of the universe and yet retain a strong concept of the *sacredness* of anything? Still, Kant's attempt is one of the great "nice tries" in the history of philosophy. What is special about persons, suggested Kant, is neither immortal souls nor their role in the divine order of the universe. It is rather their *rationality.* That is what makes them unique and morally special; that is the property that makes them truly free or autonomous (in a way unlike any other creature) and confers upon them the special moral status Kant calls "dignity." That is why human beings have rights that can trump all claims of utility.

Since moral judgment clearly presupposes rationality in some sense, Kant is surely correct in seeing rationality as an important component of any plausible moral theory.[6] However, important as rationality is, it seems very doubtful that it will bear the enormous weight that Kant seeks to place on it—the weight of being the very *essence* of morality and of the moral status of any creature who is to count as a proper object of moral concern and respect. Several serious problems emerge when rationality is called upon to play this role. Consider, as a very fundamental problem for Kant, the concept of rationally itself. What is Kant going to count as rationality? Is it simply, as Hume and Hobbes had argued, the ability efficiently to choose means most likely to lead to those ends set by our passions? Surely not, for this instrumental concept of rationality fails both to carve out a special uniqueness for human beings (watch an ape put sticks together to reach a desired object) and it fails to avoid an ultimate analysis of values in terms of desires and preferences—the very utilitarian model that Kant wants to avoid. Thus Kant is forced to suggest that rationality as autonomy involves some kind of mysterious contra-causal influence of a noumenal self that is not a part of the empirical world. But now we have a metaphysical thesis just as open to skeptical doubt as are those theological claims that were earlier rejected. But if faith is good enough here, why was it not good enough there?

Suppose we grant Kant his claim about human rationality. It still seems possible easily to doubt that this is the primary attribute that confers moral uniqueness and preciousness on those who possess it. It certainly, for example, will not track well on the Christian doctrine of ensoulment and thus will represent a rather weak attempt at a secular equivalent for that doctrine; for it seems to entail results that the Christian doctrine explicitly seeks to avoid. On Kant's view, unlike the Christian view, worthiness of respect as a person would seem to be a matter of *degree*—not something owed equally to all members of the human species. People differ in their degree of rationality; is the moral respect owed them thus to differ accordingly? Some people (the severely retarded, infants, the senile, the comatose) are not rational at all; do they thus get *no* moral respect as persons? (May we kill and eat them, hunt them for sport, and perform medical experiments on them so long as all of these activities are performed without causing pain to the victims?) Christianity is a doctrine of moral egalitarianism; Kantianism, whatever Kant's actual intentions, seems to entail radical moral inegalitarianism and thus must be very defective as a secular equivalent of the Christian moral view.

Finally, consider how easy it is to doubt the moral centrality of rationality even in clear cases where it is present. We may grant that some persons possess rationality to a high degree and that most persons probably possess it at some threshold level for what is required to count as autonomous. Such persons are special, of course, but is it obvious that this specialness has strong *moral* implications—that it and it alone is what makes persons sacred and worthy of respect and rights? Why is not love and kindness and a tendency toward acts of charity just as good a candidate for moral specialness? Is it because kindness grows out of our empirical animal nature whereas rationality is a part of our noumenal nature? Perhaps. But then can it be seriously maintained that this metaphysical doctrine is not open to serious skeptical doubts—doubts at least as serious as those to which religious belief may be subjected?[7]

Because of these problems, I am inclined to suspect that the Kantian enterprise is doomed to failure. The rich moral doctrine of the sacredness, the preciousness, the dignity of persons cannot in fact be utterly detached from the theological context in which it arose and of which it for so long formed an essential part. Values come to us trailing their historical past; and when we attempt to cut all links to that past we risk cutting the life lines on which those values essentially depend. I think that this happens in the case of Kant's attempt—and no doubt any other attempt—to retain all Christian moral values within a totally secular framework. Thus "All men are created equal (and) are endowed by their Creator with certain unalienable rights" may be a sentence we must accept in an all or nothing fashion—not one where we can simply carve out what we like and junk the rest.[8]

Of course, we have all read Plato's *Euthyphro* and we know all about the gap between "is" and "ought," the naturalistic fallacy, and the open question argument. Thus we all know that there is no airtight *logical* guarantee of the objective value of human dignity even if we grant that it is commanded by God or is a part of the divine plan. "I know that God has given humans rights but I still do not hold those rights to be valuable" is not a formal contradiction. This is granted. On the other hand, can anyone seriously doubt that the religious worldview, if accepted, gives one a *relevant reason,* even a *powerful reason,* in favor of accepting human sacredness and respecting any moral and legal rights based on it—that such rights and dignity claims are at least more plausible when located in such a general worldview than when utterly detached from it? Perhaps it could be argued that it is more a matter of rhetoric than of logic, but it at least seems that a theologically rich language of public discourse about human rights and the place of human beings in the universe would carry more persuasive power than a language that attempts to preserve talk of such rights in the absence of any such profound commitments.

Writers such as Rawls, Dworkin, and Nozick seem to think otherwise; for they all seem to pride themselves on offering theories that, in their view, require no controversial metaphysical assumptions at all. In his latest book Dworkin expresses total indifference to the issue of whether, in John Mackie's phrase, moral values are part of the "fabric of the universe." And, in his earlier *Taking Rights Seriously,* he dismisses any attempt to understand his rights theory in any metaphysically complex way:

> Individual rights are political trumps held by individuals. Individuals have rights when, for some reason, a collective goal is not a sufficient justification for denying them what they wish, as individuals, to have or to do, or not a sufficient justification for imposing some loss or injury upon them. That characterization of a right is, of course, formal in the sense that it does not indicate what rights people have or guarantee, indeed, that they have any. But it does not suppose that rights have some special metaphysical character, and the theory defended in these essays therefore departs from older theories of rights that do rely on that supposition (*Taking Rights Seriously,* Introduction).

I think this line will not work. If individuals have trumps "for some reason," then we surely need to know for *what* reason. What justifies this special ability to block utility and majoritarian preference? If it is the dignity of persons, then we need to know—not just a slogan—but what this comes to: what it is about persons that confers dignity upon them. Surely it must be something special about them (and something different from the mere sentience that utilitarians find basic), and I simply do not see how one could begin to articulate an account of this specialness without entering the world of metaphysics—and controversial metaphysics at that. Otherwise the account will remain at the level of vacuous generality.

Consider, for example, the trouble Robert Nozick gets into (in *Anarchy, State, and Utopia,* Chapter 7) in seeking to defend a version of Locke's theory of the legitimate original acquisition of property without availing himself of any of the theological assumptions on which Locke based his own theory. Nozick, like Locke, wants initial acquisition to be limited in order to prevent one person from taking all property (even what he cannot use and which will waste and spoil) and leaving all others with nothing at all. Thus he accepts what he calls "The Lockean Proviso" that there be "enough and as good left in common for others" because only in this way can we "ensure that the situation of others is not worsened." He then develops a complex and clever theory of what constitutes the worsening of another's situation. What he does not explain, however, is why anyone is morally required to *care* whether or not another's situation is worsened. If nature is unowned and I am bound by no antecedent moral rules of property ownership with respect to nature, why may I not simply say, "Lucky me I got it all first and unlucky you who came too late"—and let it go at that? What right do you have with respect to unowned and morally virgin nature?

I do not think that Nozick can answer this question. Locke, however, can and does. And his answer is based upon the claim with which he begins his entire discussion of original acquisition: "*God, who hath given the World to Men in common,* hath also given them reason to make use of it to the best advantage of Life, and convenience. The Earth, and all that is therein, is given to Men for the Support and Comfort of their being. And though all the Fruits it naturally produces, and Beasts it feeds, belong to Mankind in common . . . no body has originally a private Dominion, exclusive of the rest of mankind, in any of them [italics added]." (*Second Treatise,* Section 26). We now see the origin of the Lockean Proviso: God created the world *ex nihilo* (and thus owned it) and has given it to persons for their collective ownership. The world is owned by all, and *that* is why no one person may legitimately make off with all of it. This view is, of course, controversial to the same degree as any theological claim is controversial; but it is at least a *reason* that renders the Lockean proviso intelligible. Without it, the proviso simply hangs in midair—another illustration of what can happen when a moral doctrine is cut off from all its traditional roots.

What I have been suggesting is that the doctrines of human dignity and natural rights, currently fashionable among liberal theorists, may not sit so well with the contempt for religion (or at least for any philosophical or political role for religion) that is also currently fashionable among liberal theorists. Liberal theorists have a self-destructive tendency to be charmed by views that undermine their own central doctrines—for example, a failure to realize that the liberal virtues of value pluralism and value tolerance may undermine the absolutism about human rights upon which liberalism ultimately depends—and this may be simply another exemplification of that tendency.

Suppose that I am correct in the above claim—correct that the liberal theory of rights requires a doctrine of human dignity, preciousness and sacredness that cannot be utterly detached from a belief in God or at least from a world view that would be properly called religious in some metaphysically profound sense. What options does this leave us? There are, I think, only four: (1) Seek to adopt and encourage, insofar as this is in one's volitional control, the religious world view that these important moral doctrines require;[9] (2) Accept a weaker theory of human moral rights—for example, one based on calculations of expected utility;[10] (3) Join the Critical Legal Studies Movement, junk all the talk about rights as so much bourgeois nonsense, and try to reconceive the law and the function of the courts—not as adjudicators of rights—but in some new and probably more overtly political way;[11] (4) Accept a theory of constitutional rights (for example, a theory mandating respect for the Framers' intentions) without any pretense that this theory rests on a secure moral foundation. These are all interesting possibilities and, if space allowed, I would want to say considerably more about each of them.

For those, such as I, who find it very difficult—perhaps impossible—to embrace religious convictions, the idea that fundamental moral values may require such convictions is not one to be welcomed with joy. This idea generates tensions and appears to force choices that some of us would prefer not to make. But it still might be true for all of that.[12]

Notes

1. For a fuller discussion of this shift toward relativism on the part of Rawls and Dworkin, see Thomas C. Grey's "Advice for 'Judge and Company'" (a review essay on Dworkin's *Law's Empire*), *New York Review of Books*, 12 March, 1987. There are, of course, legal theories of constitutional rights (the late Justice Hugo Black's perhaps) that make no pretense of being founded in morality or in moral philosophy. My primary focus in this Afterword is on those theories—for example, Dworkin's—that do purport to be so founded.

2. See Ronald Dworkin, "The Bork Nomination," *New York Review of Books*, 13 August, 1987.

3. The most recent exploration of the possibility of generating moral rules from models of rational self-interest is David Gauthier's important book *Morals by Agreement* (Oxford: Oxford University Press, 1986).

4. For a fuller discussion of the different moral visions of human nature that lie behind utilitarianism and Kantianism, see Chapter 2, "Moral Theory and its Application to Law," in *The Philosophy of Law: An Introduction to Jurisprudence*, by Jeffrie G. Murphy and Jules L. Coleman (Totowa, NJ: Rowman and Allanheld, 1984).

5. Some, of course, would argue that one can take claims about the natural rights

and the inherent dignity of persons as themselves foundational—arguing that they are more plausible than any theory one might use either to support or undermine them, perhaps even arguing that they are self-evident or obvious. This position is difficult to maintain, however, in the face of the fact that the philosophical world now contains large numbers of intelligent and sophisticated utilitarians, egoists, skeptics, and relativists—none of them finding the Kantian tradition even plausible, much less self-evident.

6. But *why* is it important? In itself? Instrumentally, because we take satisfaction in the use of this faculty and in its products? Because it allows us properly to fulfill a portion of our role in the divinely ordered framework in which it operates?

7. For a somewhat fuller discussion of the relation between Kantian ethics and religious morality, see Jeffrie G. Murphy, "Kantian Autonomy and Divine Commands," *Faith and Philosophy*, vol 4, no. 3, July 1987: 276–281.

8. If this is true, then there may be interesting implications for judicial review—for example, courts should perhaps be reluctant to interpret the constitution in ways that undermine religion since, if religion is undermined, constitutional rights that depend for their foundations on a religious worldview may be undermined too.

9. Could one attempt a move similar to Kant's famous (or notorious) "moral proof" for the existence of God? Kant basically argued as follows: We have no knowledge of God (that He exists or does not exist); certain moral principles presuppose a belief in God; therefore a rational person is justified in *postulating* the existence of God. The demands of morality here take precedence over our normal metaphysical bias in favor of Occam's Razor. Perhaps this is an idea worth exploring.

10. It is possible that utility would be best served by embracing, as a public morality, something other than utilitarianism—for example, it is logically possible (perhaps even empirically likely) that the general welfare would be better served if people were taught to aim, not at the general welfare, but at respecting the natural rights of persons. Natural rights (perhaps even a belief in God) would then represent socially useful fictions. This suggestion raises interesting theoretical possibilities, but it should be noted that it clearly collides with the liberal belief that the true ethical foundations of a society should be transparent to all citizens in that society.

11. It is ironic that most of the critical legal studies scholars who support this political conception of the courts are from the political left and have a radical (often socialist) political agenda that they want the courts to pursue. In fact, of course, this political conception of the courts is much more likely to serve the interests of the political right and the enactment of their political agenda.

12. Kent Greenawalt was kind enough to read and comment on an earlier draft of this esssay. I am grateful for his comments and have attempted to address the concerns he expressed.

Selected Bibliography

Aristotle, *Constitution of Athens and Related Texts,* trans. Kurt von Fritz and Ernst Kopp. New York: Hafner Press, 1974.

Bailyn, Bernard. *The Ideological Origins of the American Revolution:* Cambridge, MA: Belknap Press, Harvard University Press, 1982.

Beck, Lewis W. *A Commentary on Kant's Critique of Practical Reason.* Chicago: University of Chicago Press, 1960.

Becker, Lynn. "Electronic Publishing: First Amendment Issues in the Twenty-First Century," *Fordham Urban Law Journal* 13 (1985).

Bentham, Jeremy. *An Introduction to the Principles of Morals and Legislation.* New York: Hafner Press, 1948.

Bobbitt, Philip. *Constitutional Fate.* New York: Oxford University Press, 1982.

Borden, Morton, ed. *The Antifederalist Papers.* East Lansing, MI: Michigan State University Press, 1965.

Boyle, Francis Anthony. *Defending Civil Resistance Under International Law.* Dobbs Ferry, NY: Transnational, 1987.

Bronaugh, Richard N., et al., eds. *Readings in the Philosophy of Constitutional Law.* Dubuque, IA: Kendall/Hunt, 1983.

Byrne, Edward M. *Military Law.* Annapolis: Naval Institute Press, 1981.

Cairns, Huntington. *Legal Philosophy from Plato to Hegel.* Baltimore: John Hopkins Press, 1967.

Carmen, Ira H. *Cloning and The Constitution.* Madison: University of Wisconsin Press, 1985.

Carter, Lief H. *Contemporary Constitutional Lawmaking.* New York: Pergamon Press, 1985.

Chafee, Jr., Zechariah. *How Human Rights Got into the Constitution.* Boston: Boston University Press, 1952.

Collins, Hugh. *Marxism and Law.* New York: Oxford University Press, 1987.

Corwin, Edward S. *The Constitution and What It Means Today.* Princeton, NJ: Princeton University Press, 1958.

Corwin, Edwin C. *The "Higher Law" Background of American Constitutional Law.* Ithaca, NY: Cornell University Press, 1979.

Cranston, Maurice. *John Locke.* London: Oxford University Press, 1957.

Curry, Thomas. *The First Freedoms: Church and State in America to the Passage of the First Amendment.* New York: Oxford University Press, 1986.

Dicey, Albert V. *Introduction to the Study of the Law of the Constitution,* 10th ed. New York: St. Martin's Press, 1961.

Doren, Carl Van. *The Great Rehearsal.* New York: Penguin Books, 1986.

Ducat, Craig R., and Chase, Harold W. *Constitutional Interpretation,* 4th ed. St. Paul, MN: West, 1988.

Dworkin, Ronald. *Law's Empire.* Cambridge, MA: Belknap Press, 1986.

———. *Taking Rights Seriously.* Cambridge: Harvard University Press, 1977.

Edelman, Martin. *Democratic Theories and The Constitution.* Albany: State University of New York Press, 1984.

Ely, John Hart. *Democracy and Distrust.* Cambridge: Harvard University Press, 1980.

Feinberg, Joel, and Gross, Hyman. *Philosophy of Law,* 3d ed. Belmont, CA: Wadsworth Publishing Co., 1986.

Fotion, Nicholas, and Elfstrom, Gerard. *Military Ethics.* Boston: Routledge and Kegan Paul, 1986.

Friendly, Fred W., and Elliot, Martha J. *The Constitution: That Delicate Balance.* New York: Random House, 1984.

Friedman, Leon, ed. *The Law of War: A Documentary History,* 2 vols; New York: Random House, 1972.

Gauthier, David. *Morals by Agreement.* Oxford: Oxford University Press, 1986.

Golding, Martin P. *Philosophy of Law.* Englewood Cliffs, NJ: Prentice-Hall, 1975.

———. *Legal Reasoning.* New York: Alfred A. Knopf, 1984.

Graham, Jr., George T., and Graham, Scarlett G., ed. *Founding Principles of American Government,* rev. ed. Chatham, NJ: Chatham House Publishers, 1984.

Greenawalt, Kent. *Discrimination and Reverse Discrimination.* New York: Alfred A. Knopf, 1983.

Grey, Thomas. "Origins of the Unwritten Constitution: Fundamental Law in American Revolutionary Thought," *Stanford Law Review 30* (May, 1978) 843–893.

———. *The Legal Enforcement of Morality.* New York: Alfred A. Knopf, 1983.

Grundman, Adolph H. *The Embattled Constitution.* Malabar, FL: Robert E. Krieger Publishing Co.,1986.

Harman, Gilbert. *The Nature of Morality.* New York: Oxford University Press, 1977.

Hart, H.L.A. *The Concept of Law.* Oxford: Clarendon Press, 1961.

———. *Essays in Jurisprudence and Philosophy.* New York: Oxford University Press, 1983.

Henkin, Louis. "Constitutional Rights and Human Rights," *Harvard Civil Rights— Civil Liberties Law Review.* 13, no. 3 (Summer 1978) 593–632.

_____. *Foreign Affairs and The Constitution.* New York: Foundation Press, 1972.

_____. *The Rights of Man Today.* Boulder, CO: Westview Press, 1978.

Hegel, G.W.F. *The Philosophy of Right.* Trans. T.M. Knox, Oxford: Oxford University Press, 1942.

_____. *The Phenomenology of Mind.* Trans. J.B. Baillie. New York: Harper Torchbooks, 1967.

Hegel's Political Writings. Trans. T.M. Knox. Oxford: Oxford University Press, 1964.

Hobbes, Thomas. *Leviathan: Parts I & II.* Indianapolis: Bobbs-Merrill Co., 1958.

Hume, David. *A Treatise on Human Nature.* L.A. Silby-Bigge, ed. Oxford: Clarendon Press, 1960.

_____. *Essays: Moral, Political, and Literary.* Eugene F. Miller, ed. Indianapolis: Liberty Classics, 1985.

Hutson, James. "The Creation of the Constitution: The Integrity of the Documentary Record," *Texas Law Review* 65, no.1 (1986)

Jacobsohn, Gary J. *The Supreme Court and The Decline of Constitutional Aspiration.* Totowa, NJ: Rowman and Littlefield, 1986.

Kammen, Michael, ed. *The Origins of the American Constitution.* New York: Penguin Books, 1986.

Karst, Kenneth L. "Paths to Belonging: The Constitution and Cultural Identity," *North Carolina Law Review.* 64, no. 2 (January, 1986) 303–377.

Karys, David. ed. *The Politics of Law.* New York: Pantheon, 1982.

Knox, T.M., "Hegel and Prussianism," *Philosophy* XV, no. 1 (January, 1940).

Koch, Adrienne, ed. *Notes of Debates in The Federal Convention of 1787 Reported by James Madison.* Athens, OH: Ohio University Press, 1966.

Locke, John. *Two Treatises of Government.* Thomas I. Cook, ed. New York: Hafner Press, 1947.

_____. *An Essay Concerning Human Understanding.* Peter Nidditch, ed. Oxford: The Clarendon Press, 1975.

Lyons, David. *Ethics and The Rule of Law.* New York: Cambridge University Press, 1984.

MacDonald, Forrest. *Novus Ordo Seclorum: The Intellectual Origins of the Constitution.* Lawrence, KS: University Press of Kansas, 1985.

MacIntyre, Alasdair, *After Virtue.* Notre Dame: University of Notre Dame Press, 1981.

MacKinnon, Catherine A. *Feminism Unmodified.* Cambridge: Harvard University Press, 1987.

Macpherson, C.B., ed. *Property: Mainstream and Critical Positions.* Toronto: University of Toronto Press, 1983.

Mackie, J.L. *Ethics: Inventing Right and Wrong.* New York: Penguin Books, 1977.

Marcuse, Herbert. *Reason and Revolution.* Boston: Beacon Press, 1960.

Marx, Karl. *Critique of Hegel's Philosophy of Right.* Trans. Joseph O'Malley. Cambridge: Cambridge University Press, 1970.

McIlwain, Charles H. *Constitutionalism: Ancient and Modern.* Ithaca: Cornell University Press, 1983.

Mill, John Stuart. *Three Essays.* Introduction by Richard Wollheim. New York: Oxford University Press, 1978.

Montesquieu, Baron de. *The Spirit of The Laws.* Trans. Thomas Nugent. New York: Hafner Publishing Co., 1949.

Murphy, Jeffrie G. and Coleman, Jules L. *The Philosophy of Law: An Introduction to Jurisprudence.* Totowa, NJ: Rowman and Allanheld, 1984.

Nozick, Robert. *Anarchy, State, and Utopia.* New York: Basic Books, 1974.

Paton, H.J. *Groundwork of the Metaphysics of Morals.* New York and Evanston: Harper Torchbooks, 1964.

Pennock, J.R., and Chapman, J.W., eds. *Authority Revisited: NOMOS XXIX.* New York: New York University Press, 1987.

———. *Constitutionalism: NOMOS XX.* New York: New York University Press, 1979.

Perry, Michael. *The Constitution, The Courts, and Human Rights.* New Haven: Yale University Press, 1982.

Pool, Ithiel de Sola. *Technologies of Freedom.* Cambridge, MA: Belknap Press, 1983.

Porty, Richard. *Philosophy and the Mirror of Nature.* New Jersey: Princeton University Press, 1979.

Rakove, Jack N. *The Beginnings of National Politics: An Interpretive History of The Continental Congress.* Baltimore: The John Hopkins University Press, 1979.

Rawls, John. *A Theory of Justice.* Cambridge: Harvard University Press, 1971.

Reck, Andrew. "The Philosophical Background of the American Revolution," *Southwestern Journal of Philosophy,* V (1974) 179–202.

Reiss, Hans., ed. *Kant's Political Writings,* Cambridge: Cambridge University Press, 1970.

Richards, David A.J. *The Moral Criticism of Law.* Encino, CA: Dickenson Publishing Co., 1977.

Ritter, Joachim. *Hegel and The French Revolution.* Cambridge, MA: The M.I.T. Press, 1982.

Rosenbaum, Alan S., ed. *The Philosophy of Human Rights: International Perspectives.* Westport, CT: Greenwood Press, 1980.

Roth, John, and Whittemore, Robert C., ed. *Ideology and The American Experience.* Washington, D.C.: The Washington Institute, 1986.

Rousseau, Jean-Jacques. *Of The Social Contract.* Trans. Charles M. Sherover. New York: Harper and Row, 1984.

Spencer, Martin E. "Plato and The Anatomy of Constitutions," *Social Theory and Practice,* 5, no. 1 (Fall, 1978) 95–130.

The Theodosian Code. Trans. Clyde Pharr. Princeton, NJ: Princeton University Press, 1952.

Tully, James. *A Discourse on Property: John Locke, and His Adversaries.* Cambridge: The University Press, 1980.

Tully, James, ed. *James Locke: A Letter Concerning Toleration.* Indianapolis: Hackett Publishing Co., 1983.

Tushnet, Mark. "Critical Legal Studies and Constitutional Law: An Essay in Deconstruction," *Stanford Law Review,* 36 (January, 1984) 623–647.

———. "The Dilemmas of Liberal Constitutionalism," *Ohio State Law Journal* 42 (1981) 411–426.

———. "The U.S. Constitution and The Intent of The Framers," *TIKKUN,* 1, no. 2 (1986).

Unger, Roberto. *The Critical Legal Studies Movement.* Cambridge: Harvard University Press, 1986.

Wills, Gary. *Explaining America: The Federalist.* New York: Doubleday, 1981.
_____. *Inventing America: Jefferson's Declaration of Independence.* New York: Double-
day, 1978.
_____. *The Federalist Papers.* New York: Bantam Books, 1982.
White, Morton, *Philosophy, The Federalist, and The Constitution.* New York: Oxford
University Press, 1987.
Wood, Gordon S. *The Creation of the American Republic.* New York: Norton and Co.,
1969.

Index

ABOUT THE EDITOR

Alan S. Rosenbaum is Associate Professor of Philosophy at Cleveland State University. He is the author of *Coercion and Autonomy: Philosophical Foundations, Issues and Practices* (Greenwood Press, 1986), and has edited *The Philosophy of Human Rights: International Perspectives* (Greenwood Press, 1980). His articles have appeared in numerous philosophical and professional journals.

ABOUT THE CONTRIBUTORS

Leslie Armour is Professor of Philosophy at the University of Ottawa, Canada. His most recent books include *The Industrial Kingdom of God* (ed.) (University of Ottawa Press, 1982); *The Idea of Canada and the Crisis of Community* (Steel Bail-Humanities Press, 1981); *The Faces of Reason: Philosophy in English Canada, 1850-1950* (Wilfred Laurier Univ. Press, 1981). He has published a wide variety of papers in the most prominent journals of philosophy and other professional publications.

Richard A. Falk is currently Professor of International Law in the Center of International Studies at Princeton University and he has served as its director. He serves on the editorial boards of such prominent publications as *The Nation; World Policy Journal;* and *American Journal of International Law.* He has written and/or (co-)edited over 25 books, including *International Law: A Contemporary Perspective* (Westview Press, 1985); *Indefensible Weapons: The Political and Psychological Case Against Nuclearism* (Basic Books, 1982); and *The End of World Order* (Holmes & Meier Pubs., 1983). His articles have appeared in some of America's most prestigious scholarly journals, law reviews, magazines, international publications, and newspapers.

Milton Fisk is Professor of Philosophy at Indiana University. His books include *Ethics and Society: A Marxist Interpretation of Value* (New York Univ. Press, 1980); *Nature and Necessity: An Essay in Physical Ontology* (Indiana Univ. Press, 1973); and *A Modern Formal Logic* (Prentice-Hall, 1964). His many articles have appeared in the leading philosophical journals and as chapters in edited volumes.

Peter A. French is Lennox distinguished Professor of the Humanities, Professor of Philosophy, and Chair of the Department of Philosophy at Trinity University, Texas. His books include *Collective and Corporate Responsibility* (Columbia Univ. Press, 1984); *Corrigible Corporations and Unruly Laws* (Trinity Univ. Press, 1985); *Puzzles, Paradoxes, and Problems* (St. Martin's Press, 1986); *Ethics in Government* (Prentice-Hall, 1983); and *The Scope of Morality* (Univ. of Minnesota Press, 1980). He is senior editor of *Midwest Studies in Philosophy,* a major professional journal. He has lectured widely in the United States and throughout Europe. Among his numerous awards, the Governor of Minnesota in 1982 presented him with the state's Certificate of Honor for Outstanding Contributions to Education.

Mary J. Gregor is Professor of Philosophy at San Diego State University. She is the author of a number of authoritative books and articles on the writings of Immanuel Kant, including *Kant: The Doctrine of Virtue* (Harper & Row Torchbooks, 1964); *Kant: Anthropology from a Pragmatic Point of View* (Martinus Nijhoff, 1974); and *Laws of Freedom* (Blackwell, 1963); and forthcoming, a translation of Kant's *Metaphysik der Sitten* for Cambridge University Press.

Guy Lafrance is Professor of Philosophy and Chair of the Department of Philosophy at the University of Ottawa, Canada. His most recent books include *Gaston Bachelard. Profils épistémologiques* (University of Ottawa, 1987); *Pouvoir et Tyrannie* (Univ. of Ottawa, 1986); and *Trent-Rousseau Studies* (Univ. of Ottawa, 1980). He has published chapters in books by others and many articles in French, German, Canadian, and American professional philosophical journals.

Jeffrie G. Murphy is professor of Philosophy and Law at Arizona State University. He serves on the Editorial Boards of 2 leading journals, *Law and Philosophy* and *Philosophical Studies.* His most recent (co-)authored and edited books are *Forgiveness and Mercy* (Cambridge Univ. Press, 1988); *The Philosophy of Law: An Introduction to Jurisprudence* (Rowman & Allenheld, 1984); *Evolution, Morality, and The Meaning of Life* (Littlefield, Adams, &

Co.,1982); *Punishment & Rehabilitation* (ed.); and forthcoming, *Retribution Reconsidered* (D. Reidel). His many articles appear in such distinguished philosophical journals and law reviews as *Journal of Philosophy; Columbia Law Review;* and *Virginia Law Review.*

Andrew Reck is Professor and Chair of Philosophy at Tulane University. He has published approximately 100 articles (including chapters in books). His books include *Speculative Philosophy* (Univ. of New Mexico Press, 1972); *Recent American Philosophy* (Pantheon Books, 1964); *Introduction to William James* (Indiana Univ. Press, 1967); and *The New American Philosophers* (Delta Books, 1970).

Jeffrey Reiman holds a joint appointment at the American University as a Professor of Philosophy and Justice in the Department of Justice, Law, and Society, and the Department of Philosophy and Religion. He is the author of *The Rich Get Richer and The Poor Get Prison: Ideology, Class, and Criminal Justice* (Macmillan Press, 1984) (2nd ed.); *In Defense of Political Philosophy* (Harper & Row, 1972); and numerous articles on issues in ethics, political and legal philosophy, including recently "Justice, Civilization, and the Death Penalty" in *Philosophy and Public Affairs* and "Law, Rights, Community, and the Structure of Liberal Legal Justification" in Pennock and Chapman, eds., *Justification: NOMOS XXVIII* (New York Univ. Press, 1986).

Wade Robison is Professor of Philosophy at Kalamazoo College and is currently the president of the Hume Society. His most recent publications include three (co-)edited books: *McGill Hume Studies* (Austin Hill Press, 1979); *Profits and Professions: Essays in Business and Professional Ethics* (Humana Press, 1983); and *Medical Responsibility: Autonomy, Informed Consent and Euthanasia* (Humana Press, 1979). Also, his articles appear in many philosophical journals and as chapters in other scholars' edited works.

Peter G. Stillman is Professor of Political Science at Vassar College. He serves as the Secretary of the Hegel Society of America and on the editorial boards of *Out of Minerva* and CLIO (Annual Philosophy Issue). He has published many articles and book chapters on Hegel and Marx, and has recently edited *Hegel's Philosophy of Spirit* (State Univ. of New York Press, 1987).

Rosemarie Tong is Associate Professor of Philosophy at Williams College. Her recent books include *Ethics in Policy Analysis* (Prentice-Hall, 1985) and *Women, Sex, and the Law* (Rowman & Allenfeld, 1984); *Reproductive and Genetic Technology* (Rowman & Allenfeld); and *Introduction to Feminist Thought* (Westview Pubs.), are forthcoming. She has published a number of articles in professional journals and serves as Associate Editor of *American Legal Studies Journal.* In 1982, she was presented with the Teacher of the Year Award by the American Philosophical Association.

Mark Tushnet is Professor of Law at the Georgetown University Law Center. He served as a law clerk to Justice Thurgood Marshall of the United

States Supreme Court. He is the author of *Red, White, and Blue* (Harvard Univ. Press, 1988); *The NAACP's Legal Strategy Against Segregated Education, 1925-1950* (Univ. of North Carolina Press, 1987); *The American Law of Slavery, 1810-1860: Considerations of Humanity and Interest* (Princeton Univ. Press, 1981); and he is co-author of two casebooks, *Federal Jurisdiction: Policy and Practice* (Michie Co., 1984) and *Constitutional Law* (Little, Brown & Co., 1986). His numerous articles on constitutional law and history have closely identified him as a leading participant and spokesman for the Critical Legal Studies Movement.